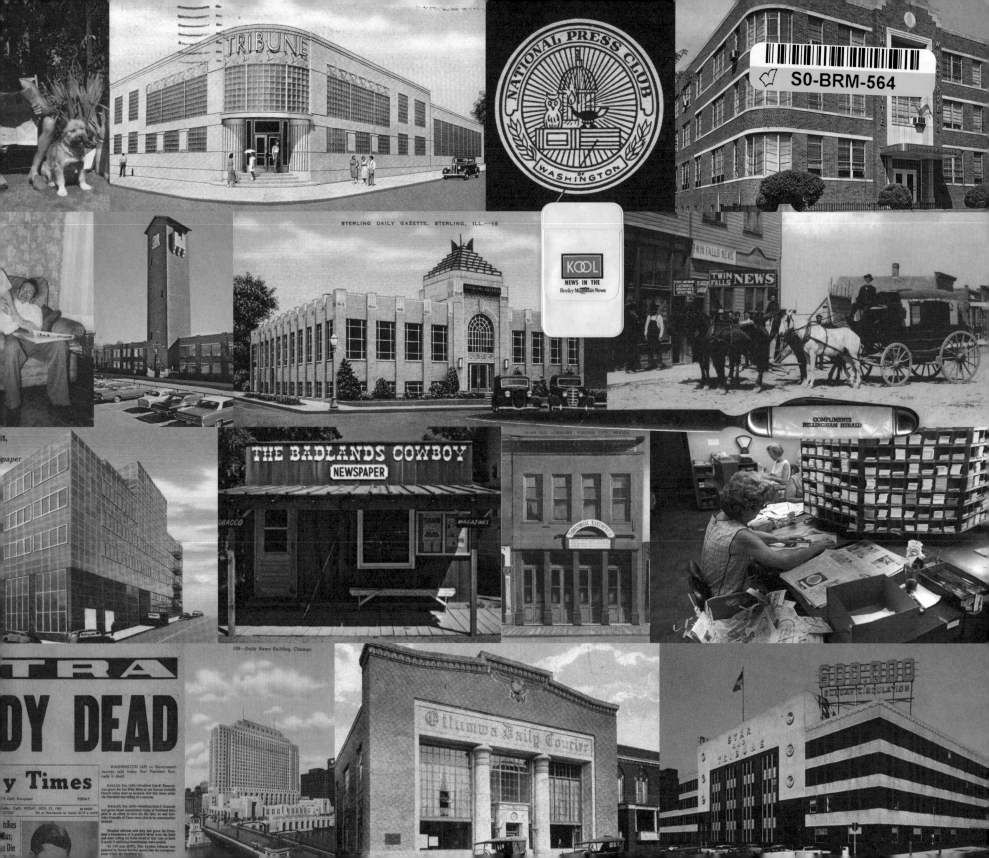

DON'T STOP THE PRESSES!

DON'T STOP THE PRESSES!

TRUTH, JUSTICE, AND THE AMERICAN NEWSPAPER

Patt Morrison
Foreword by Dean Baquet

ANGEL CITY PRESS

To my colleagues in this fellowship of newspapering.
Although they are stretched thin in harried, depleted newsrooms,
or have departed from shuttered newspapers altogether,
they work with diligence, passion, conscience, and honesty,
knowing that they serve the public weal and the founding principles of this democracy.

Page 2: Picnic, May 1947.
Opposite: Dog delivers the news. Undated.

CONTENTS

Opposite: Baby "reads" the news. Undated.

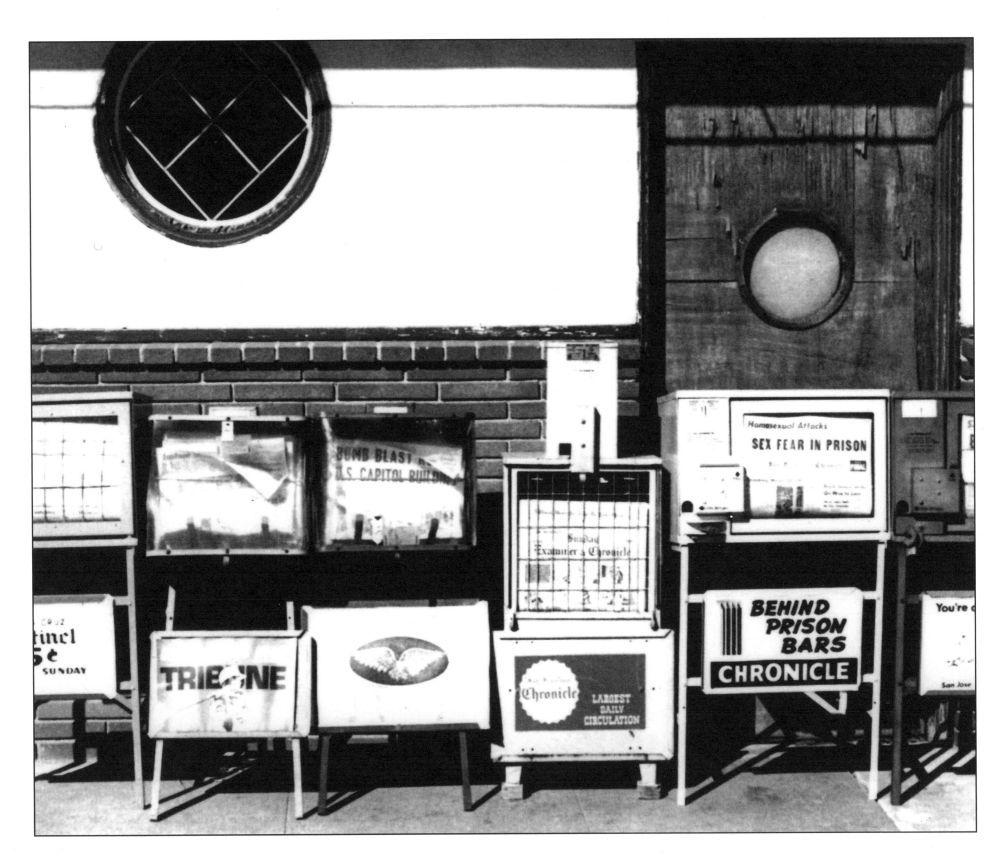

FOREWORD

Newsrooms developed an inferiority complex twenty years ago. That's when the business model that sustained them—that paid for foreign reporters, big news bureaus, and the latest technology—started to crumble.

Advertisers could take their goods elsewhere. Readers had other options for news, weather, and sports. Sometimes those options were even better than the traditional newspaper, which was by necessity static. Most of the great media families that walked the earth—the Chandlers, the Bancrofts, the Knights—sold their companies or lost control of their empires to cost-cutters who didn't understand or care about the mission of journalism.

But something equally powerful has happened with the election of Donald Trump. As Americans seek the truth, they are finding a whole lot of it is coming from those great old newsrooms like the *Los Angeles Times*, the *Washington Post*, and, of course, my own, the *New York Times*. As Americans look for tough-minded, independent coverage of Washington and the world, they are finding that no one does a better job of it than traditional newsrooms, with their standards and constant striving.

American newspapers are flawed, of course. We were slow to change. And for years we lost touch with our readers. Our critics are right in pointing out that we could be more than a little arrogant. We did not listen and we somehow could not accept the changes the digital age was forcing upon us, even though most of them were good.

We still have so much to learn, and many of our newsrooms will not survive, either because of brutal budget cutting that has made it hard for them to offer unmatched coverage, or because their communities simply cannot afford them.

But for those that survive—and the successors that will inevitably spring up in the coming years—the role has never been clearer than it is now.

And it has never been more evident than in this year, when the glories of journalism have been on display, when the newsrooms Patt Morrison's timely book summons to mind woke up to find themselves once again vital to Democracy.

Think of what we know about Donald Trump only because of newsrooms. The *Post* broke the story of his phony claims to being a big philanthropist. The *Times* chronicled Russian meddling in American elections.

But it goes far beyond Trump, and the story of the dramatic changes he has made to government and society. It is also because a confident and independent press has broken the stories of powerful men who abuse women. In recent months news organizations across the country have taken on powerful men—sometimes our own newsroom leaders and stars.

The *Times* may have started it with the stories of Bill O'Reilly and Harvey Weinstein. But every big news organization has gotten into the act. The *Los Angeles Times* has produced hard-hitting reporting about its homegrown entertainment industry. The *Times-Picayune*, not surprisingly, has gone after the chefs who are its local celebrities. And the *Post* blew up the Alabama Senate race with the story of abuses by Republican nominee Roy Moore.

From where I sit, these are not just stories. This is the stirring of newsrooms that are once again feeling their power, their ability to influence events. It is an important event, really, a moment the country and our industry should relish. If the late 1990s were the beginning of the storm that tore apart the nation's newsrooms, changing them forever, then it is possible that 2017 will be seen as the year a settling wind set in.

—DEAN BAQUET
New York, 2018

Opposite: In the San Francisco Bay Area, an array of newspaper vending machines sell five different daily newspapers.

CHAPTER 1

PUBLISHING UNWELCOME TRUTHS SINCE 1690

ook around you, at everyone you see—at your kitchen table, at a restaurant, in a store or an airport, on the street. Next: imagine taking every smartphone and tablet and laptop out of everybody's hands, and replacing them with a newspaper.

Now you have an inkling of how American life looked in the great age of newspapers, when every day—and sometimes twice a day—the spread of millions of copies of a few ounces of ink and paper, changed the course of lives and nations.

Today, whether by ink or by bytes, it still does.

In dozens of languages, the paper—the printed newspaper—is still a classroom and a boardroom and a playroom. It amuses and entertains; it provokes and outrages; and above all, it puts us in the know, and in the same room with the truth.

Newspapers have always been how Americans talk to and about one another—to the family four blocks over, or about the stranger in the far-off world. Papers speak in the pages of store-

front weeklies in tumbleweed prairie towns, the local dailies that cover hometown doings with gusto and heart, and the influential journals published in powerful cities. Newspapers are neighbors, and they make neighbors.

The American newspaper was born, uniquely, in a country that was already literate. America desperately wanted, and depended on, news to establish itself as a nation. Any new settlement of a few hundred people didn't consider itself a real town until someone had lugged a printing press over mountains or across deserts to print a newspaper.

When one precious copy made it through to some way-the-hell-and-gone gold-mining town, miners who slavered for news forked over as much as a dollar apiece to gather and hear the loudest fellow among them stand on a tree stump and bellow out every single article. In Delphos, Kansas, in 1879, the cyclone that flattened much of the town also whirled away the contents of the brand-new weekly newspaper, the *Delphos Herald*. But the editor,

Opposite: Postcard, April 1912. Readers are eager for news of the sinking of RMS *Titanic*, April 1912.

A reader with *USA Today*, the flagship newspaper of the Gannett newspaper chain. When it debuted in 1982, it got the nickname "McPaper" for its fast-read layout of super-short stories, big, bright graphics and large photos, but the format has since been picked up by newspapers nationwide. Undated.

David Loudon, rummaged through the wreckage and salvaged enough lead type and paper to put together an issue of the newspaper in the town square, running it off on a press he cobbled together in the ruins of the newspaper building.

Why do we *need* newspapers? Because democracy cannot survive without news. That's the Founding Fathers talking. The press's mission—its job description—is uniquely set out in the First Amendment of the Bill of Rights: "Congress shall make no law…abridging the freedom of speech, or of the press…."

In a democracy, the people exercise the power, and to do their jobs as citizens, they need reliable, regular information. Before he became "the most trusted man in America," CBS News anchorman Walter Cronkite was a Texas newspaperman and United Press war correspondent. Here's what he had to say about real news: "A democracy ceases to be a democracy if its citizens do not participate in its governance. To participate intelligently, they must know what their government has done, is doing and plans to do in their name . . . . This is the meaning of freedom of the press. It is not just important to democracy; it *is* democracy."

In the Stephen King novel *Under the Dome*, a Homeland Security official who needs to find a local man in a hurry calls up the town's newspaper editor. "In my experience," he tells the newswoman, "town politicians know a little, the town cops know a lot, and the local newspaper editor knows everything."

Not always *everything*, naturally, but readers have always relied on a newspaper's ability to discover information that isn't easy for them to come by. People depend on newspapers to help them decide who gets their votes, what schools to send their kids to, whether to open a business, where to go on vacation, how to invest.

Ordinary Americans can't skip work or leave the kids to devote weeks to investigating whether bids for a new town sewer are legit, to look into suspicious campaign contributions to a new state senator, or to track how the prices of life-saving prescription drugs are being manipulated. That's the work that reporters do every day, on their behalf. Alice Ollstein, a reporter for the online news site Talking Points Memo, overheard a veteran reporter explaining the job to a little girl visiting Capitol Hill in 2018: "The whole country can't be here watching Congress, so someone has to be here to tell everyone what's going on."

A newspaper is paper and ink that is stronger than steel. It is the fish-wrap warrior of free speech. It is the people's intelligence service, dedicated first and foremost to informing, to watching, to warning about, to holding accountable to the public's eye whoever possesses power and influence over others.

And even if the day comes that the "paper" part disappears, and the newspaper exists only online, it will still be as necessary in the twenty-first century as it was in the eighteenth.

Paradoxically, in this online age of the so-called obsolete newspaper, a website that wants to look credible and authoritative may put up Old English or Gothic type font for a masthead—just like a newspaper—and adopt a name like the *Times* or the *Examiner*, to sound like a solid, old-school newspaper.

If you picked up a newspaper from two hundred years ago—you can buy one on eBay, with change back from fifty dollars—the topics and the names would be strange to you, but the format would be instantly familiar, and for good reason: it works.

The devoted newspaper reader and senior media writer for *Politico*, Jack Shafer, believes that the printed newspaper page "is an amazingly sophisticated technology for showing you what's important, and showing you a lot of it.... I'd argue that even the serendipity of reading in newsprint surpasses the serendipity of reading online, which was supposed to be one of the virtues of the digital world."

There's a telling little scene in the 1987 romantic comedy *Roxanne*. C.D. Bayles (played by Steve Martin) buys a newspaper from a coin-operated newspaper rack. He scans the headlines, doubles over in horror, jams more coins into the vending machine, and stuffs the newspaper back inside.

Now why, readers wonder, is so much real news also bad news? Everyone feels that way sometimes—*doom! gloom! disaster!* every darn day, right? But news—thankfully—is about the exceptions. When the

Russian paper *City Reporter* in Rostov-on-Don tried publishing just good news for a day in 2014, with headlines like NO DISRUPTION ON THE ROADS DESPITE SNOW, its readership dropped by two-thirds. News is about things that don't go as planned. It isn't news when your governor doesn't embezzle. It isn't a surprise when schoolrooms fill with students every day. You shouldn't be stunned when safe water comes out of the kitchen faucet each morning, which is why the Flint, Michigan, water crisis became such big news.

Any day you open your paper and *don't* read that the sun still rises and sets, the tides still ebb and flow, and the sky is still blue—in the big picture, that's actually a good news day.

If you're thinking, "Why should I care about any of this? I don't get my news from a newspaper," you're probably wrong.

Here's why:

Back in February 1979, during Jimmy Carter's presidency, farmers who were angry that interest rates and crop prices were bankrupting them converged on Washington, D.C., to protest. The tractorcade messed up traffic something fierce, and *Los Angeles Times* reporter Paul Houston saw a woman stuck in the tangle leap out of her car and shout at the farmers, *I don't need*

Snapshot of a multi-tasking man on a toilet reading the newspaper and petting the dog. 1958.

you farmers! I get my food at the grocery store!

Newspapers today are like farmers. People think, Oh, I don't need newspapers—I get my news from Facebook or Twitter. But Facebook is only the messenger, not the message. Facebook doesn't have reporters at city hall; Twitter isn't covering the Pentagon. Track back some online news story you read, through all the links and clicks, and odds are that it originally came from a newspaper, very possibly a hometown paper like your own.

Whether it's read on phones or tablets or laptops, almost every scrap of real news comes from real reporting and editing. And most of that still comes from real newspapers—the big national news outfits, with hundreds of editors and reporters, or a hometown paper that reports on prep sports or the library fundraiser or a local soldier on a foreign battlefront or the corrupt doings of some town pol.

So where *does* the Internet get the news that it spreads but doesn't report?

Baltimore is a case study. In 2010, a Pew Research Center journalism project dug into the city's news ecosystem and found that 95 percent of stories—new, actual information—came from that derided "old media," meaning mostly newspapers, followed by local TV news. It turned out that the "new media"—like Twitter and blogs—were little more than an alert system for passing along reporting others had done.

So the danger for our communities and our democracy is that, as newspapers are forced to prune staff and stories, if they have to close altogether, as more of them are doing, more government and business press releases praising their own "achievements" get posted uncritically online as news—with no context, with no press conference questions, with no reporter-researched story pointing out something like, "However, over the past six years, the numbers have shown something different . . .."

That's real news. Real news is what Alex S. Jones (the journalist, not the conspiracy-minded radio host) calls the "iron core of news." He means the solid, substantive information that makes up the owner's manual of democracy.

What's the definition of journalism? One is *the first draft of history.* Another goes like this: *Journalism is printing what someone else does not want printed; everything else is public relations.* Credit for the first known version of that goes to Kansas's *Atchison Globe*, in 1894: "There are but two classes of people in the world—those who have done something and want their names kept out of the paper, and those who haven't done anything worth printing and want their names put in."

Benjamin Franklin, a newspaperman himself, understood the nature of news: "If all printers were determined not to print anything till they were sure it would offend nobody, there would be very little printed."

Real news may not be as entertaining as the sleazy details of a celebrity divorce. And it takes elbow grease to report and verify. That's why journalists love the true-to-life scene in the movie *All the President's Men*: Robert Redford and Dustin Hoffman, as reporters Bob Woodward and Carl Bernstein, park their butts on hard chairs in the Library of Congress and thumb through literally hundreds of checkout slips to fact-check their story about the

Four women read a Sunday paper. *Parade* magazine began appearing as a Sunday supplement in 1941. ca.1950

Watergate scandal.

Reporters unearth real news in the minutes of the local planning commission, the annual reports of influential businesses, the arrest logs of the police, the fine print in a statehouse budget, or the costs of combat waged with billions of tax dollars—all the painstaking pieces of the stories.

This raw material is analyzed and evaluated by reporters and editors who know their subjects. Every newspaper story passes through several sets of hands and eyes—and the bigger the story, the more hands and eyes assess and question it. Hours, and sometimes days or months, can pass before an editor finally hits the *publish* button. It is not a perfect system, not by a long shot, but every day, by fits and starts and setbacks, it grinds its way toward the perfect. John Steinbeck planted the seeds

Three generations of men are engrossed in the newspaper *al fresco.* ca. 1915

of his magisterial novel *The Grapes of Wrath* in a 1936 series on migrant workers that he wrote for the *San Francisco News.* Two decades later, in 1956, he wrote this:

> What can I say about journalism? It has the greatest virtue and the greatest evil. It is the mother of literature and the perpetrator of crap. In many cases it is the only history we have and yet it is the tool of the worst men. But over a long period of time, and because it is the product of so many men, it is perhaps the purest thing we have.

You hear the phrase *curated media!* tossed at newspapers as an insult—as if "curated" means "censored." But *curated* is a badge of honor, a synonym for fact-checked. It's why newspapers get quoted more often than many online sites that call

themselves news: if it's in a newspaper, it's a good bet that someone fact-checked it first.

A hundred fifty years ago, readers could choose newspapers that mirrored their class and their politics, from dignified broadsheets, to lurid screamers, to populist pot-stirrers. Today, newspapers crowd into the middle of the road politically, but people tend to drift into their own corners when it comes to the information they read or watch or listen to. Read something you don't agree with, and you may decide it's biased—"fake news." That's human nature. We like what we agree with.

In 2017, a Knight/Gallup survey discovered that even when a factual and accurate story made a politician or a political group look bad, 40 percent of Republicans said it should "always" be called "fake news." During the Reagan years, the *Journal of Personality and Social Psychology* monitored people who self-identified on opposite sides of an issue—in this case, a massacre in Lebanon—and watched identical TV news stories on the topic. Afterward, each side was firmly convinced that the news stories were biased against its point of view and in favor of the opposite side.

Now, a newspaper's daily to-do list is simple: watch to see what's changing, find out why, and keep a skeptical eye on the

people in power. That's exactly what the Founders intended newspapers to do. They remembered that before there was a United States and a Constitution, newspapers could not do that.

Four hundred years ago, in 1617, the royal governor of Virginia thanked God that Virginia had no publishers operating without government license, "for learning has brought disobedience." As the British Crown itself once cautioned the colonial governor of Massachusetts, "Great inconvenience may arise by the liberty of printing."

Bring it on!

A little girl settles down to read the newspaper. 1962.

CHAPTER 2

REAL NEWS: WHO, WHAT, WHERE, WHEN, HOW

Millions read newspapers every day, have read them for years, without knowing much about the recipe, the alchemy of just who puts together this twenty-four-hour diary of a day and how they do it. What kind of job-opening ad would a newspaper list to fill a desk in its newsroom?

WANTED: NEWSPAPER REPORTER/EDITOR

QUALIFICATIONS:

- *A fast, fluent writer.* What's the use of knowing something to tell if you don't know how to tell it? Newspaper people use the language interestingly and accurately. As Mark Twain put it, "The difference between the almost right word and the right word is really a large matter—'tis the difference between the lightning-bug and the lightning."

- *Curious.* Journalists drive their families and friends nuts by constantly wondering aloud, "Would that be a good story?" As a little boy in the Depression-era Bronx, future news-legend Gabe Pressman published a weekly family newspaper, the *Hot News*, with grabber headlines like COUSIN TEDDY CUTS TOOTH. A whimsical bulletin-board note put up years ago at the *Orange County Register* read "Jack and Jill went up the hill," and the staff scribbled the sort of questions journalists would ask if Jack and Jill were a real story: "What were they doing at the well?" "Which hill?" "Was the water source clean/tested?" "Why did Jack go home vs to urgent care to mend his head?" "Did we talk to neighbors at the bottom of the hill?" "Seems counterintuitive to go UP a hill to get water?"

- *A Wiki-brain.* In 1921, the stupendously smart *New York Times* managing editor Carr Van Anda was editing a story about a lecture Albert Einstein gave at Princeton. He found a mistake in one of Einstein's equations. Einstein acknowledged the slip-up with thanks. Not everyone in journalism has to be a Van Anda, but all journalists carry between their ears gigabytes of information that outstrip Google. Having all that helps them to write stories that assess where the latest development fits into the

Opposite: Weeks after the December 7 attack on Pearl Harbor, *Honolulu Star-Bulletin* newsroom windows were blacked out; staffers were ready for news. January 1942.

big-picture context of that story. Plus, these are the people you want on your trivia-night team.

- *Skeptical.* The old newsroom commandment goes: If your mother says she loves you, check it out. Good reporters and editors are like Toto in *The Wizard of Oz.* While others stand shivery-kneed before official smoke and bluster, they're yanking back the curtain to find out what's really behind all that noise. By nature, they're contrarians, not true believers. The news itself is contrarian. What makes news is the exception, not the usual. Journalists also have to play by rules that their neighbors, even their own spouses, don't. Reporters can't have a personal stake in a story. An education reporter can't cover his child's school. Even reporters and editors who don't cover politics can't donate to campaigns or candidates. Some political reporters don't vote, because they believe voting means subliminally preferring one candidate over another.

- *Competitive.* In May 1983, *Los Angeles Times* newsman Eric Malnic—who'd been shot at covering the Watts riots in 1965—had to helicopter into Fresno, California, about sixty miles away, to cover an earthquake in the town of Coalinga, where the airspace was closed. Once he landed in Fresno, Malnic nabbed one airport taxi and paid off the rest to skedaddle. When competing reporters flew in a bit later, they were stuck looking for rides. Meanwhile, Malnic's taxi raced ahead to Coalinga. Newspapers compete against time, against other news agencies, and now against internet rumor-mongering, to get it first if they can—but first, to get it right. Being second is never as awful as being wrong.

There's no age requirement to competitiveness. In April 2016, the *Orange Street News*—whose editor and publisher, Hilde Kate Lysiak, usually covered local council meetings and drug busts in Selinsgrove, Pennsylvania—beat the competition to the story of a murder on Ninth Street. Hilde was in third grade, and her father used to be a *New York Daily News* reporter. Not everyone was impressed with her initiative. To her online critics, Hilde posted a video response: "If you want me to stop covering news,

Less than a week after graduating Vassar in 1927, H. Katherine Smith, who was blind, was hired by the *Buffalo Courier-Express*. She wrote feature columns called "Good Listener" and "Men You Ought to Know." Volunteers read her information that she couldn't get in Braille. Her dog Quinta was identified as her "sight-seeing dog" by the long-ago photographer who took this picture.

then you get off your computers and do something about the news. There, is that cute enough for you?"

- *Resourceful.* Theo Wilson covered California crimes and trials for the *New York Daily News.* During a court break in the notorious Manson case, she told the mass murderer Charles Manson to "shut up" for threatening reporters. This New York gal never learned to drive and took cabs everywhere. One day in 1976, she called a taxi to take her from her home in Hollywood to cover the kidnapping of a bus full of children—in someplace called Chowchilla, 250 miles away. Like water,

Press credentials like this Kansas license plate, along with identifiers worn around the neck, make it easier for law enforcement and firefighters to recognize accredited journalists authorized to cross police and fire lines.

In August 1880, six years after the town of Kingman, Kansas, was founded, the staff of the *Mercury* assembled for this image. The paper was founded in 1878, and Kingman—population about 350—became a two-newspaper town when the *Citizen* started up a year later.

corrections ever? For a 2017 *New York Times* piece about a dog rescuing a drowning fawn: "An earlier version of this article misidentified the breed of Storm the dog. He is a golden retriever, not a Labrador retriever. (He is still a good boy.)"

The *Los Angeles Times*'s 1938 stylebook laid out the ideal standard: "Be so accurate that the fate of a human life can rest with safety upon the facts you assemble." Because sometimes, it might.

Theo Wilson, the *New York Daily News* reporter, in November 1966. Not too long thereafter, she moved to Los Angeles to cover the city's flashy crimes and trials. In retirement, she started a little newspaper for the Hollywood Hills, and after she died, her corner of the neighborhood was named Theo Wilson Square.

reporters find their way around obstacles in their path.

- **First-rate nitpicking skills.** The best reporters and editors never think good enough is good enough. Only deadlines can wrench from their hands something they've cross-checked for facts and proofread for details like correct prepositions (did the murder happen *in*, or *on*, or *near* the property?). People whose careers are spent calling out public figures who do wrong have to be maniacs about getting things right themselves. Getting it wrong means being embarrassed in print twice—first by the mistake and then by the printed correction. One of the best

Are journalists Donald Trump's "enemy of the people?" Hardly. Fair play, the rule of law, democracy—real newspeople get a little moist-eyed about these principles. Newspaper investigations bust the chops of conniving public officials, and the double-dealing rich and mighty, when they screw over the public by not playing by these rules, or by tilting the playing field their way.

Journalism is not a hobby. Professional journalists make a livelihood by reporting, writing, photographing, or editing for a newspaper, magazine, broadcast, or online site that regularly publishes or airs fact-checked, contextualized news; curated current information; and researched analysis from credible, informed sources.

The *La Crosse Tribune* in Wisconsin

was founded in 1904 after a local electric company monopoly was cheating citizens without so much as a peep out of the two existing local papers, whose owners had a hefty interest in the power companies. In Tennessee, the *Knoxville News* was the new paper in town in 1921, and it wasted no time proving that city and county governments were rotted through, top to bottom—hospitals, jails, cops, water and sewer systems—all of it as crooked as an M.C. Escher skyline.

Real journalists—not the commentariat who use the word as a shield for doing partisan hack jobs—have at some point worked shoe-leather stories about fires and floods, covered courts, cops, plane crashes, or city hall. They've written obituaries, slogged through piles of public records or business filings, phoned sources for interviews, fact-checked on deadline, and hung out in state capitals or city halls to buttonhole some politician for comment. And then they've done it all again the next day.

So that's what makes good reporters. What makes good stories? What reporter doesn't long to be the first to file a story from the moon?

Closer to home, every day, stories come from city hall, the White House, the courts, business boardrooms, and school boards. Police are the taxpayers' most visible employees, and every paper covers their deeds and misdeeds. Crime has always been a big part of newspapers' coverage, and most mainstream papers were

pretty deferential to the police versions of events. But as newspapers in the civil rights era of the 1960s began to cover police abuses of minority Americans and of antiwar protests more skeptically and aggressively, the chummy relationship between police and some police reporters became an arm's-length one. But those arms still aren't long enough for some Americans' liking.

The most-read item in some local newspapers is the police blotter. It's a compiled log of police calls that reads like part law enforcement, part gossip, and all about a town. "It's like watching the *Jerry Springer Show*," one reader told California's Grass Valley *Union*. "You feel better about your life after you've read it." Here's a choice sample, from Colorado's *Greeley Tribune* on April 11, 2013, at 12:21 p.m.: "A caller in West Greeley reported there was a very large, black bird in the back yard with a wingspan of 2 feet. The caller said the bird was not being aggressive but was scary because of its size. Officers found the bird was actually a barbecue cover."

A typical press identification card, this was issued in 1969 to a Pearl River, New York-based staffer for the *Bergen Record*, a New Jersey newspaper. Its crackerjack investigative teams have uncovered misdeeds like the 2013 "Bridgegate" abuse of power scandal, which got two members of Governor Chris Christie's administration sentenced to federal prison.

The comings and goings of ocean liners and their glamorous passengers were already major news before World War II, so the arrival of the German passenger airship *Hindenburg* drew an eager crowd of newsmen and newsreel photographers to New Jersey on May 6, 1937. The airship caught fire as it landed, and thirty-six people died. Here, the press crowds into a briefing room for official updates on the disaster, with names of survivors listed on the blackboard.

Story ideas also come from what reporters and editors see around them, and what readers tell them about. That's why newsrooms need to be as diverse as the Americans who read their stories, by gender identity and sexual orientation, race, ethnicity, faith, and geographic and economic backgrounds. That's why newsrooms of the past were sometimes as narrow and straight as the neckties worn by the white guys who populated them. It didn't occur to them that their coverage was inadequate by omission, and sometimes biased by commission.

At the *San Francisco Chronicle* in the 1980s, a gay man named Randy Shilts was the first journalist at a major paper to

Georgia Democratic governor Jimmy Carter holds an impromptu airborne press conference on September 11, 1976, during his campaign for president. Covering presidential candidates is an indispensable but expensive obligation of newspapers, and it isn't a free ride. Flying on campaign planes can cost double the standard airfares, or more. During George H.W. Bush's 1988 presidential campaign, the *Washington Post* said that a campaign aide came through the plane with a credit card reader to get reporters' credit information, in case their home offices dragged their feet about paying. In 2009, the White House Correspondents' Association calculated the news media's tab for covering presidential trips at $18 million, not including covering vice presidents' or cabinet members' travels. As news agencies cut expenses everywhere, including politics and the president, fewer ears and eyeballs are monitoring and questioning the men and women at the top.

report groundbreaking, comprehensive stories about a mysterious, fatal disease that was the emerging AIDS epidemic. New newsroom demographics, along with more civic-minded journalism and public interest, are remaking newspapers into the "mirror" that newspaper names suggest they are.

Potential stories arise 24/7. A question from a worried parent to a journalist at their kids' soccer game helps to unearth a story about a consumer scam. Someone recognizes a reporter in a car repair shop waiting room and passes along a tip about layoffs coming at a local business. One unfilled pothole is not a story, but when neighbors see a crew from a company owned by the mayor's brother unexpectedly repairing the street—that might be news.

Every day, too, journalists' email overflows with press releases from a public relations industry built on getting out a positive message about a company or a product via the press. Just about every business of any size, every university, every celebrity, every elected official—even the pope and the queen of England—have PR people. You could fill a day's paper with nothing but their press releases, but a journalist's correct reaction to every press release is "Really?"

Some press releases turn out to be newsworthy: a medical journal has details of a solidly tested breakthrough for lupus, let's say. But reporters are wary with reason, and they don't take these at face value. A splashy press release about a study that indicates more sugar is better for you comes from a place we'll call the American Edible Energy Institute. Sounds authentic, right? But a reporter does some checking and finds that the American Edible Energy Institute is, in fact, an operation dreamed up and bankrolled by candymakers solely to spin sugar into PR gold. Some industries, most notoriously "Big Tobacco," have set up institutes and foundations to try to undermine legitimate research with industry-friendly slants. In this business, you can never lift up too many rocks.

The newspaper's advertising department earns a lot of the money that the newsroom spends, and the wall between advertising and reporting is supposed to be airtight, so that an advertiser can't influence coverage of its industry by threatening to yank its ads. The war between these two "souls" of a newspaper can claim its share of victims.

In 1982, according to David B. Sachsman and Warren Sloat in their book *The Press and the Suburbs*, a big advertiser in a New Jersey city announced a "financial reorganization" via press release. The general manager of the *Trenton Times* promised the advertiser that the press release would run verbatim, and the editor told the business reporter—who was on his first day on the job—to run the press release word-for-word, no cuts, no additions. But the reporter followed the journalism rule to check it out, and duly reported that this was actually a Chapter 11 bankruptcy. He

A monstrous landslide in Seattle in December 1921 summoned scores of rescuers to search for a missing family. As they dug, a second landslide rolled toward them. Ernest D. Tyler, a reporter for the *Seattle Star*, became front-page news in his own paper because he saw the second slide coming and ran to warn the diggers, who scrambled out of the mudslide's path. "A moment later, Tyler was buried in an avalanche of mud. He was rescued by diggers and managed to tell the *Star* of his experience over the telephone." It's a reminder that journalists are people first and last.

was fired for insubordination. About a dozen other journalists quit in solidarity, and the paper had to scramble to clear up what became a public embarrassment about whether advertisers were dictating the news. Newspapers need advertising money to survive, but even more, newspapers need credibility to attract readers—and more advertising.

Just by starting with that question—"Really?"—reporters have turned up impostors who claim to have seen combat or won medals when they did not. In 2011, a *Chicago Tribune* reporter decided to check out a burn surgeon's horrific testimony of babies burned to death be-cause of non-flame-retardant upholstered furniture.

Over a year's work, reporters discovered not only that there were no babies who died as the surgeon described, but that he was being paid by a chemical industry front group running a campaign to keep flame-retardant requirements on the books, without evidence that the rules prevented house fires. In fact, the chemicals could potentially harm human fertility and be linked to cancer.

How do editors decide who should cover what? If you think of a newspaper as a sports team, you can understand assignments for reporters and editors.

If a football metaphor works, here's this: publishers are the team owners; top editors are the coaches crafting team strategy; news and assignment editors are the quarterbacks calling the plays for reporters to carry out; and copy editors are the defensive line, checking and vetting to keep mistakes and confusing writing from getting through.

Baseball fan? In baseball, a player doesn't play every position. A shortstop is not also a catcher. So, too, newspapers have beats, like baseball positions. Beats are subjects so important that reporters are assigned to them—city hall, a local sports team, police and courts, health care, national security, business, consumer issues, agriculture, high tech. Beat stories are a newspaper's bread and butter, and the bigger the newspaper, the more beats there are. At a smaller paper, the same reporter may cover city hall and also get sent out to cover a fire. Bigger newspapers may have beat reporters who are music or movie critics, consumer reporters, political reporters, and book reviewers.

Beat reporters cultivate sources. A source isn't someone sinister or secretive. A source is just a knowledgeable person whom a reporter contacts for expert insights and to act as a "sounding board" on something the reporter is looking into. Usually sources are quoted by name; far more rarely, and only when editors agree to it, are they cited anonymously.

Reporters have to figure out a Goldilocks relationship with a source—not too near, not too far. Sources want to put their spin on things. Especially when a person demands anonymity, a reporter must balance that source's motives with the value of getting important news to the public. Reporters have to be wary of getting "played."

Into the 1950s, the Los Angeles Police Department issued this kind of badge to newspapers' police beat reporters. Instead of the officer rank, the badge read "reporter."

In 2004, the *New York Times* public editor wrote critically about the paper's occasionally "credulous" coverage of allegations of weapons of mass destruction in Iraq. A source who lies damages the paper's relationship with readers. At the other end of the spectrum, journalists need to be careful that the valuable and vital journalism equation of giving voice to both sides doesn't create false equivalency, giving one point of view a weight it doesn't merit, like climate-change denial.

Once in a while, when newspapers are in possession of sensitive information about crime or national security, reporters and editors may negotiate with law enforcement and security officials about what *not* to print. In 2017, a *Washington Post* story about the consequences of President Trump revealing closely held secrets about an Islamic State (ISIS) plot to Russian diplomats withheld "most plot details . . . at the urging of officials who warned that revealing them would jeopardize important intelligence capabilities," the paper noted.

Most of the work government does is public information—government information that belongs to the public. Yet reporters looking for even the most basic public records sometimes run into pushback and foot-dragging from government employees who refuse to follow the law, and from lawmakers in cities and states who try to keep everything they do se-

cret—whether it's the salaries of college campus cops in Arkansas, or financial statements about Iowa casinos, information that had been public for decades until legislators gave gambling lobbyists what they wanted and walled off the data.

In January 2018, the Clark County, Nevada, coroner was not only ordered to turn over all the public records about the 2017 Las Vegas massacre that the *Review-Journal* had been trying for six months to get, but the judge told the coroner to pay the newspaper for the legal costs of having to go to court in the first place.

It took the *Journal News* in New York about two years of legal appeals to force counties across the state line from Newtown, Connecticut, to obey the law and hand over public records, the names and addresses of pistol-permit holders. (An editor's note pointed out that the reporter on the story also owned a gun, a .357 Magnum.) The paper had to hire armed guards because of some menacing responses, and furious bloggers posted some of the paper's journalists' addresses online in retaliation.

A human chain rescues reporter William Dredge, center, who sank into a hole as he was covering a 1954 mudslide in the San Gabriel Mountain foothills above Los Angeles. Hauling Dredge to safety are flood-control workers on the right, and, on the left, newspaper reporter Nieson Himmel, keeping a grip on his hat. Beginning in the "noir" era of the 1940s, Himmel became a legendary Los Angeles crime reporter. Sometimes partnered with a 500-pound photographer called "Tiny" Rutherford, he cruised the city for news. Himmel knew the players in the city's mobbed-up underworld, and covered the notorious, unsolved 1947 mutilation murder of a young woman who went by the moniker "The Black Dahlia." In L.A.'s car culture, Himmel never actually owned one. He rented a vehicle by the day, and when he'd filled it to the gunwales with junk-food wrappers and old newspapers, he turned it in for another.

Reporters don't write stories just by emptying the contents of their notebooks onto their computer screens. About 40 percent of those notes make it directly into the story, but the other 60 percent shape the story, too. Writers must research and analyze what shouldn't appear in a story as much as what should, before ever striking a key on the keyboard.

So putting a stake in the heart of rumor and untruth is as critical as writing up legit information. It takes thirty seconds to tweet a rumor, but hours of diligent work

Acres of newsprint were spent covering and debating evolution around the 1925 Scopes trial, a test case for a Tennessee law that criminalized the teaching of evolution in public schools. In Nebraska, the *Hastings Daily Tribune* took advantage of hot news and made a souvenir pocket mirror with this provocative image and inquiry on its flip side.

to track down the truth or untruth of it. Proof, verification, confirmation: those are the standards that, like evidence of a crime, sort real from rumor. If some astounding thing you read online isn't in the newspaper, it's likely because there's no truth to it, or it didn't meet the newspaper's standards for being demonstrably, provably true.

On any given day, from Pennsylvania to North Dakota to Arizona, the front pages of America's newspapers can print such a different array of stories that you can hardly believe they're all covering the same twenty-four hours in the same country.

And with good reason. News is weighted by geography, too. On the day the top story in an Oklahoma paper is about a fracking-generated earthquake, the top story in a Colorado paper is about the state marijuana law. Hometown newspapers' first job is reporting the news of the place where *you* live. It takes a story of hefty national import—a president's diplomatic misstep, a terrorist threat—to bump

the news of a fire in the local factory off the front page.

The local paper has been there all season, covering the Cinderella high school team that sweeps the state finals, and it's been there writing the blow-by-blow, day-by-day stories about that new water-saving rule your city will have to follow.

Over and over, reporting changes lives and saves lives—in local papers along with the big-name mastheads. In a 2016 Pulitzer Prize–winning series, investigative reporter Eric Eyre of the *Charleston Gazette-Mail* laid out the details of drug wholesalers' ferociously protected data and the toll of opioid painkillers on West Virginia: the highest opioid death rate in the nation.

Eyre found that in two years, companies had shipped *nine million* hydrocodone pills to a single drugstore in the village of Kermit, population 392. No wonder the drug sellers didn't want anyone to know that. Things began changing in West Virginia—and in Washington—because of those stories.

Turn that formula around, and a big national story can focus on something as intimate as one soldier's life and death.

A Delta Force commando named Joshua Wheeler was the first American soldier to die in combat against ISIS. He was killed in 2015 as he was helping to free seventy condemned prisoners. A *Washington Post*

story reminded readers that beyond his gravestone at Arlington National Cemetery were Wheeler's fourteen tours of duty; a marriage; four sons; and five brothers and sisters he had looked after as they grew up, cooking them breakfast, fixing the ponytails in his sister's hair before she went to school. A newspaper story made him everyone's brother, everyone's dad, everyone's husband.

Every newspaper's best-known names are usually its columnists, experienced reporters promoted to write regularly, with personality and style, about their insights on politics, sports, or culture and lifestyle matters.

They're the wise men and women in Washington, D.C., who make sense of the clanking machinery of government, the local lifestyle columnists who can find something profound and touching in the middle-school bake sale, and the sports columnist who likens this season's tough high school basketball schedule to the labors of Hercules.

The household god of sports columnists, Red Smith brought pure literature to the playing field with this description of a 1951 baseball playoff game: "Pennants are waving, uplifted fists are brandished, hats are flying. Again and again the dark clubhouse windows blaze with the light of photographers' flash bulbs." Smith's Pulitzer Prize was of lesser renown compared to the fact that, in his 1950 novel *Across the River and Into the Trees*, Ernest Hemingway wrote that one of his characters "was reading Red Smith, and he liked him very much."

Some of newspapers' most beloved journalists aren't the Beltway big names. They're rip-snorting local columnists like Mike Royko, who worked at three Chicago newspapers—and at each of them, gleefully barbecued the city's besmirched political system and its bulldozer of a mayor, Richard J. Daley.

Columnist Molly Ivins made Texas politics her target-rich beat. For ten years of her career, she wrote stingingly of the state's elected mugs and thugs for the *Dallas Times Herald*. (Her short gig as a reporter at the *New York Times* that began in the late 1970s was a doomed mismatch between the solemn "newspaper of record" and the six-foot-tall woman who worked in bare feet and jeans.) Her description of a big New Mexico chicken killing and cookout holiday as a "gang-pluck" never made print, but the fact that she even wrote it made it clear she was not *Times* material.

The *San Francisco Chronicle*'s beloved Herb Caen made "three-dot journalism" his trademark. Almost every day for almost sixty years, Caen strung together a handful of short, witty, insightful items that gave

TOP COLUMNISTS AND THEIR SPIN

News reporters cover the news, straight up and down. Columnists put their own style and spin on topics. Spokane's *Spokesman-Review* sent out this promotional parade entry, probably for the city's Lilac Festival parade, in the year or two before the event was suspended in 1943 due to the war. Aboard the "Calling all stars to write for the *Spokesman-Review*" truck, a switchboard operator sits at a dummy switchboard under an arch decorated with the faces of the paper's columnists. Few of them are remembered now, but then, they were nationally renowned.

Cartoonist Rudolph Dirks created the *Katzenjammer Kids* and later the *Captain and the Kids* comic strip. J.N. "Ding" Darling was a double Pulitzer Prize-winning editorial cartoonist whose drawings advocating wildlife conservation caught the eye of President Franklin Roosevelt, who named him to head the forerunner of the U.S. Fish and Wildlife Service. There's a wildlife refuge in Florida named for him. Dr. Irving S. Cutter's syndicated column was called "How to Keep Well." Irvin S. Cobb wrote with insight and humor about public affairs. He had a cigar named after him, and he hosted the 1935 Academy Awards. "Mrs. Roosevelt," Eleanor Roosevelt, wrote her "My Day" column from 1935 until shortly before she died, in 1962. Emily Post's columns really did help socially uncertain Americans learn good manners and conduct, and her family has continued her work. "Ripley's Believe It or Not!" was Robert L. Ripley's syndicated cartoon panel showcasing the world's bizarre and astonishing events and people.

J. Edgar Hoover used his newspaper column to thump his chest about Americanism in particular and the FBI in general. Myrtle Meyer Eldred's "Your Baby and Mine" column laid the groundwork for all sorts of advice columns on child-rearing. The influential journalist Dorothy Thompson, second only to Eleanor Roosevelt in "most admired American woman" polls, wrote penetrating columns on international affairs from the hot seat of Europe for more than twenty years.

San Francisco a small-town intimacy.

The sober work of national political columnists, from Walter Lippmann in the 1920s to David Brooks in 2017, has been influential in every marble building in Washington, D.C. Their columns appear in the opinion-editorial section of newspapers—which operate independently of the regular news staff, something readers don't always understand. It's here that newspapers make political candidate endorsements, too.

Angry readers who don't like an editorial can vent in letters to the editor, or make their points by canceling their subscriptions. But in the Bronx, New York, the weekly *Riverdale Press,* with a circulation of about 10,000, got firebombed in 1989 for its editorial defending people's right to read Salman Rushdie's controversial novel *The Satanic Verses.* Its offices were wrecked, the telephones melted by the heat, but it still managed to put out a paper, with a front-page editorial headlined "We shall not be silenced."

Just the job title "foreign correspondent" sounds like a life of potent cocktails and potentates, but the correspondent's life

For half the twentieth century, Herb Caen's sprightly columns in the *San Francisco Chronicle* delighted the City by the Bay. His farewell gift was his funeral fireworks display—the *pièce de résistance* was a blazing likeness of his manual typewriter, his "loyal Royal."

is stressful and sometimes grim. From counting drone strikes to counting Imelda Marcos's shoes in the name of accuracy, working overseas to bring the world's stories to Americans safely buffered by geography and bulwarked by the nation's economic and military powers is no cream-puff task.

Correspondents' stories humanize the world, putting readers right there with women demanding to drive in Saudi Arabia, Poles arguing over whose accounts to tell in their World War II museum, Africans buying castoff American clothes and inadvertently crashing the traditional textile industry.

Early foreign correspondents covered a war and then hustled back home. In 1838, the *New York Herald* publisher James Gordon Bennett Sr. signed up a half-dozen men to write about Europe—*in* Europe. Adolescent America was coming to realize that its cotton export market depended on matters thousands of miles away, that something as far-off as the Crimean War could affect the fortunes of wheat farmers in Minnesota, and that Americans needed to read news about it.

Bennett's son hired an Englishman for one of the most renowned stunts in

newspapering—and the payoff quote that may not actually have been uttered. He sent Henry Morton Stanley to find what had become of David Livingstone, an antislavery crusader and African explorer who had vanished from Western eyes. In October 1871, Stanley found Livingstone and greeted him with four words he may have dreamed up later, to doll up the story that became a worldwide sensation: "Dr. Livingstone, I presume?"

The foreign correspondent had no more pugnacious, truth-to-power role model than newspaperman George Seldes.

American political conventions draw thousands more journalists than there are delegates. Credentials are issued to cover the doings, like these from the Democrats' 1988 convention and the Republicans' 1984 convention. Still more coveted are floor passes that allow reporters access to the convention floor to talk to the delegates, candidates, and wheeler-dealers. Most major special events, from tech conventions to concerts, issue similar press passes.

In 1947, Portland's *Oregon Journal* added a helicopter, the *Newsroom Dragonfly*, to its news-gathering arsenal. Photos taken from it were a competitive sensation. When the airborne news crew hovered above a fire in the building of the competing newspaper—*The Oregonian*—one *Oregonian* employee was quoted in a book about the helicopter saying, "Here comes that *Journal* helicopter like a vulture. I'll bet it pours gasoline on the fire." That same year, in December, the helicopter was being piloted by the associate publisher, a World War II veteran, when it crashed, killing him and his passenger. The paper folded in 1982.

In 1918, Seldes was nearly court-martialed by the Allies—French premier Georges Clemenceau flat-out wanted him publicly executed—for daring to interview Germany's defeated commander Paul von Hindenburg after World War I. The interview was spiked, buried, and never published. Then, Seldes was kicked out of Soviet Russia by Lenin, and thereafter booted from Italy by Mussolini.

It was a trifecta for the contrarian reporter who wound up coming home to publish a newsletter, *In Fact*, full of stories that other newspapers wouldn't print, most of them sent to him by the unhappy reporters who wrote them.

Keeping a foreign bureau staffed—even if it's only one seasoned, resourceful correspondent—is monstrously expensive.

KING OF HEADLINES

The cigarette, the hat, the typewriter, the telephone—the United Press wire service's White House correspondent Merriman "Smitty" Smith is the spit and image of the no-guff reporter.

Here, Smitty's up all night updating reports of President Eisenhower's heart attack in Denver in September 1956. In 1945, when President Truman announced the end of World War II to White House reporters, Smitty hurtled to the press room, fell, broke his collarbone, got up, and ran to his phone to dictate the extraordinary news.

In 1963, Smith would cement his reputation as a reporter not to be crossed. On November 22, in Dallas, Texas, Smitty, working for the underdog United Press, and his unfriendly rival, Associated Press reporter Jack Bell, were riding in a press "pool" car not far behind the presidential limo.

In a story for the American Journalism Review, UPI colleague Patrick J. Sloyan recounted that at the bark of gunshots at 12:30 p.m., the epic battle between Smith and Bell began for control of the then-rare radiophone mounted in the car.

Smitty, a gun owner who recognized the sound as gunfire, was closer to the phone. He grabbed it and demanded to be connected to the UPI Dallas office. As Bell hammered at his back to get the phone, Smith dictated into the crackly line the shocking bulletin that would clatter across the teletype into the nation's newsrooms at 12:34 p.m.:

"Three shots were fired at President Kennedy's motorcade in downtown Dallas." Five minutes after that, after seeing JFK's body and talking to a Secret Service agent, Smith dictated the flash that the president had been wounded "perhaps fatally."

Four minutes, nine minutes, sound like an eternity today, but it was lightning-speed then, and for the A.P. competition, it might as well have been nine years.

UPI's Smitty would win the Pulitzer Prize for his assassination coverage, the biggest beat of his, or just about any reporter's, career.

Newspapers used to hand out promotional items— coffee mugs, pens, calendars, sewing kits, and matchbooks like this one from Oregon's short-lived *Portland Reporter*. The newspaper began in 1960, after a strike against Portland's two major papers. Operating a seventy-year-old printing press named "Little David" (as in David and Goliath), the *Reporter* ran up some respectable circulation numbers against the two non-union papers, thanks to its local news coverage by a unionized staff. Five years into the occasionally bloody newspaper wars, the *Reporter* closed up shop. Newer, cheaper printing technology won, and labor lost. This would be the story at newspaper after newspaper, where technology looked even more alluring as newspapers moved from private ownership to publicly traded companies, and the pressure for bigger profits rose. Fresh off the paper's Watergate triumph, the *Washington Post*'s striking pressmen and its management engaged in a brutish showdown that management won—a tipping point for newspapers' relationships with pressmen and printers' unions.

The *Brooklyn Eagle* was a powerhouse afternoon paper for more than a century, edited for a couple of years by poet Walt Whitman. Badges identified *Eagle* newsboys; in 1953, one carrier collecting for subscriptions spilled his tips, and a hollow 1948 nickel cracked apart, revealing a square of microfilm hidden inside. The clue cracked a major KGB spy case.

A regular peacetime one-newspaper-reporter bureau can run about three hundred thousand dollars a year. That's why newspapers have closed so many foreign bureaus, sometimes resorting to "parachuting" in a stateside reporter to cover a huge story, or depending on freelancers, either reliable local journalists or on-the-fly American reporters who get paid little and travel light.

Just as going to war is a nation's most solemn responsibility, covering that war is one of journalism's heaviest duties. Reporters monitor the "lives and treasure" at stake, on behalf of Americans whose taxes and reputation pay for them. But oh, the price tag.

The *New Yorker* calculated that it cost the *New York Times* three million dollars a year to maintain its wartime Baghdad bureau. Security, translators, drivers, and local assistants who help correspondents navigate local laws and obstinate local officials; the costs add up—all to get the story, and to get the story out.

Correspondents find their way through thickets of paperwork and harassment meant to stop them from doing their jobs, and across front lines of warring factions.

Paul Watson, a Pulitzer Prize–winning correspondent, wrote in the *Los Angeles Times* about plunging back into Kosovo in 1999, where he was threatened at gunpoint and arrested three times:

While covering more than a dozen wars and uprisings in countries like Somalia, Rwanda, Afghanistan, Iraq, and Indonesia, I developed a sort of war mantra to help ease the panic. "Your fear is what they want," I keep repeating in my mind. "Do not give it to them."

When Iraq invaded Kuwait in 1999, the *Washington Post*'s Caryle Murphy was the only newspaper reporter there. Her name didn't even appear on some of her stories, as her editors tried to help keep her safe on hostile turf where Americans were being hunted down.

In 1978, Greg Robinson, a photographer from the *San Francisco Examiner*, was among the people shot to death on an airstrip in Jonestown, Guyana, on the orders of a lunatic cult leader named Jim Jones, whose followers then committed suicide by the hundreds. Two San Francisco newspaper reporters who'd gone to cover the story were shot and wounded.

Not every dangerous job comes with a uniform.

❦

It took a while for newspapers to be able to print photos, but they made up for lost time.

The first newspaper image that wasn't just another engraved version of a photograph was a halftone of a New York shantytown, "direct from nature," that ran in the *Daily Graphic* in New York on March 4, 1880. The illustrated newspaper took advantage of the skepticism of the *New York Herald*'s publisher, James Gordon Bennett Jr. His art director, Stephen Horgan, suggested the new technology to Bennett, but a Bennett adviser told him Horgan was an idiot. Horgan went right over to the *Graphic* and on to renown.

Smaller cameras and bigger newspapers made newspaper photography an indispensable part of telling the story. The legendary New York noir/realist newspaper photographer Arthur Fellig got the nickname Weegee (like Ouija board) for his otherworldly intuition for finding news.

Actually, Weegee kept a police scanner and a portable darkroom in his car. The police scanner became standard equipment for newspapers, and technology pushed photo processing from souping rolls of film in noxious chemicals to split-second digital push-button transmission. More nimble, mobile photography made combat-and-conflict photographers their own genre, a daring breed often stepping into harm's way to tell a story with a picture.

A newspaper photographer is no casual passerby with a camera and a moment of luck. A photojournalist sees what others don't. Hundreds of people may witness an incident and record it on a camera phone, but a photojournalist can frame it and preserve it and tell a story with it.

The Pulitzers officially acknowledged photography's importance in 1942, and the first photography prize went to a *Detroit News* photographer for a shot of a melee between strikers and strikebreakers at a Ford plant. The lensman, Milton Brooks, said, "I took the picture quickly, hid the camera under my coat and ducked into the crowd. A lot of people would have liked to wreck that picture."

One of the most shocking newspaper front pages ever printed shows the surreptitious 1928 death-chamber shot of condemned murderer Ruth Snyder. She was blindfolded and shackled to the electric chair as thousands of volts rocketed through her body.

To get the picture, the *New York Daily News* brought in a ringer, a photographer from its sister paper in Chicago. Tom Howard strapped a one-shot camera to his ankle and took his seat in the witness gallery. As the switch was thrown, he "pointed and clicked"—aimed his toe and pushed a plunger. For his unsettling image, he got a one-hundred-dollar bonus, and photographers have been banned from executions ever since.

The best news photos can distill a moment in a nation's life—poignant, comic, heroic. Babe Ruth had already retired from baseball by 1948, but he put on the Yankee pinstripes one last time. The Pulitzer Prize–winning composition by *New York Herald Tribune* copy editor Nat Fein—sent off to Yankee Stadium at the last minute to sub for a sick photographer—was shot from behind the Bambino's back: the barrel body, the wearied legs, cap in hand, facing one final, worshipful crowd.

On February 25, 1945, the black-and-white photo of Americans triumphantly raising the Stars and Stripes over the savage battleground of Iwo Jima appeared on

Perhaps the twentieth century's first "trial of the century" was the 1903 Gillespie murder case. Newsmen from across the Midwest poured into Rising Sun, Indiana, after a socially prominent woman was shotgunned to death in her own front parlor. Here, reporters from more than a half-dozen newspapers pose outside the courthouse. One day, as photographers were taking pictures, one defendant, the dead woman's brother, socked a photographer. In a pro-press ruling, the judge refused to ban photographers from snapping pictures.

the front pages of Sunday papers, lifting the nation's spirits. It was taken two days earlier by Joe Rosenthal, an Associated Press photographer. Though his lousy eyesight kept him out of the military, he still had the photojournalist's friends, good timing and good instinct. The photo inspired a Marine memorial statue and a poster that sold two hundred million dollars in war bonds.

At the opposite emotional end of Rosenthal's picture was another Pulitzer Prize–winning flag picture, this one by Stanley Forman from the *Boston Herald American* in 1976. It captured the moment a white man viciously wielded a flagpole to attack a black man during protests over Boston's school desegregation. The disturbing image is called *The Soiling of Old Glory*.

Newspapers take photo ethics seriously, especially now, with the temptations of Photoshop. In the 1940s and 1950s, and even the 1960s, obviously staged photos—cutesy holiday and kids and pets, bikini babes—were a newspaper standby. But these days, staging or manipulating photos can get photographers fired—and it has.

Whether it's for a million readers or a thousand, the operating rules for reporters and editors are pretty simple. Laurie Ezzell Brown, whose family has published the *Canadian Record* in Texas for more than a century, laid them out when she spoke at a 2008 journalism convention:

Is it true and factual? Have I asked the right questions? Have I given the truth every chance to tell itself? Have I listened? Is it honest? . . .. Can I live with the consequences? . . .. When I am accosted in the produce section of the grocery store, bleary-eyed from lack of sleep and longing for the comfort of a home-cooked meal, can I defend it? Is it fair? Did I choose a truth and then find the facts I needed to support it? . . .. The hardest part of community journalism is also the most rewarding part. We live within what we write about . . .. We look our stories in the face every day. We meet them eye to eye. And if we deny their humanity, if we feel no compassion, then we have failed to grasp the story's essence, and will fail the story's telling.

The still-harrowing front page of the *New York Daily News* on January 13, 1928. A photo taken on the sly showed Ruth Snyder at the moment she was electrocuted for her husband's murder, and the single word, in 172-point type, DEAD!

THE PEN AND THE SWORD

This job can get you killed. Hundreds of journalists have been shot, blown up, kidnapped, and murdered in the line of duty, covering wars, conflicts, battles, and skirmishes.

Why? Why take risks just for a story?

This memorial plaque to correspondents and artists killed in the Civil War—before combat photographers operated nimbly at the battlefront—was installed in a Maryland park in 1896. A tribute but also a bit of an ego exercise by war correspondent George Alfred Townsend. In 2003, the names of four journalists killed by terrorists and in the Iraq war were added.

Wartime news is probably the most-read news of all. When newsprint ran out during the Civil War, a few Southern papers printed some editions on wallpaper. The day Union forces took Vicksburg, Mississippi—July 4, 1863—the soldiers in blue printed up the next day's paper, describing their victory and adding, "For the last time, it appears on 'wall-paper.'"

If the Greek dramatist Aeschylus was right—that truth is the first casualty of war—what is the war correspondent's role? Chronicler or critic, or something of both? Journalists and their second-guessers ask the same question, for different reasons: can reporting plain facts affect the war effort and the home front? When does that justify suppressing them? Or is writing forthrightly a form of patriotism?

Julius Caesar realized when he wrote his wartime chronicles that war is waged on two battlefields: one on the ground and the other on paper—in the modern age, in the news media. That's why the military pushes its own story lines so hard, and why reporters push back, to sort through the "fog of war" for real news.

THE REVOLUTIONARY WAR

In the run-up to revolution, colonial newspapers readily took sides. In 1770, the

This October 1966 ad from the American Newspaper Publishers Association shows a photojournalist "somewhere in Vietnam." It touts the rigors of a newspaper career and describes the "newspaperman" as someone who "contributes to keeping people informed, and no society can remain free without information."

Boston Gazette and Country Journal—a paper that would go on publishing until 1904—was gung-ho for independence. Britain's Stamp Act, imposed on every page of paper used in the colonies, particularly threatened newspapers, so some of them, including the *Gazette*, defiantly printed a skull and crossbones in the spot where the official royal stamp had appeared.

Isaiah Thomas, publisher of Boston's *Massachusetts Spy*, saw firsthand the battles of Lexington and Concord in April 1775. Then, on a printing press he smuggled out of Boston because the authorities had it in for him, he printed his reporter's account: numbers, names, details, and this order he heard from the British commanding officer, as chilling as any video clip today: *Disperse ye damn'ed rebels! Damn you, disperse!*

For a newspaper to back one side or the other was to risk more than a tax. When James Rivington's influential *Gazetteer* declared for the royalists, colonials stormed his New York print shop, trashed the place, and stole the metal type. Soon, they were bragging that they had melted it down for bullets.

It was more than clear to the fledgling republic that newspapers were worth their weight in powder and shot; no wonder press freedom found its way to the top of the Bill of Rights.

THE CIVIL WAR

In the 1860s, newspapers became both indispensable and plentiful. When brothers', fathers', husbands' lives turned on the events of a moment, newspapers went into overdrive to cover them fast enough and fully enough.

So it sometimes happened that readers could learn from a daily newspaper that a loved one was dead, weeks before that soldier's chipper letter made its way from the front telling the folks that he was just fine. Via newspapers, war now came to the mailbox and the doorstep—except for

The *New York Herald* sent as many as forty journalists at a time into the field during the Civil War. This "rolling headquarters" conveyance also advertised the paper's presence.

those papers hostile to the Union cause. Then, they could be officially banned from the mail altogether.

Reporters were right there with the troops, northern and southern. "Embedded" is the word now. They could send their stories by telegraph. The telegraph's immediacy, brevity, and clarity—adjectives cost money, after all—changed newspaper reporting and writing as much as television coverage of the Vietnam War changed journalism a hundred years later.

But telegraph lines were in the military's hands, so telegraph stories were subject to censorship. Then as now, the military didn't trust reporters, not even those whose publishers sided with the

Union. Yankee general William Tecumseh Sherman regarded war correspondents as men who "pick up news for sale." He once court-martialed a *New York Herald* reporter—President Lincoln overruled him on that one—and when the *Herald* reported that the Union had cracked a Confederate code, Sherman threatened to have a different *Herald* reporter executed as a spy.

Both reporters and readers can thank General Joseph Hooker for one enduring journalistic tradition: the byline, the writer's name atop the story. It began as a punishment, not a privilege. Until the war, most news accounts appeared anonymously or under coy fake names (Ben Franklin used Silence Dogood and

Harry Meanwell, among many). But Hooker wanted to know whom to blame for stories he hated. So he issued General Order No. 48: reporters accompanying the Army of the Potomac would publish "over their own signatures."

One of his fellow generals, George Meade, pulled a stunt that every general since has probably envied. A mildly critical account by *Philadelphia Inquirer* reporter Edward Crapsey irked Meade so much that he mounted Crapsey backwards on a mule and had him paraded through camp with a placard reading LIBELER OF THE PRESS slung around his neck. (Crapsey's colleagues avenged him by keeping Meade's name out of print as much as possible.)

Shades of a Twitter future: during the 1863 Battle of Gettysburg, soldiers could actually read about the battle as they were still fighting it. On July 3, an enterprising kid named Cullen Aubrey rode from his family farm to the local train station, loaded up copies of the July 1 issue of the *Philadelphia Inquirer* with its headline THE GREAT BATTLE!, and sold them to the eager soldiers.

Newspapers were not yet capable of printing the images that photographers were beginning to bring back from the battlefields, but pictures would in time change the public's attitudes about war.

News of the homefront delivered to the battlefront, and the reverse, became speedier during the Civil War, thanks to reader demands and amped-up technology. Here, a newspaper vendor sells papers from Philadelphia, New York, and Baltimore near a Union Army camp.

THE SPANISH-AMERICAN WAR

This was as much a war between newspapers as between nations, a "correspondents' war" waged by publishers like W.R. Hearst and Joseph Pulitzer.

One correspondent was Stephen Crane, who had written his Civil War novel *The Red Badge of Courage* before ever witnessing combat. In 1896, a newspaper syndicate's offer of seven hundred dollars enticed him to set off to cover the war in Cuba. He survived the sinking of his ship in Florida; it was the closest he got to Cuba.

One man who earned a national reputation during the Spanish-American War knew better than his Civil War military predecessors how to court the press. Theodore Roosevelt wanted to be governor of New York, and making nice with reporters could make that easier.

In 1898, at the makeshift Texas camp where he trained his Rough Riders, Roosevelt complained insincerely that press photographers were "always taking pictures," according to the book *Teddy Roosevelt at San Juan: The Making of a President.* A sign at the camp entrance said it all: ALL CIVILIANS, EXCEPT REPORTERS, PROHIBITED FROM CAMP.

WORLD WAR I

American newspapering in the First World War was notable not so much for what reporters wrote as for what the government wrote to try to be louder than the press. Its Committee on Public Information was a bold propaganda initiative.

It published stirring songs and posters and a daily *Official Bulletin* filled with news promoting the war effort, from the British wool yield results to the training of "high-minded" citizen soldiers. It was sent to every newspaper, post office, and government agency in the country.

At the same time, the U.S. government allowed only eighty American journalists to go abroad to cover four million American men in uniform. Military censors worked with vigor to keep anything critical—stories or photos—out of the papers, which were trying to navigate a "voluntary censorship" of war-related news.

Where the war divided public opinion, the government was quick to try to muffle the divisions. The *Milwaukee Leader*'s owner was a prominent socialist named Victor Berger. He was elected to Congress even after he was convicted under the Espionage Act, when the *Leader* refused to add its voice to a pro-war chorus. The newspaper was banned from the U.S. mail, and the government raided its offices and seized the names of its subscribers.

The Committee on Public Information was disbanded shortly after the war, but by then, the government had realized it could use advertising and promotion to get around the press. So, too, twenty-first-century politicians have learned to use social media to their own ends, including bending, inflating, ignoring information, then challenging journalists to prove them wrong.

One of the styles of military-issued uniform patches issued to war correspondents during World War II. Correspondents sometimes wore identifying armbands, as well; they dressed in military uniforms bearing no rank designation. Most journalists held the honorary rank of captain, which governed treatment by the enemy if they were captured.

In November 1918, a happy crowd displays papers reporting events leading to an end of the world war. It was not called World War I until there was a second world war.

WORLD WAR II

Phillip Knightley, who wrote *The First Casualty: The War Correspondent as Hero and Myth-Maker from the Crimea to Kosovo*—the indispensable book about war reporting—said that the military's notion of ideal war coverage was summed up by a World War II censor's answer to the question of what to tell Americans about how the war was going:

"I'd tell them nothing until the war's over, and then I'd tell them who won."

(In 1983, President Ronald Reagan did just that when he ordered the invasion of the Caribbean island of Grenada—with no reporters accompanying American troops. He didn't even tell Prime Minister

Newspaper racks in Los Angeles during World War II also encouraged advertising spare rooms for rent to cope with a wartime housing crunch as workers thronged to jobs in defense plants.

Margaret Thatcher, and Grenada was part of the British Commonwealth.)

That "iron lid" doesn't work for a wartime government, which needs the press in order to try to manage wartime perceptions on the home front and elsewhere. And the press, in turn, needs to make sure it's not being played for puppets.

The "Good War" still put government and newspapers at odds. Reporters and editors were patriots, too, but that didn't mean they were pushovers. Journalists worried that censorship would be abused in order to hide military bungles and cover brass butts, not just keep information out of enemy hands.

Thousands of U.S. reporters and photojournalists covered the war, all of them necessarily accredited by the military. The Office of Censorship was headed by a well-regarded journalist who put the burden of "voluntary censorship" on newspapers.

The arrangement didn't ban stories outright, but it counted on editors' and reporters' desire not to get in trouble, nor to be the ones who put American lives at risk. The censorship office had the power to punish a paper that overstepped. Even society reporters whose burbling party stories listed the names of military guests got a rap on their white-gloved knuckles.

War stories also had to have an official voice. Military authorities were the gatekeepers for military news. Newspapers and news services submitted thousands of stories to the Office of Censorship to make sure that line wasn't crossed. In fact, a number of newspaper editors worried that self-censorship was more rigid and problematic than what the government might impose.

But the censorship could also come off as silly and overbearing, as Michael S. Sweeney described in his book *Secrets of Victory: The Office of Censorship and the American Press and Radio in World War II*. First Lady Eleanor Roosevelt, in her newspaper column "My Day," happened to mention the weather in the city she and her husband had recently visited. Then, in her Au-

gust 17, 1942, column, she wrote that she had received a "very stern letter" from the Office of Censorship, telling her that she should no longer spill the beans in print about "whether it rains or whether the sun shines where I happen to be."

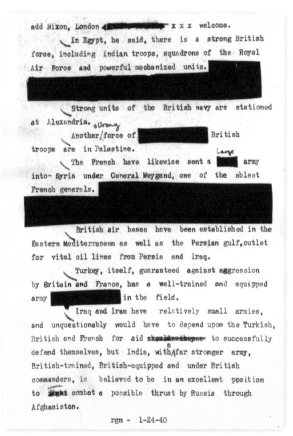

A news dispatch—sent to the International News Service in New York in January 1940 by London correspondent Robert G. Nixon—shows the extent of censorship imposed during the war, with sentences literally snipped out. This story was sent more than a year and a half before the United States joined the war effort and imposed its own censorship on journalists.

For photojournalists, censorship and standards of taste meant that some of their images were not printable. Censors would not approve any images that showed identifiable dead American soldiers, or those who had been mutilated or savagely wounded. When photos of dead American soldiers finally did appear in 1943, they were government-approved, meant to illustrate heroic sacrifice. One approved photo showed three poignantly sculptural bodies on the sand of Buna Beach in the Pacific.

In the end, as Sweeney wrote, at 5:28 p.m. on August 15, 1945—V-J Day, when the newspapers brought out the huge headline font known as Second Coming type—the head of the Office of Censorship closed the office door and hung an Out of Business sign on it.

THE VIETNAM WAR

Of course, censorship wasn't out of business. There were always more wars for reporters to cover and more stories for censors to try to stop.

The slow build to war in Vietnam, the fragmented battle lines, and the force of technology made World War II–style censorship impossible, and in any case, strict official censorship would have called Americans' attention to what was already an iffy undertaking.

Early on in the war, Homer Bigart,

The *Milwaukee Journal* sent John Stallard to cover the Vietnam War. In this 1966 photo, Stallard reports using his portable typewriter perched on a makeshift desk, his helmet close at hand.

who'd won Pulitzers covering World War II and the Korean War, wrote so incisively and critically for the *New York Times* about the poorly conceived, badly run conflict that the South Vietnamese government threw him out after six months.

In Vietnam, stories by reporters who accompanied the troops, along with the novelty of TV footage of foxhole-level combat, took Americans into a first-person soldiers' war.

That war ran athwart what reporters were being told in Washington and at the "Five O'Clock Follies," the U.S. government briefings each afternoon in Saigon.

The military's language didn't match

journalists', either. Civilian deaths were "collateral damage," for example, and reporters wouldn't go along with it. In 1974, Air Force Colonel David Opfer complained, "You always write it's bombing, bombing, bombing. It's not bombing, it's air support."

That was right after the United States had accidentally bombed a Cambodian village, and every available pen and camera could bear witness to it. The *New York Times* saw a sobbing Cambodian man cry out to reporters, *All my family is dead! Take my picture, take my picture! Let the Americans see me!*

That story would not have passed

The single most famous photograph of the Vietnam War was taken by Associated Press photographer Nick Ut on June 8, 1972, and quickly appeared in newspapers around the world. A South Vietnamese Air Force pilot, who evidently mistook a group of fleeing people for the enemy, dropped a napalm bomb. Nine-year-old Kim Phúc's two cousins died, and she ran screaming as the napalm—a substance like jellied gasoline—burned away her clothing and seared her skin. Ut took the photo and then poured water over the critically burned girl before getting her to a hospital. "I cried when I saw her running," Ut told an AP colleague. "If I don't help her—if something happened and she died—I think I'd kill myself after that." Four days later, assessing how the image would heighten anti-war sentiment in the country, President Richard Nixon suggested on the White House tapes, "I'm wondering if that was fixed." His chief of staff, H.R. Haldeman, replied obligingly, "Could have been." Shades of "fake news" and rumor mongering. The unforgettable, authentic picture won the Pulitzer Prize.

World War II censors. But it showed that this war's news stories were inextricable from civilians' stories. Vietnam landed on the breakfast tables of millions of newspaper readers daily, but rarely with more impact than Associated Press photographer Nick Ut's image of Vietnamese children, burned by American napalm, running down a road. The image became a turning point in the endgame of a war that still rests uneasily on the national soul. And never again would U.S. military and political leaders allow that kind of free-range war coverage.

IRAQ AND THE WAR ON TERROR

Almost no combat photos were published from the first Gulf War in 1991. Instead, TV viewers saw a fireworks show, a "video game" of distant missile strikes and luminous tracer fire in night skies, as if no human beings were involved.

Good luck to the reporters who wanted meatier stories. A top military aide put out a classified mandate: reporters "will be escorted at all times. Repeat, at all times." These were even stricter rules than in World War II. Every interview would happen in front of officers, and every story would be run past censors. Editors let readers know that by labeling their stories like a cut of beef: "reports reviewed by military censors."

Sometimes, when newspapers had the chance to challenge the "antiseptic war" storyline, the journalists themselves failed. Freelance photographer Ken Jarecke's stunning image of an Iraqi soldier burned to death—frozen in place like a Pompeii volcano victim as he crawled from his tank—was pulled off the wire by the Associated Press editors, so almost no American newspaper editors, and certainly no readers, saw it then. It was as if taste, not news significance, mattered most. What had changed since 1943, when Thomas Dickson, the acting photo editor at the *New York Daily News*, told *Newsweek*, "I personally try to select pictures that will go down well when I have my coffee in the morning"?

The gut-level power of a photo of a uniformed corpse had been well known since 1862, when Mathew Brady's photographs of Civil War battlefields went on display in a New York gallery. "We see the list [of dead] in the morning paper at breakfast, but dismiss its recollection with the coffee. There is a confused mass of names, but they are all strangers; we forget the horrible significance that dwells amid the jumble of type," the *New York Times* wrote of the display. "Mr. Brady has done something to bring home the terrible reality and earnestness of war. If he has not brought bodies and laid them in our dooryards and along the streets, he has done something very like it."

That's exactly what no government wanted: the image of a soldier's coffin on the home front. A 1991 Gulf War policy that lasted until 2009 banned photographs of flag-covered coffins returning home. In 2004, an employee of a military contractor took a photo of coffins she had helped to load onto a plane in Kuwait, and she allowed the *Seattle Times* to run it. She hoped to show military families the care that their loved ones' bodies received. Instead, she was fired from her job.

After 9/11, the second Gulf War turned into a home-front war for Washington journalists searching out the truth of accounts about weapons of mass destruction (WMD), whose supposed existence George W. Bush's administration used to justify the 2003 military assault on Iraq.

The *Washington Post*'s legendary editor Ben Bradlee called this the "heart" of journalists' dilemma, and their vulnerability: that sources themselves may lie, or may not know, or may know just enough to create problems. The *New York Times* later assessed the shortcomings of its Iraq coverage, noting that "editors at several levels who should have been challenging reporters and pressing for more skepticism were perhaps too intent on rushing scoops into the paper."

The more control the military and government exercise, the fewer opportunities exist for reporters to challenge the accuracy of what they're told. But the more vital it becomes to do so.

Independent answers were hard to come by, either out of Washington or out of Iraq, where reporters were embedded with military units that gave them tiny, human snapshots of the American GI's war, but not larger proofs of its assertions.

In his autobiography *War Reporting for Cowards*, correspondent Chris Ayres concluded that the "true genius of the embedding scheme" was that it "turned me into a Marine," an extension of the group of guys who protected his life every day.

Only after the war were the WMD allegations discredited once and for all, and as with every war and every political campaign, the press undertook a round of self-criticism, determined to learn from what happened this time—what did it not know, and why did it not know it?—so as not to get fooled or hoodwinked again.

KILLED IN ACTION

The body of the most beloved of World War II correspondents, Scripps-Howard columnist Ernie Pyle. He was killed by enemy machine-gun fire on April 18, 1945, on the Japanese island of Ie Shima. Less than two weeks after Pyle died, a B-29 superfortress bomber was dedicated, bearing his name and a sketch of his familiar face on the fuselage

Abraham Lincoln, who was no slouch at troweling on the flattery when it suited him, once told a gaggle of reporters: "You gentlemen of the press seem to be pretty much like soldiers, who have to go wherever sent, whatever may be the dangers or difficulties in the way."

That bit was no flattery. Reporters and photographers the world over risk their lives in the line of duty. Newspapering, like an army, has its own "killed in action" list.

The 77th Infantry Division raised a makeshift wooden memorial to Ernie Pyle on the spot where he died. A permanent stone memorial was installed after the war.

However long the list grows—and it lengthens all the time, as American reporters do their work on the elusive battlefields of Asia and the Middle East—Ernie Pyle's name is almost always at the top. Throughout World War II, Pyle didn't write about the generals; he wrote about the ordinary men on the front lines, and his columns in the Scripps-Howard newspapers made him a friend to millions of readers on the home front and the battlefront. On the slope where he was shot and killed on the island of Ie Shima in the East China Sea, soldiers put up a wooden marker: "At this Spot the 77th Infantry Division Lost a Buddy / Ernie Pyle / 18 April 1945."

Correspondent Webb Miller had more wars on his resume than a three-star general. He covered General John J. Pershing's Mexican border skirmishes with Pancho Villa, both world wars, and, on foot, the Italian invasion of Ethiopia. He interviewed Hitler and Mussolini without mishap, although, as a young reporter at the *Chicago American*, Miller was hogtied, thrown in the trunk of a car, and kidnapped on the orders of the Morton Salt millionaire be-

cause he tried to interview the Salt King's daughter, who had eloped with a jockey. In 1940, Miller was found dead along a train track in wartime London. Three years later, the U.S. Navy began naming its Liberty ships after war correspondents. The first was the SS *Webb Miller*.

The first monument to reporters killed in battle was a memorial arch built by a Civil War correspondent in Maryland. In classic High Victorian sentimentality, George Alfred Townsend's tribute to his dead colleagues loaded symbol upon symbol—the messenger god Mercury, a pen triumphing over a sword. Since then, the arch has added names, like *Boston Globe* reporter Elizabeth Neuffer, killed in a car crash covering the second Gulf War in 2003, and the *Wall Street Journal* correspondent Daniel Pearl, murdered by terrorists in Pakistan in 2002. In Arlington National

Cemetery, an oak tree flourishes, planted "in memory of journalists, who died while covering wars and conflicts, for the American people. One who finds a truth lights a torch." The glass panels of the Newseum's Journalists Memorial in the nation's capital list the names of more than 2,300 journalists worldwide who have died on the job, in peacetime and in war.

War zones are the likeliest place for American reporters and photographers to be killed, but the home front isn't always safe turf, even though the battlefield might seem as unthreatening as city hall.

Tactically, murdering a reporter to stop news stories is about as counterproductive as killing a cop to stop a criminal investigation. It almost guarantees that the dead reporter's colleagues will rise up against the killers. In 1976, *Arizona Republic* investigative reporter Don Bolles was blown up in his Datsun, supposedly by some of the corrupt business forces he had been writing about. His last words were "John Adamson . . . Emprise . . . Mafia." Outraged members of the year-old Investigative Reporters and Editors project took up where Bolles had left off, assembling their findings in the Arizona Project, a chronicle of the Grand Canyon State's organized crime, fraud, and corruption.

In 2007, a newspaperman named Chauncey Bailey was shotgunned on an Oakland, California, street. He was killed by a hit man who was also a handyman at a Black Muslim bakery, whose financial and personnel problems Bailey had been covering for the weekly *Oakland Post*. Once again, journalists carried on. The Chauncey Bailey Project pledged "You can't kill a story by killing a journalist." The day a jury convicted one of his killers, a prosecutor acknowledged a debt to the Chauncey Bailey Project.

Between the world wars, reporters and editors in the Midwest were assassinated by cabals of politically connected gangs who didn't like their exposés on corruption. In Ohio, Don Mellett and his *Canton Daily News* won the Pulitzer in 1927, but by then Mellett was dead, assassinated as he parked his car in his garage.

In a then-politically crooked Minneapolis, three newspapermen were gunned down over the course of about a decade. Scandal-sheet publisher Arthur Kasherman—who wrote in the unhinged, "even a stopped clock is right twice a day" fashion of some modern-day fringe bloggers—reported manically about public corruption.

Chauncey Bailey, editor of the weekly *Oakland Post*, was gunned down on August 2, 2007, in Oakland, California. to silence his reporting. UC Berkeley established a graduate fellowship in Bailey's memory, and the Chauncey Bailey Project was created by journalists to carry on the story that got Bailey killed, and to prove the maxim that "You can't kill a story by killing a journalist."

He was shot to death on a Minneapolis street in January 1945, the day he had written that an illegal craps game was taking in seventy-five thousand dollars a month.

Walter Liggett, who had worked at several big New York City newspapers, went back to his native Minnesota to write about politicians colluding with organized crime. In December 1935, he was machine-gunned to death near his own back door, in front of his wife and daughter.

Howard Guilford, co-publisher of Minneapolis's *Saturday Press*, was murdered by a shotgun blast through his car window in September 1934. In big type and capital letters, his newspaper had been naming names of politicians who turned a blind eye to "vile hooch," gambling, and prostitution because they were beholden to "Jew gangsters." Distasteful as that tone was, the *Saturday Press* gave journalism a legal landmark. A Minnesota law allowed officials to stop sheets like the *Saturday Press* from publishing, but the United States Supreme Court decided in 1931 that such censorship—prior restraint—was almost always unconstitutional. The

Saturday Press was one reason that, nearly forty years later, the Nixon administration could not stop newspapers from printing the *Pentagon Papers*.

MURDERED AND MARTYRED

In many countries, reporters' and editors' lives are snuffed out with grisly frequency. Groups like the Committee to Protect Journalists and Reporters Without Borders tally the "deliberate violence against journalists." Regimes, too, target reporters for death. In Mexico, journalists covering drug wars and corruption are assassinated in the streets, or kidnapped, tortured, and beheaded.

Once in a while, foreign politics reaches out to kill reporters working in the United States. As far as most Americans are concerned, the Vietnam War ended in 1975, but some South Vietnamese partisans just switched continents. Over nine years, from 1981 to 1990, from Virginia to San Francisco to Houston, five Vietnamese American journalists were assassinated by what the investigative news outlet ProPublica called a death squad named VOECRN, the Vietnamese Organization to Exterminate Communists and Restore the Nation. The FBI concluded that the death squad was made up of extremist former South Vietnamese military officers who decided to fight, in this country, the anti-Communist war they had lost in Vietnam.

None of those five murders has been officially solved: the gravestone of newspaperman Nguyen Dam Phong, shot seven times in the driveway of his Houston home, reads: "Killed in pursuit of truth and justice through journalism."

YOU DIRTY RAT!

In June 1930, as bootlegging, bribery, and blackmail were running Chicago, *Tribune* crime reporter Jake Lingle was shot to death at a commuter train stop.

The cutthroat world of Chicago newspapering didn't agree on much, but this time it sang in chorus: the bullet from the muzzle of the .38 that killed Lingle was really about muzzling the press.

Chicago threw him a flashy funeral, with military bands.

Oops. Lingle, it turns out, was on the take. How else could a sixty-five-dollar-a-week newspaperman afford a chauffeur and a swanky apartment? When Lingle was killed, he was on his way to the racetrack with fourteen hundred dollars in his pocket and a racing form in his hand.

The killing went officially unsolved, but Al Capone, who gave Lingle a diamond belt buckle as a thank-you for all the favors, had finally decided that his "head got too big for his hat."

With probably the most famous "oops" front page in American journalism, the *Chicago Daily Tribune* jumped the gun to call the 1948 presidential election—erroneously—for Republican Thomas E. Dewey. The upset winner, incumbent Democratic president Harry S. Truman, shows off the paper at a St. Louis train stop.

FAKES, FRAUDS AND EFF-UPS

Publish tens of thousands of words on deadline every day, and something, somewhere, sometimes, is going to get messed up.

The "we goofed" daily corrections pages can be so meticulous that they come off as parody:

The *New York Times* corrected a 2012 story about the suspected ringleader of an attack on the American compound in Benghazi with this: the paper "misidentified the beverage that Ahmed Abu Khattala was drinking at the hotel. It was a strawberry frappe, not mango juice, which is what he had ordered."

The *Michigan Chronicle* apologized in 1995 for messing up the nickname of the matriarch of a congressman's family. She was "'Big Ma,' not 'Big Mouth' as reported." And the *Oakland Tribune* ran a correction in 1985 after a reporter quoted someone as referring to "the Iron Ass" when the actual quote was "the INS"—the federal Immigration and Naturalization Service.

The *Boston Globe* cringed in March 1980 when a jokey placeholder headline on an editorial about a lackluster economics speech by President Jimmy Carter, MORE MUSH FROM THE WIMP, made it into 160,000 copies before someone changed it to the more dignified ALL MUST SHARE THE BURDEN. *Wimp* became a new entry in the American political lexicon.

Standards of professional rigor, fact-checking, and competition that keep reporters on the up-and-up nowadays were a while in coming. In the meantime, newspapers were not above churning out fantasy for fun and profit. None was better at it than Mark Twain, who worked as a reporter from Philadelphia to California with sometimes more fondness for fiction than facts. At Nevada's *Territorial Enterprise*, he followed his phony 1862 account of the discovery of a petrified man with an equally imaginary 1863 story of a man who massacred his six children and scalped his wife in his despair over losing all of his money in utilities. Twain later wrote that the petrified-man story was meant to make the "pompous" new coroner look "ridiculous," and the murderous family-man story was really a "deep, deep satire" about utility companies' shady dealings. Too deep, maybe. In both cases, Twain blamed readers for not getting the joke. He soon left newspapering, and both journalism and fiction were probably the better for it.

Another Nevada fantasist was Twain's drinking buddy and fellow teller of tall tales, Lyin' Jim Townsend. On one occasion, when Townsend had to go out of town for three weeks, he is said to have thoughtfully written up the "news" in advance.

Newspapering's most flamboyant stunt—so blatant that the Smithsonian included it in a science-fiction exhibition—was probably the 1835 Great Moon Hoax. The six-part series in the *New York Sun* wrote of the "discovery" on the moon of waterfalls, unicorns, and bat-people. The stories tossed in a few scientific-sounding terms along with the name of a renowned astronomer, Sir John Herschel. Herschel was in Africa when the stories appeared. He didn't find out that his good name had been abused until later, and he was much displeased when people pestered him about the hoax, as if it were real. As for the reporter, he wanted to boost circulation, sure, but also to satirize by exaggeration the preposterous astronomy theories of the time. Really, he figured, who could possibly believe his account that a seven-ton telescopic lens even existed, let alone spotted winged mini-moon men?

Plenty of people, as it turned out.

The same was true nearly forty years later, when the *New York Herald* panicked New Yorkers with alarming headlines about a killing spree by animals who broke out of the Central Park Zoo. Not until the end of the ten-thousand-word concoction did readers learn that the story was "a huge hoax, a wild romance, or whatever other epithet of utter untrustworthiness our readers may choose to apply to it."

In an odd way, the anger and hysteria that fake stories created prove that people do expect to read facts in newspapers. Even silly April Fool's stories sow confusion, which is why most papers forbid them—they mess with newspapers' credibility.

On April 1, 1978, an outdoors writer at an Erie, Pennsylvania, paper quoted a federal researcher (rather obviously named Ayper Ilfu) about a ban on monofilament fishing line because it caused cancer in brook trout. Overwrought anglers fought to buy out the stock. "I tell you, it was brutal," one tackle shop owner told the Associated Press. The writer was fired.

In 1899, four reporters, each working for a different Denver paper, concocted a humdinger. The story they'd all planned to cover didn't pan out, so they all agreed

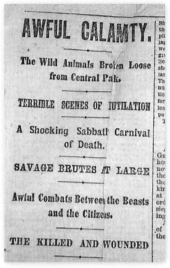

A headline from the 1874 *New York Herald*'s hoax story about a killing rampage by animals escaped from the Central Park Zoo. The writer described—in gory detail—seeing the dismemberment of four children by a lion, among other horrors. Like the "War of the Worlds" radio hoax more than sixty years later, the *Herald* story panicked some readers. Parents hurried to schools to fetch their children, and the police superintendent sent off citywide action orders before he realized the story was fake.

to fake it. "It won't hurt anybody," one of them argued. "So what the devil?" Over several convivial beers, they chose a country far enough away that no one could fact-check their hoax—China—and a sensational storyline: that some American engineers who'd stopped briefly in Denver were on their way to tear down the Great Wall of China at the behest of the Chinese government. Four decades later, the fake story, which had been reprinted far and wide, suddenly gave birth to another hoax: that it had fueled the Boxer Rebellion.

Although the deadly serious coverage of the Civil War and World War I had sobered up newspapers and their readers, on more frivolous topics the cheerfully dishonest art of fabrication soldiered on. The future Oscar-winning screenwriter Ben Hecht was a reporter for the *Chicago Daily Journal* during the Prohibition era, when he and his pals recklessly ornamented, elaborated, and just plain made stuff up. On a slow news day, Hecht dug a raggedy trench in a Chicago park,

planted some broken dishes alongside it, and wrote a story that ran under a huge headline, EARTHQUAKE IN CHICAGO!

Larky fictions still popped up into the 1950s and 1960s. In the *Arkansas Gazette*, a made-up character with the triple-threat name Omo Fevers Bartlett slipped occasionally into print, once as a victim of an Alpine snowstorm.

If you went by Los Angeles newspapers in the 1950s and 1960s, Victor Frisbie was a regular man-about-town. Legend holds that Frisbie's "father" was a *Los Angeles Examiner* reporter who covered the 1950 Rose Parade from inside a phone booth, calling in trenchant "quotes" from the nonexistent Mr. Frisbie. Not long after, the reporter was killed crossing a street, and his colleagues supposedly honored his memory by making sure Victor Frisbie survived in print now and again.

A man who became a well-known *New York Times* columnist almost didn't. In 1966, a college intern at the paper, Clyde Haberman, slipped a fake name into a list of commencement prizes, and an editor told young Haberman he would never work for the *Times* again.

Forty years later, when that editor died, Haberman—long since back on the *Times* payroll—declared that the editor was right to fire him. If journalism has a mortal sin, Haberman wrote, "it is the willful publishing of an untruth. Sure, we get things wrong, but it is generally as the result of human fallibility, not deliberate transgression. You don't make things up and put them in the paper. It's as simple as that."

Why does this matter? What's the harm in a few practical jokes? Unlike lawyers or doctors, reporters don't have to pass exams to qualify for their jobs. Instead, they get tested every day, every time their names appear on stories, every time the paper is published. Simply put, from a *New York Times* editor named Jonathan Landman: "Accuracy is all we have. It's what we are and what we sell."

And yet the belief persists that reporters just make things up, willy-nilly. Apart from the ethics and the sheer impracticality of fabrication, the truth is that reality is so richly strange that there's no need to make stuff up. After a *Boston Globe* columnist resigned in 1998 for ginning up people and quotations, a fellow *Globe* columnist wrote sorrowfully: "Sadly, a lot of readers apparently think she didn't do anything the rest of us don't do routinely." Several careers have come to their end for transgressions like that of the *Chicago Sun-Times* critic who left a performance early and then filed a review. She was canned.

Once in a while, reporters' judgment simply deserts them—and by extension, their readers.

In 1919, as Americans were terrified by the specter of Bolsheviks and anarchists, the *Philadelphia Public Ledger* published stories extensively quoting the bogus anti-Semitic *Protocols of the Elders of Zion*, forged in tsarist Russia. The *Ledger* snipped out references to Jews, substituted Communists, and called it a Red Bible, a "guidebook of world revolutionists." The likely source was a U.S. military intelligence officer who was vehemently anti-Jewish and anti-Bolshevik. Carl Ackerman, the reporter who wrote the stories, went on to become the third director of Columbia University's journalism school.

A corrections page can't address newspapers' deeper fumbles on mishandling or misperceiving stories. Media critics'

There were times when photographers staged photos, and posed pictures of cute kids seemed harmless enough. But this image, from February 1959, is in appalling taste. Someone put the *Chicago Daily News* in the hands of James and Nancy Kaye, whose parents had just died in the crash of an American Airlines plane described in the headlines. The caption: "Neither seem to fully comprehend the closeness of the tragedy."

jobs were created to do that. In 1974, the *Los Angeles Times*'s David Shaw ushered in a vigorous style of media self-criticism. He won a Pulitzer Prize in 1991 for a series dismantling the news media's often uncritical coverage of the McMartin preschool child molestation case.

The most flagrant modern individual reporting sin of both omission and commission was arguably committed by the Pulitzer Prize–winning *New York Times* correspondent Walter Duranty. His coverage of Soviet Russia in the 1930s was arrogant, credulous, and complicit, and it went disturbingly easy on Stalin—particularly Duranty's refusal to acknowledge the extent of the politically engineered famine that killed millions in Ukraine. Seven decades later, a professor asked by the newspaper to investigate the coverage suggested that Duranty's Pulitzer be revoked by the prize committee "for the greater honor and glory of the *New York Times*." It was not.

A few fakers—best-known, for the worst reasons:

● Foster Winans, a *Wall Street Journal* columnist, was convicted in 1985 of federal

The *Chicago Sun-Times* went with a source who had it wrong and announced that former president Gerald Ford would be 1980 Republican presidential nominee Ronald Reagan's running mate. Reagan chose George H.W. Bush instead.

charges of insider trading for leaking information to a stockbroker before it ran in his column. Thirty years later, a former Securities and Exchange Commission chairman said the case was "a painful reminder that trust is the glue that holds our system together."

● Janet Cooke, a *Washington Post* reporter, won a 1981 Pulitzer for a story about an eight-year-old heroin addict, a story she admitted making up to satisfy the high-pressure demands of the job. The paper returned her Pulitzer.

● Jack Kelley, a *USA Today* foreign correspondent, resigned in 2004 after a team investigating his work concluded that he had made up stories, quotes, and sources over about a dozen years, had plagiarized other writers' work, and had tried to cover up his own fabrications.

● Jayson Blair was a young *New York Times* reporter who faked and plagiarized his way through dozens of stories and then tried to cover his tracks when his editors started investigating. He resigned in 2003 and wrote a scorching, finger-pointing memoir.

● Veteran *Chicago Herald-American* science reporter Hugh Stewart turned rumor into a news story: a local woman was pregnant with sextuplets. This was astounding news in 1951, before fertility drugs were commonly used, and it would have one-upped the sensational birth of the Dionne Quintuplets in 1934. After other papers couldn't track down any such woman, Stewart insisted he couldn't reveal his source. When he finally did, the source turned out to be his twelve-year-old niece, who had heard a tale about it at camp. Stewart said his editors "were right in firing me. I was awfully goofy."

MYTHS OF NEWSPAPER REPORTERS

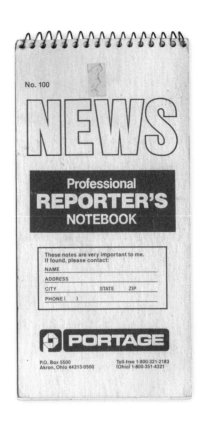

Everyone has some notion—usually a cartoonish one—of what newspaper people do. Some myths about reporters and editors doing their jobs:

- **They are rich.** You're confusing newspaper people with network TV people. Big-city editors and columnists—especially popular sports columnists—can pull down six figures, but the median salary for an American newspaper journalist in 2016 was a princely $37,820. Why should you care? Because if poverty wages can thin out the staffs of papers—especially small, hometown papers—the voices of ordinary Americans are silenced, and public officials, without reporters' eyes on them, can get away with murder.

- **They are on the take.** You might think so, with those sorry salaries, but would reporters dress the way they do if it were true? No, car companies do not give journalists free wheels; Apple does not hand out free phones in the newsroom in exchange for flattering coverage. Even if it tried, the staff would be fired for taking them. (*El Nuevo Herald*, the *Miami Herald*'s Spanish-language counterpart, fired three journalists in 2006 after discovering that they were being paid by the Bush administration's Office of Cuba Broadcasting to criticize Fidel Castro on

U.S. government-financed radio and TV.)

The fact is, journalists, like people in other underpaid lines of work, find intangible rewards in the job itself—the "backstage pass;" first-hand access; the responsibility and the thrill of being witness to and chronicler of important events; and most of all, knowing that a story you write could improve people's lives, could awaken voters or legislators to some wrongdoing, could change public policy, could expose the bad guys and reward the good guys.

- **They pretend to be other people to get stories.** It used to happen. Reporters pretended to be doctors or detectives to get inside interviews. The renowned Nellie Bly posed as an insane woman to write exposés that helped to end the abuse of lunatics in nineteenth-century New York.

More defensibly, the *Chicago Sun-Times* bought a tavern, named it the Mirage, and set up shop to chronicle the shakedowns, kickbacks, and payoffs that officials routinely demanded of a business. The paper's stunning twenty-five-part series in 1977 led to indictments and city hall-shaking reforms, but it lost the Pulitzer because some judges decided that the deception—newspaper

people pretending to own a bar to get a story—was unethical.

Nowadays, the "undercover" tactic is banned. And press organizations have reason to protest whenever government officials pose as reporters, because the ruse endangers journalists' lives and reputations. One FBI agent pretending to be an Associated Press (AP) reporter in 2007 was memorably clueless about what real reporters do. The agent identified himself as an AP staff publisher—there is no such job—to trap a teenaged bomb-threat suspect into an "interview."

- **They write stories to sell papers.** A hundred years ago, maybe. Now, almost every newspaper is pre-sold by subscription, whatever the headlines. And rather than online come-on clickbait like WHAT DID TRUMP TELL FELLOW GOLFERS ABOUT THE WHITE HOUSE?, newspapers just spill the beans up front, with forthright headlines like TRUMP TELLS GOLFERS WHITE HOUSE IS A "REAL DUMP."

- **They make stuff up.** If they were that imaginative, journalists would all be writing thrillers and selling them for top dollar to movie studios.

- **They suck up to the powerful.** Oh yeah? Just ask the powerful how much they love their clippings. Reporters are all about keeping watch on how the powerful everywhere use their power—or misuse it. When journalists fail at anything, it's usually that they don't ride the powerful hard enough.

- **The media is . . .** Stop right there. *Media* is the plural of *medium.* News outlets are many, not one. And they are mightily different. The *National Enquirer* is not the *Boston Globe,* any more than *Frontline* resembles *TMZ.* If you must refer to them collectively, like a parliament of owls, or a pod of whales, better "the mainstream news media," because mainstream is a good thing—it means not occupying the extremes. Or better yet, simply "the press."

- **They libel people.** Just because you don't like facts that are written about you doesn't make them libelous. News stories can contain unpleasant facts, but they *are* facts. The Founders saw for themselves that speaking fearlessly about public officials is crucial to democracy. Some of them who became president weren't happy when the tables turned, but there you are. The nation's courts keep making important rulings that backstop free speech and the work of a free press. In other countries, journalists are imprisoned and killed—not for libel, but for telling the truth.

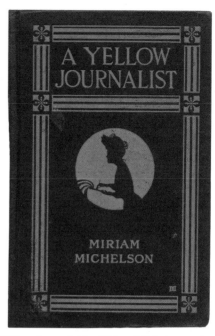

The caricature of the tough, fast-yapping newspaper reporter is itself caricatured here in his-and-hers posters created by artist M. Norman and printed by *More* magazine, a monthly journalism review published from 1971 to 1978.

A Yellow Journalist by Miriam Michelson, takes its title from the era of sensationalized "yellow journalism." The 1905 novel is about a bold San Francisco "girl reporter" who risks life and limb in derring-do adventures and cuts legal and ethical corners, all to get the story—and her man.

- **They never tell you the whole story.** A newspaper is not an encyclopedia. And no story is ever truly complete, because the world never stops. Journalists don't have historians' luxury of time and distance. They get as much accurate information as possible, and if something doesn't check out by deadline, either it won't make it into print or it waits for the next day's paper.

- **They never admit when they are wrong.** Wrong! The little errors get corrected quickly; the big "misses" take a while. Just before the 2016 presidential election, a Florida paper, the *Daily Commercial*, agreed with readers' complaints that it

"hasn't done enough to mitigate the anti-Trump wave in the pages of this paper."

In 2006, the *Charlotte Observer* issued a apology for its own failed coverage of an 1898 white riot, a racist coup d'état that ousted duly elected black and white officials in the town of Wilmington and killed many African Americans.

In 2000, the *Hartford Courant*, Connecticut's biggest newspaper, investigated itself and apologized, with a banner headline, for publishing ads in the eighteenth and nineteenth centuries advertising slaves for sale.

What you can't run a correction for is the two-hundred-year-long arc of

"missed" stories that newspapers began to realize in the last decades of the twentieth century: how entire segments of the population—women, minorities, the rural poor, the urban poor, immigrants, citizens of the Midwest or Deep South—were inadequately reported on.

- **They're biased.** You can argue that everyone is biased. Newspeople, though, work hard to recognize institutional and individual biases and rid their stories of them. Objectivity? It's like the number *pi*—you can't actually reach it, but you can get closer and closer to it. But fairness and open-mindedness? They're a newspaper's stock in trade.

Municipal Building,
Newspaper Row and City Hall Park,
New York City.

CHAPTER 3

ALL IN THE FAMILIES

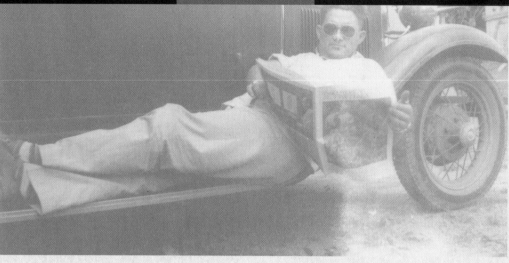

A few of them were the Silicon Valley grandees of their age. They were farsighted, shrewd, convinced of their own genius, and most of all, oh-so eager to flex their power with the most potent information tool that humankind had then devised: ink on newsprint.

And all while wearing frock coats, not hoodies.

Famous publishers are rare birds. Most American newspaper publishers have been of drab plumage: ordinary, hometown men and women with more influence than income. They've sometimes been journalists, or business people more familiar with ledgers than news stories. They've been printers who just happened onto newspaper publishing as a sideline.

Back in colonial America and out in the frontier, the publisher was likely to be something of a one-man band, cranking out the pamphlets and books and advertising flyers that were his bread and butter, or maybe the lord of an ink-smeared, printshop manor of no more than a few people, some of them his own relatives.

Then and now, at smaller papers it's the publisher who can wind up getting the angry email from a subscriber when a paper goes into a puddle, the furious phone call from a local car dealer and advertiser who wants the car critic fired over a harsh review of the new models, or the starchy letter from a politician unhappy that the newspaper's editorial—a separate operation from the news coverage—didn't praise his latest proposal.

Always, though, publishers have figured it's worth it. Because even in the mid-1980s, some sixty million daily newspapers were bought every day in this country. And that doesn't count weekly papers, the go-to news source for small towns.

Throughout the first half of the twentieth century, some Americans read two or even three papers a day. Americans got into the newspaper habit early. Colonial newspapers helped to bring the new American nation into existence, and afterward, they held a mirror up to the new government. Newspapers schooled new Americans in their new lives.

Opposite: An early twentieth-century postcard of the grand newspaper palaces clustered in New York City.

Naturally, along with the statesmen and the visionaries, there have been scoundrels and troublemakers, mediocrities and fools among newspaper publishers. The best managed to set high and daring standards for American journalism, even before the ink was dry on the Constitution of the United States.

BEN FRANKLIN would become the young nation's most famous printer and publisher, but his elder brother, James, beat him to the starting line.

JAMES FRANKLIN, as founder of the pre-revolutionary *New England Courant*, helped to lead the charge against royal British authority. He got tossed in jail for shaking his inky fist at Boston's colonial rule and wound up banned from his own newspaper. The year James Franklin died, in 1735, American newspapers got their first patron saint, John Peter Zenger, a man who wasn't originally a journalist at all.

JOHN PETER ZENGER was a German immigrant who had been making a living printing batches of religious tracts. He began printing the *New-York Weekly Journal* in 1733, and its backers used its pages to rumble up New York's detested royal governor. Predictably, all hell broke loose, but it was poor Zenger who was arrested for seditious criminal libel. The public hangman was ordered to burn every copy of the journal.

The public burning of copies of the *New-York Weekly Journal* for its supposed libel of the royal government started a larger, symbolic fire for free speech and the free press in the American colonies. The jury acquitted the printer, John Peter Zenger.

It looked like a slam-dunk case against Zenger until Ben Franklin's friend appeared for the defense. This lawyer, Andrew Hamilton, was the unsung hero. In that courtroom, in August 1735, he appealed to the jury's seedling patriotism: this case wasn't about "one poor printer." It was nothing less than "the cause of liberty." Hamilton laid down what became a bedrock principle of American journalism: that the words themselves must be "false, malicious, and seditious, or else we are not guilty"—that truth is still a defense against libel.

In that courtroom, against all colonial law and evidence, Hamilton knocked the wind out of the British rule that "the greater the truth, the greater the libel." Jurors hoisted their middle fingers to the King's majesty and found Zenger not guilty. The courtroom spectators *huzzaed* like mad, and Hamilton went home to a salute of cannon fire.

Not for the last time, in momentous times, newspapers had chosen sides in a pitched battle with authority. And not for the last time, American people—and eventually American law—sided with them.

Think "publishers" and the names William Randolph Hearst and Joseph Pulitzer rise to the top of the multitudes—a pair of flamboyant moguls who battled each other from fancy buildings along New York's Newspaper Row, at Park Row near City Hall. In the searing forge of the late-nineteenth century's press innovations, you'll find these two among the prime movers, if not always the highest-minded, of American newspapering. Hearst and Pulitzer were as mismatched a pair as you could find. But they would not have become power players without a rule-breaking publisher old enough to be their grandfather—James Gordon Bennett Sr.

JAMES GORDON BENNETT SR.— more later about the junior Bennett—was a Scotsman who founded the *New York Herald* in 1835, working at a desk made from a plank laid across a couple of barrels. He had almost nothing in common with the high-principled political journalism of earlier newspapers, full of hefty debates about politics and finance, nor with earlier editors like Benjamin Franklin Bache, Ben Franklin's grandson. (Bache, a firebrand on the printed page, was nicknamed Lightning Rod Junior after his grandfather's invention. His relentless mockery of President John Adams got him thrown in jail, illegally.)

Bennett was the paper-and-ink incar-

nation of his showman contemporary, P.T. Barnum. (Fittingly, Bennett built his new *Herald* building on the site of Barnum's old museum.) The point of a newspaper, Bennett made clear, "is not to instruct, but to startle and amuse."

At a penny a paper, he did.

Bennett's newspapering was born just as the country's sense of its own identity was reborn. Technology was raising up new, brash cities, and it built new, swifter

James Gordon Bennett Sr. was the Scottish-born founder of the influential *New York Herald*. He and his spendthrift son instituted a number of modern newspaper practices, not all of them laudable, like salacious crime stories.

printing presses to churn out newspaper stories about plain, warts-and-all people— the Andrew Jackson model of American, sometimes unlettered but not ignorant, cocksure, ambitious, and the equal of any other man, or he'd know the reason why. Bennett was happy to feed their appetites, and to whet them. He made the newfangled telegraph a tool of daily journalism, and he sent correspondents to Europe and to the Civil War battlefronts.

All by himself, Bennett shattered a dignified journalistic taboo. He was the first newsman to cover, in R-rated detail, a "love nest" murder, the 1836 killing of a prostitute named Helen Jewett. Then, murders like that were two-a-penny in New York, but nice people didn't talk about them, and nice newspapers certainly didn't write about them.

Yet, there were Bennett's stories, lingering salaciously over Jewett's "dreadful bloody gashes," her burned pillows "black as cinders," the portrait of Lord Byron on the wall, and the books of poetry beside the bed of sin. Eighty years later, the *Herald* was still dishing out headlines like LITTLE WIFE BEAT SIX-FOOT BLONDE IN DIVORCE RAID. By then, some other newspapers—and eventually some television news—had followed its lead.

HORACE GREELEY, the publisher of the rival *New York Tribune*, fractured a different journalism tradition—and founded a new one—ten years after Bennett's irresistibly lurid story. On February 27, 1846, the *Tribune*'s Washington correspondent, writing a "letter from Washington" under the pen name Persimmon, laid out in grotesquely accurate detail exactly what an Ohio Democratic congressman named William Sawyer did on the House floor every day at two o'clock. The honorable gentleman carried his lunch to "a window back of the Speaker's Chair," spread it out on a "greasy paper," ate it with gusto, wiped his hands on his sleeves, his trousers, even his own bald head, then used "a jackknife for a toothpick" before tossing the greasy paper out the window and going back to the people's business.

Naturally, when Sawyer read this story, he was livid. But he also, foolishly, blew an ember into a forest fire by asking the House clerk to read the story aloud on the floor of Congress. His colleagues loyally voted to boot *Tribune* correspondents out of the press gallery, but the damage was done. Fellow congressmen sniggered about Sausage Sawyer, and a paper back home in Ohio took malicious delight in calling him "a brute in manners and a booby in brains." Embarrassed at home and mocked around the nation, Sawyer did not run for reelection in 1848.

This was publisher Greeley's sly, long-game power play: Greeley flat-out hated slavery. During these years of volcanic debate over whether new American states would be slave or free, Sawyer was on Greeley's opposite side. Sawyer had speechified about the "revolting" prospect of racial equality, and he complained sarcastically that some stranger visiting Congress "would very naturally suppose that Congress was instituted mainly for the benefit of Negroes."

As a surgical exercise in the power of the press, the Persimmon story was brilliant. Its cinematic vividness cut short the congressional career of a pro-slavery voice, without ever mentioning the word *slavery*. The personal became political. A *Washington Post* reporter visiting a congressman's office decorated in *Downton Abbey* style was asked by a congressman's aide why he was rushing to write up a "gossipy piece" about the office. Presently, the congressman was indicted for misspending taxpayer money on it.

The Civil War made the newspaper a daily necessity for every American. Any battle, any order from Washington, D.C., could mean life or death for a loved one. Americans who had begun reading newspapers as faithfully as they ate breakfast—and sometimes with breakfast—kept doing it after the war was over.

Without a war to cover, newspapers still had to give paying customers something to read. William Randolph Hearst delivered—and how.

WILLIAM RANDOLPH HEARST was born in California, the only child of a strike-it-rich mining millionaire who didn't see any reason why bird shouldn't be spelled *b-u-r-d*. Hearst built a coast-to-coast publishing empire and a hilltop California castle that he called The Ranch, and packed it with movie stars and the treasures of Europe.

Hearst took up newspapering by wheedling his father into giving him the *San Francisco Examiner*, which he majestically called the Monarch of the Dailies (modesty got you nowhere in the newspaper game). Then he bought the *New York Journal* and started filling in the miles between them, buying newspapers across the country to build a massive chain that could editorialize with one voice. (This was the M.O. of the big publishers. They bought, traded, sold, and folded newspapers to consolidate their own power and to drive others out of business—before newspaper strikes and competition from other newspapers and from television beset the empires they had built.)

Sometimes Hearst made sure that voice shouted *Vote for Hearst!* He won a New York congressional seat and miraculously lasted two terms, even though he missed

WILLIAM RANDOLPH HEARST AND SON.

Hearst gets my vote and ought to get yours

William Randolph Hearst, the pioneering publishing magnate and sometimes political candidate, with one of his four sons. The note on the cabinet card reads, "Hearst gets my vote and ought to get yours."

168 out of 170 votes in his first year. He lost his bids for New York's mayor and governor, and for the Democratic presidential nomination. But in newspapers, he realized, lay lasting power. He believed that, despite his dabbling in moviemaking. Movies had made Douglas Fairbanks one of the most famous faces in the world, and he once asked Hearst why he didn't give up newspapers for films. Hearst's answer: "I thought of it, but I decided against it, because I realize that you can crush a man with journalism, and you can't with motion pictures." Maybe *Citizen Kane* made him rethink that.

JOSEPH PULITZER was a Hungarian who'd made it to the United States by signing up to fight in the Civil War. At one point, down to his last seventy-five cents, he shoveled coal, dug graves, and waited tables on his way to becoming the fastidious New York power broker who ran the *New York World* from the copper-domed headquarters that was, for a time, New York's tallest building.

Pulitzer had leveraged himself from the bankrupt *St. Louis Dispatch* to owning the *World*. Using small words and big illustrations, the *World* was probably the nation's first million-circulation paper. It ran a color Sunday edition with graphics so dazzling that present-day author and newspaper lover Nicholson Baker cashed in some of his retirement money toward rescuing a full set of those Sunday papers that the British Library wanted to be rid of. It was, Baker was certain, "rarer than a Shakespeare First Folio or the Gutenberg Bible."

Hearst and Pulitzer were geniuses at promotion. To Hearst, publishing a newspaper without promoting it was as pointless as "winking at a girl in the dark." Between them, they gave new generations of urban newspaper readers lively, thrusting coverage, sensational and populist journalism that didn't always scruple about playing fast and loose with the facts.

At the same time, in stories that ran alongside sensational, exotic tales of sex fiends and foul play, Pulitzer's *New York World* crusaded passionately against civic and corporate graft, corruption, and tax cheats on behalf of the "little man" who paid a penny or two to read about who was doing him wrong.

As for William Randolph Hearst, his politics gradually swung from progressive to conservative. But his newspapers were always, as Arthur James Pegler, one of Hearst's own journalists, said, "like a screaming woman running down the street with her throat cut."

Just as it does today when it comes to the bottom-feeding swamps of social media, America's intellectual class gave an eye-roll to this kind of journalism. Henry Ward Beecher—whose sister Harriet wrote *Uncle Tom's Cabin*—was an immensely famous moral arbiter after the Civil War, a nineteenth-century Billy Graham. Such newspapers, he warned, practiced a kind of cultural "cannibalism . . .. Rome had her gladiators, Spain her bullfighters, England her bear-baiting, and America her newspapers." By the time he wrote that, Beecher had been sued by his assistant for having an affair with the man's wife, and the new-style newspapers had torn the pious preacher to shreds.

Crippled by lousy eyesight and painful hearing, Joe Pulitzer eventually insulated himself in soundproof spaces aboard his yacht, *Liberty*, or in his "Tower of Silence" at his home. His staff, in modulated voices, read the *World* stories aloud to him. Three thousand miles away, in his wide-windowed study high up on the Enchanted Hill, a barefoot W.R. Hearst was said to spread each day's issue of his many newspapers out on the floor, the better to compare them side by side, as he turned the pages with his bare toes.

The pen-to-pen combat between Pulitzer and Hearst was as bloodthirsty as any stories that ran in their papers. After Pulitzer launched newspapering's first comic strip, *The Yellow Kid*, Hearst's *New York Journal* hired the cartoonist away, as he would steal other stars on Pulitzer's staff and other ideas that had made the *World* a groundbreaking newspaper. Story for story, they dueled it out, and even the tiniest development in a big story justified a new street edition with noisy new headlines.

If Pulitzer's paper ran big headlines, Hearst's ran bigger ones. Pulitzer did have some queasy doubts about his own screaming headlines. A Pulitzer manager named Don C. Seitz remembered that the boss was "greatly offended" by the blar-

JOSEPH PULITZER
The New York World.

Joseph Pulitzer revolutionized newspapering and battled fellow publisher William Randolph Hearst for readers with crusading stories and innovative features.

ing headlines in his evening paper, telling Seitz to collect the huge lead type, "place it in the furnace and melt it up." Too late. As Seitz understood, symbolically, "it would not stay in the furnace [because] it had shown what people wanted"—big, brief, brassy storytelling.

JAMES GORDON BENNETT JR. was a contemporary of Hearst and Pulitzer in New York. The profligate playboy son, Bennett inherited the publishing empire of his formidable father. He blew

his engagement to a society girl when he showed up drunk at her New Year's Eve party and peed in the fireplace. He fled abroad on his yacht, living in seagoing luxury, sometimes keeping a cow onboard for fresh cream, and running his newspaper from the high seas or the south of France.

Like other rich men, big-city publishers could afford to indulge their personal passions and crusades, and Bennett was in good company on that score. Hearst built the world's largest private zoo on his California hilltop (he and his mistress, the actress Marion Davies, were animal lovers), and he enlisted the pages of his newspapers for his campaign against vivisection (experimenting on live animals).

Bennett the Younger's primary cause was owls. He loved them so much that editorials in the *Herald* demanded that they be legally protected. Bennett loved owls so much that he wanted one as his mausoleum, a two-hundred-foot-tall owl to be built on a New York hilltop pedestal; inside the owl, his own coffin was to hang suspended from chains, forever, for the public to visit.

Perhaps it's a blessing that Bennett's architect, Stanford White, was shot dead by his ex-lover's husband before the project got any further than the conceptual, because on the New York skyline, the owl

The idiosyncratic tastes of the flamboyant publisher of the *New York Herald*, James Gordon Bennett Jr., were vividly clear in his 1895 newspaper building, from the Italian Renaissance style to more than two dozen bronze owls around the roofline. The newspaper and the building are commemorated now only in the name on the map: Herald Square.

tomb would have stood higher even than the Statue of Liberty.

NEWSPAPER DYNASTIES

THE OCHS-SULZBERGER FAMILY is the most enduring. It's run the *New York Times* for more than a century, through five generations. (During New York's deadly Civil War riots over new draft rules, a part-owner of the *Times* took his turn defending the building with a Gatling gun mounted on the newspaper's rooftop. His name was Leonard Jerome, grandfather of future British prime minister—and newspaper war correspondent—Winston Churchill.)

THE MEYER-GRAHAM FAMILY—four generations of them—ran the *Washington Post*. In 1933, Eugene Meyer bought

the paper. Five years later, his daughter Katharine graduated Vassar and took a twenty-four-dollar-a-week job as a cub reporter for the old *San Francisco News*, covering labor unions on the waterfront. But in the way of things then, it was her husband, Philip Graham, not she, who came to run the *Post* after Eugene Meyer died. Philip's suicide in 1963 made Katharine Graham one of many women publishers who found themselves sitting in their late husbands' vacant chairs. Her son Donald took over as publisher when she died. The publisher title took an eight-year detour out of the family after Donald gave up the chair in 2000, but it returned in 2008 in the person of Katharine Graham's granddaughter, Katharine Weymouth. She left the job a year after the *Post* was bought by

Amazon founder Jeff Bezos in 2013.

As publisher of the *Washington Post*, Katharine Graham was one of the most important women in the country. In 1972, she put her paper and her fortune behind the newspaper's historic Watergate investigation. One night, when reporter Carl Bernstein phoned Attorney General John Mitchell for comment on a *Post* story about a secret spy fund that Mitchell had helped to run for Richard Nixon's re-election, Mitchell screamed: *Katie Graham's gonna get her tit caught in a big fat wringer if that's published!* (The *Post* published his quote but left out "her tit.")

Dynasties, royal or publishing, are only as durable as the changing economy, the times—and the heirs. Around the country, other family newspaper dynasties flourished and sometimes fell. Keeping publishing power in the family made it easier to wield power with confidence and not answer to the nitpicking of shareholders. It was a compelling reason to make newspapering a family affair. But it wasn't always reason enough. Over time, families have broken up and sold off their holdings, and family-founded media companies that actually have lasted have often survived by adding broadcast and web properties.

Calamity did its damage, too.

THE BINGHAM FAMILY owned the influential Bingham news-media empire, including the Pulitzer Prize–winning *Louisville Courier-Journal* and *Louisville Times*, as well as broadcast companies. One heir, Worth Bingham, died at age thirty-four when a surfboard slung across the back seat of his convertible clipped a parked car, swung around, and broke his neck. Three decades later, his son died of a heroin overdose.

THE OTIS-CHANDLER FAMILY lost control of its *Los Angeles Times* after four generations. The Otis-Chandler dynasty began in 1881 with the stone-fisted General Harrison Gray Otis, who was followed by his son-in-law, Harry Chandler. Harry's son Norman, and Norman's son Otis (Otis was the only son; his father was one of two sons), each carried on as publishers. The newspaper left the family in 2000, when its properties merged with Chicago's Tribune Company.

E. W. SCRIPPS AND ROY HOWARD formed a newspaper chain—with the double-barreled company name of Scripps-Howard—that altered the power and reach of newspapering by pioneering the newspaper syndicate. Scripps believed a chain of centrally owned-and-run small newspapers, with local content plus syndicated news stories and features, was a match for any big-city newspaper. Scripps once remarked that if he wanted to start a newspaper, he could do it with a payroll of two: an editor and a reporter. Anything else, he could get from the papers in his syndicate.

Scripps cherished no illusions about himself. He called himself a "damned old crank," indifferent to the public's regard. In his early years, when he began his empire with the *Cleveland Penny Press*, and a competitor tsked-tsked that he had a mistress, Scripps and his lady friend showed up together publicly to call the man's bluff.

This red-headed Illinois farm boy didn't love much—certainly not his fellow man, and his fellow woman only slightly better—but he loved the sea, and when he died aboard his yacht off the coast of Liberia, his body was dropped overboard, per his instructions.

Scripps's legacy was oceanic, too. He and his half-sister and business partner, Ellen, a proper Victorian lady who taught herself to become an expert in seaweed and sea mosses, donated the funds to create the Scripps Institution of Oceanography. It's a paradox of newspaper dynasties that long after the newspapers have passed into strangers' hands, the founders' names still ornament charities around the nation.

Roy Howard, Scripps's other business partner, was the Scripps-Howard chain's powerhouse and workhorse. A long-ago Indiana newspaper delivery boy, he never stopped being a reporter, even as he ran United Press, later United Press International. (UPI—"One Up on the World"—is the news agency that played a scrappy number two to the massive Associated Press, hiring legendary reporters

James W. Scott, floridly depicted on a cigar box lid, founded the *Chicago Herald* in 1881. The son of a printer, Scott was said to have thoughtfully outfitted the *Herald's* composing room with an ice-water cooler and 348 electric lights.

like Walter Cronkite and the beloved war correspondent Ernie Pyle.)

THE McCORMICKS AND ME-DILLS, the First Families of Midwestern newspapering, ran a great many things in Chicago and beyond. The M&Ms, along with the Pattersons, were Midwestern Brahmins, publishing and political colossi, interrelated by blood and power. The Medill/McCormick/Patterson family tree branched out to the inventor of the revolutionary agricultural reaper, two pioneering women publishers—one of whom founded New York's *Newsday*—and a scion of fortune who left Chicago to start the *New York Daily News* and introduced the modern tabloid to these shores.

Of all the characters in American newspapering, it would be hard to find someone more, well, *colorful*—the genteel word newspapers use to describe the more prosperous run of eccentrics—than the twentieth-century paterfamilias, "the Colonel," Robert McCormick, who put his stamp on the *Tribune* and the region.

The Colonel's grandfather, Joseph Medill, had used the *Tribune* to help to make Abraham Lincoln president, and he never let anyone forget it: "We made Abe, and by God we can unmake him," he believed. The Colonel ran the *Tribune* in the twenti-

A classic pre-World War I illustration of two men going at it in a political argument, one armed with a newspaper to prove his point.

eth century. He bent the Republican politics of Lincoln into a more hysterical kind of isolationism and leveraged the *Tribune* into the premier paper of the upper Midwest, and a kingmaker in GOP politics.

Apart from his politics, McCormick's pet cause, like his grandfather's, was spelling reform. And when you're the boss of a major newspaper, you don't have to crusade alone. Across its pages, the *Tribune* put its readers on a forced march through—*thru*—unorthodox spellings like *clew, fantom, ameba, iland, subpena*. Nearly twenty years after the Colonel died, the *Tribune* finally declared, as one writer put it, that "thru was through."

Both of these statements are true: never pick a fight with someone who buys ink by the barrel, and, from A.J. Liebling, the conscience of the fourth estate, "Freedom of the press is guaranteed only to those who own one."

Even though the Internet has pretty much killed off the second warning, and pixels have made the first one obsolete, modern publishers were and are, perforce, business people first. Again, from the useful Mr. Liebling: "The function of the press in society is to inform, but its role in society is to make money." Reporters and editors could report and write until the cows came home, but publishers had to make the money to pay them to do it, support the substance of their work—and, these days—pay the shareholders of the companies that own the newspapers.

Many publishers have been stalwart press champions; others have been stockholders' lackeys with spines like soggy newsprint. Publishers and owners who sang from the same hymnal as the Chamber of Commerce sometimes found themselves at odds with their own newsrooms over stories that ticked off the publisher's business buddies or country club golf pals—or the advertisers. A strong

What happened in the Sixties? The "Now" generation back "Then."
Page R-1

Dacron's VanHusen Corp. makes twin mobility twice as affordable.
Page M-5

This week's *Newscast in Print*: "Negroes— The Problem That Won't Go Away"
Page P-2

TODAY'S WEATHER QUALITY:

ACCEPTABLE

Data from Ohio State Weather Service
O.S.W.S. DEPT. OF WEATHER

DACRON Republican-Democrat

One Of America's Newspapers

OHIO LUCKY BUCKEYE
Daily Lottery
4 6 1060
WINNING NUMBER

SECTION A   ★★★★   DACRON, OHIO, SUNDAY, FEB. 12, 1978   Copyright 1978 SOUTH CENTRAL OHIO COAL, GAS, ELECTRICITY, TELEPHONE, & TELEGRAPH COMMUNICATIONS GROUP   TWENTY CENTS

Powder Room Prowler Strikes Anew

Two Dacron Women Feared Missing in Volcanic Disaster

Japan Destroyed

CLEVELAND, Feb. 11 (Combined Sources)—Possible tragedy has marred the vacation plans of Miss Frances Bundle and her mother Olive as volcanos destroyed Japan early today.

The *National Lampoon* mocked the Midwestern, middle-of-the-road Sunday newspaper with the 1978 parody *Dacron Republican-Democrat*. It was a sendup of bland, hyper-local coverage. Aggressive local newspaper coverage is the safety net of news that Americans depend on.

A vintage news vendor's apron invited readers of both political parties to "follow your favorite candidate" in Indiana's *Muncie Evening Press*. The *Press* was yet another afternoon newspaper that ended up being folded into its morning rival, in this case to form the *Muncie Star-Press*.

Left, North Dakota's *Forbes Republican* began publishing in 1906, a year after the town of Forbes was founded. Newspapers began taking the name "Republican" as an adjective of "republic," and later to signal some partisan loyalties. *Right*, a matchbook cover from the *St. Louis Globe-Democrat*. Those party-affiliated names survive as relics of bygone party affiliations.

publisher could tiptoe the tightrope: keep the advertisers mollified, keep the newsroom independent and strong. A weak publisher who caved to advertisers or politicians ultimately cost the newspaper its credibility.

Reporters love that old line from a Chicago columnist named Finley Peter Dunne, that the newspaperman's job is to comfort the afflicted and afflict the comfortable. Where things get tricky is when the publisher's friends and advertisers—like the publisher himself—are the comfortable. It takes strong character and deep pockets to bankroll a newspaper that in-

vestigates government and business misdeeds (and sometimes their own), and not all publishers have had the checkbook or the gumption to do it. So sometimes the publishers and the reporters and editors wind up on different sides of a story. Usually it doesn't play out in public, but this one did:

In 1991, Santa Fe's *New Mexican* ran a long investigative series on the consequences of neglect, accidents, and environmental and health perils from decades of work at the nearby Los Alamos National Laboratory, cradle of nuclear weapons and security research. The newspaper's own-

er/publisher, a promoter of nuclear technology, blew a gasket, fired the managing editor, and printed a twenty-seven-page rebuttal of his own newspaper's work. (Six months later, the *Washington Post* said that a Los Alamos internal review "essentially confirmed" much of the paper's series.)

The graveyard of American newspapers is full of publications that named themselves, very forthrightly, the Such-and-Such *Democrat*, or the This-Town *Republican*. It's a testament to the parties and principles that probably were the reason the papers were founded in the first place. In the country's first hundred years, many newspapers—a very good many—were started up by politicians as little more than house organs to promote the publishers' policies and political careers, as Hearst did. Publishers then also served simultaneously as mayors and legislators. It's a conflict of interest that wouldn't be tolerated today.

Alexander Hamilton, the ten-dollar-bill Founding Father, the good-looking one who got a twenty-first-century revival on Broadway in 2015, began the *New York Post* as a sober broadsheet in 1801 with money from his political sympathizers. The paper became a Rupert Murdoch–owned tabloid. James G. Blaine, who barely lost the presidency in 1884 to Grover Cleveland, owned Maine's *Kennebec Journal*, which gave him a springboard to his political career.

In a little town in Ohio, a young man named Warren G. Harding published the *Marion Daily Star*—formerly the *Marion Daily Pebble*—and he didn't sell it until just before he died in office, as president of the United States. In its pages, Harding cannily soft-pedaled his own politics to keep readers and advertisers happy—and to smooth his way to power. One of the boys delivering the *Marion Daily Star* would run for president six times, as the Socialist candidate. Newsboy Norman Thomas also grew

"The biggest newspaper in the world," the postcard brags. Perhaps the *Los Angeles Times* had more lines of classified advertising than other papers, but the office of its publisher, Harrison Gray Otis, looks modest for a man who reveled in calling the shots in the City of Angels from 1881, when he founded the paper, until he died in 1917.

up to found the American Civil Liberties Union (ACLU). In the next state over, Indiana, former Vice-President Dan Quayle belonged to the Pulliam family, a politically conservative clan that owned a small chain of newspapers. In political families, ink ran almost as thick as blood.

Newspapers weren't loath to throw their editorial muscle behind specific candidates and causes. In 1910, a half-century

before the *Los Angeles Times* began transforming itself from a right-wing trumpet to a respected national newspaper, union organizers bombed the newspaper building over the paper's anti-union stand, which only confirmed to the paper's owner that he had been right all along. For decades, the Otis-Chandler family regarded the paper as a means, not an end—a way to turn Los Angeles into a boomtown. It banged the drum for new industries like aviation and the movies, enticed newcomers to L.A. with special sunshine-and-flowers editions, and enriched itself on the real estate and other businesses it promoted in its pages. Without General Otis and the Chandlers, there wouldn't have been a modern Los Angeles.

As the *Chicago Tribune* had done with another Republican politician named Abraham Lincoln, the *Los Angeles Times* went to bat for its man, Richard M. Nixon. Nixon's career stalled after he lost the presidency in 1960 and the election for California governor in 1962. After that, he lambasted the press in his "You won't have Nixon to kick around anymore" speech. But he exempted *Times* political reporter Carl Greenberg from his criticism. Greenberg, who covered politics as vigorously as he had once covered the crime beat, was humiliated by the "compliment" and offered to resign. His bosses told him to keep working. A decade later, after the *Times* remade itself into a moderate national force in publishing, President Nixon furiously tried to sic the IRS on Otis Chandler. "I want this whole goddamn bunch gone after," he ordered.

~~~

Newspaper publishers usually went head-to-head to compete, but in California in 1934, they disgracefully joined forces to defeat a gubernatorial candidate.

Socialist reformer Upton Sinclair, famed for the exposés of the Chicago meatpacking industry in his book *The Jungle*, was running for governor as a Democrat. California's mass-media machinery thought he was a threat and agreed to stop him. MGM cranked out phony documentaries using actors to portray "ordinary voters" fearful of Sinclair. The Hearst papers ranted against him. And a couple of weeks before the election, the *Los Angeles Times* did its nasty part. It ran a photo—a still from a recent film called *Wild Boys of the Road* (1933)—with a caption describing it as "a typical scene of a contingent of the invading bums pouring out of a freight car . . . lured by the rosy promises of Upton Sinclair."

This kind of incendiary handiwork was nothing new to Hearst. He did more than any other publisher to whip up the nation toward war with Spain in 1898, crafting imaginatively inflammatory stories and headlines like, HOW DO YOU LIKE THE JOURNAL'S WAR? (Although he probably never did send that legendary telegram to an artist he had sent to Cuba to cover the budding Spanish-American War. The artist, Frederic Remington, supposedly complained there was no war to cover. "You furnish the pictures, and I'll furnish the war," was the chief's alleged—and improbable—response.)

It was, indeed, Hearst's war, and he didn't want to sit it out. In 1898, he credentialed himself as a war correspondent, yachted to Cuba, and came ashore at the Battle of El Caney. Kitted out in straw hat and revolver, Hearst wound up kneeling beside his own wounded war correspondent, James Creelman. He took notes as Creelman spelled out his story, and then steamed away on his yacht.

In Chicago, *Tribune* publisher McCormick's notion of patriotism was even more unorthodox. As a boy at boarding schools in Europe, he hung an American flag over his bed and beat the tar out of foreign boys who tried to take it down. As publisher of the *Tribune*, he printed the flag at the top of his newspaper every single day, with the pugnacious motto, An American Paper for Americans. He called the *Tribune*, immodestly, the World's Greatest Newspaper, and when the *Tribune* bought a TV and radio station, those were the call letters: WGN.

As far as McCormick was concerned, the New Deal was a Communist deal. As the days counted down toward the presidential election of 1936, *Tribune* switchboard operators were instructed to answer the phones with, "Good morning, *Chicago Tribune*—do you know you only have [x] days to save your country?"

For President Franklin Roosevelt, the feeling was mutual. He never trusted the *Tribune* "any farther than you can throw a bull." Six months after the Pearl Harbor attack, a *Tribune* story headlined NAVY HAD WORD OF JAP PLAN TO STRIKE AT SEA made it clear that the United States had deciphered a Japanese code. A Chicago grand jury decided against charging the Colonel and his staff with treason, and the seething White House finally determined it was strategically wise to call as little attention to the story as possible.

Abraham Lincoln had battles to fight north of the Mason-Dixon Line, with "Copperhead newspapers," so named for the poisonous snake. The editor of one Copperhead newspaper was an ex-Ohio congressman who ranted against the war and "King Lincoln." He was sent to prison by a military court, but Lincoln, wise to the potential blowback, had the editor set free—behind Confederate lines. (Lincoln was adept at picking his fights. After General Joseph Hooker imprudently told a *New York Times* reporter that Lincoln was an "idiot," Lincoln let Hooker know, no hard feelings—so long as he won battles.)

Lincoln ordered one Copperhead paper to be reopened after General Ambrose Burnside had shut it down, but at last, after two papers ginned up a bogus story about the military draft, Lincoln shut them down

NAVY HAD WORD OF JAP PLAN TO STRIKE AT SEA

Knew Dutch Harbor Was a Feint.

Washington, D. C., June 7.—The strength of the Japanese forces with which the American navy is battling

Exactly six months after the Pearl Harbor attack, stories in the *Chicago Tribune* infuriated the White House and inflamed President Roosevelt's hostility toward the paper's publisher, because their subtext revealed that the U.S. had broken a Japanese military code. A grand jury refused to indict the reporters.

and the owners were carted off to prison.

Lincoln had no such conflict with McCormick's grandfather, publisher Joseph Medill—a Lincoln man through and through. Lincoln was an adroit handler of the press; he sent copies of his speeches to the *Chicago Tribune* and helped to make it a Republican kingmaker for a hundred years. The *Tribune*'s forerunner, the *Chicago Daily Press and Tribune*, hired a professional stenographer to record the Lincoln-Douglas debates, and soon afterward, Lincoln wrote to request copies to put "in a Scrap-book."

In November 1864, Joseph I. Gilbert, hired for the day by the Associated Press to hustle out to the Gettysburg battlefield, made his own bit of journalism history. After he jotted down shorthand notes during Lincoln's address, he asked to do what reporters now do routinely—check the president's actual speech text to make sure his own notes were right. And Lincoln, wise to the fact that the Associated Press version would get printed across the country, agreed.

Like any other reader, presidents tend to like newspapers when they think they side with them, and fume when they don't. They may hate the press, but they know they need the press—and then they hate the fact that they do. Unlike many of his elected brethren, Lincoln tended to get along better with reporters than with their publishers, but like every president who followed him, he considered newspaper leaks odious—unless he was doing the leaking.

⚜

But the journalists politicians hate the most aren't the editors or the columnists. They despise the political cartoonists.

"I don't care a straw for your newspaper articles. Most of my constituents don't know how to read. But they can't help seeing them damned pictures!" politician

Maryland, My Maryland!

THE "BRAINS"

THAT ACHIEVED THE TAMMANY VICTORY AT THE ROCHESTER DEMOCRATIC CONVENTION.

An editorial cartoon sketches out, in a single image, a thunderous point that transcend words. Edmund Duffy, a political cartoonist for the *Baltimore Sun*, won three Pulitzer Prizes, but none of them for this one, left, from December 1931, after a black man accused of killing his boss was yanked from a hospital bed by a white mob, dragged behind a truck to the courthouse and hanged. The cartoon mocked "Maryland, My Maryland," the state song of the onetime slave state, with its lyrics about "Northern scum." On the right, Thomas Nast's ink-and-paper takedown of New York's corrupt Boss Tweed. The 1871 cartoon "The Brains" is from *Harper's Weekly*. Tweed broke out of prison and went on the lam, but in Spain, in 1876, the Nast cartoon on the wanted posters made Tweed so recognizable that authorities recognized and nabbed him at once—the power of the cartoonist's pen.

William Tweed wailed.

The Pulitzer Prizes started singling out editorial cartoons for honors in 1922. The bombastic *Baltimore Sun* editor H.L. Mencken recognized the cartoonist's value, too. "Give me a good cartoonist," he said, "and I can throw out half the editorial staff." He was thinking of his new hire, Edmund Duffy, who would go on to win three Pulit-

zer Prizes for his cartoons. After one Maryland lynching in 1931, Duffy sketched the image of a hanged black man and the line, "Maryland, My Maryland!", the state's song. Furious white readers yanked *Sun* drivers out of their seats, beat them up, and set their delivery trucks ablaze.

A political cartoon could magnify a physical feature into a character flaw—Wil-

liam Howard Taft's big gut, Bill Clinton's lip-biting, Richard Nixon's five o'clock shadow. Boss Tweed was right: a few bold pen strokes could do more damage than a thousand carefully crafted words.

One political cartoonist who ended up on President Nixon's renowned "enemies list" was the *Los Angeles Times*'s Paul Conrad, whose cartoons, like the one of

Nixon nailing himself to a cross, outraged Nixon so much that he had the IRS audit Conrad's taxes for six years running.

Cartoons weren't the only reason President William Howard Taft wanted nothing to do with reporters, unlike his predecessor, Teddy Roosevelt, who hardly ever stopped talking to the press. Archie Butt, a one-time newspaperman who was a White House military aide to both Roosevelt and Taft, shared this fly-on-the-wall moment, quoted in *The Compact History of the American Newspaper*:

> Taft asked for a newspaper and his wife handed him the *New York World*.
> TAFT: "I don't want *The World*. I have stopped reading it. It only makes me angry."
> MRS. TAFT: "But you used to like it very much."
> TAFT: "That was when it agreed with me, but it abuses me now, and so I don't want it."
> MRS. TAFT: "You will never know what the other side is doing if you only read the *Sun* and *Tribune*."
> TAFT: "I don't care what the other side is doing."

Whatever their relationships with newspapers, politicians were probably happy to take them off the required-reading list. In the heat of the Spanish-American War, President William McKinley resolutely did not read the incendiary New York papers. George Washington's dignity was affronted by what some newspapers had to say about him and his presidency, and he denounced them as "infamous scribblers." After his presidency, he canceled all his newspaper subscriptions.

<hr>

In the South of the 1960s, journalist Paul Guihard, who was reporting for the French news agency Agence France-Presse, wrote that the Civil War "never came to an end." Guihard filed that story in September 1962, as he joined scores of reporters in Mississippi to cover the rioting over a federal court order to integrate Ole Miss, the University of Mississippi. It was the last story he wrote. A few hours later, Guihard was shot to death. His murder was never solved.

A hundred years after Appomattox, black Americans waged war of another kind for their civil rights. In the 1960s, national and foreign reporters swept into the South to write about segregation, protests, voter registration drives, and Freedom Riders, but you'd be hard-pressed to follow the news in most local white newspapers. In the spring of 1961, an editor of Mississippi's *Jackson Daily News* wrote that there were so many black people in Washington, D.C., "the lightning bugs are coming out in the daytime."

When Dixie's papers weren't sneering, they were resoundingly silent. In 2004, on the fortieth anniversary of the Civil Rights Act, the *Herald-Leader* in Lexington, Kentucky, was moved to run this breathtaking correction: "It has come to the editor's

WILLIAM H. TAFT, former President of the United States, has joined the staff of the PUBLIC LEDGER as contributing editor, the connection becoming effective on November 1.

Philadelphia

PUBLIC LEDGER

The National Newspaper

One Dollar will pay for the PUBLIC LEDGER daily and Sunday, delivered by mail to any address in the United States, for a trial period of six weeks. Address Box 1526-A, Philadelphia. The PUBLIC LEDGER may also be obtained at leading hotels and news-stands throughout the United States.

Just as they do now, newspapers bragged when they got big-name contributors. The *Philadelphia Public Ledger*, founded in 1836, secured the services of William Howard Taft, between his earlier job as president and future job as Supreme Court chief justice.

Publishers built large but impermanently. Left, a photo of the smoking ruins of the *Los Angeles Times* building after a union bomb exploded on the premises in October 1910, a violent coda to the power struggle between unions and the paper's publisher. Right, the Hearst Building in San Francisco, home of the *San Francisco Examiner*, was only eight years old when it burned down during the 1906 earthquake and fire. William Randolph Hearst rebuilt on the same site.

attention that the *Herald-Leader* neglected to cover the civil rights movement. We regret the omission."

There were luminous exceptions to this silence. Three of them won Pulitzer Prizes. Harry Ashmore, the executive editor of the *Arkansas Gazette*, wrote impassioned editorials about school integration in Little Rock. The *Atlanta Constitution*'s Ralph McGill won a Pulitzer for covering the rise of Nazism in Germany. At home, in spite of death threats, he wrote so ferociously that Martin Luther King Jr. mentioned him in his *Letter from Birmingham Jail* as one of "our white brothers." And Hazel Brannon Smith of Mississippi used her newspaper, the *Lexington Advertiser*, to report doggedly on civil rights developments. She stuck to her principles even after a white power group burned a cross on her lawn, even after she was convicted of libeling a local sheriff, even though advertisers boycotted her into near bankruptcy. It was not only what she wrote, but how she stood up to "great pressure and opposition" that made her the first woman ever to win a Pulitzer for editorial writing.

HOT TYPE, HOT LEAD

If your readers don't kill you, your fellow newspapermen just might.

Newspapering was never a profession for sissies or cowards, but in some cases, publishers and editors were outgunned by one another, or did some gunning down themselves. Was it personalities? Politics? Did lawsuits take too long to satisfy a man's honor? It's hard to tease out one from the other in these early newspapermen whose passions may have drawn them into the business in the first place, and whose competitiveness gave gory meaning to the term *newspaper wars*. On the casualty list of newspaperman-on-newspaperman violence were these notables:

J. CLARKE SWAYZE, editor of Kansas's *Topeka Daily Blade*, was shot to death by John W. Wilson, the son of a rival editor. The surprise is that it hadn't happened sooner. Swayze was a supporter of "Negro rights" who had already had to defend his life as a newspaper publisher in Georgia right after the Civil War. That's one reason he moved to nice, peaceful Kansas. There, it was as true in 1877 as it was in 1977 that any newspaper that landed the choice contracts to print official government business had a fat, juicy plum. Wilson's paper had that contract, and Swayze accused Wilson and his father of padding the bills. One of Swayze's two young sons was named Horace Greeley Swayze, after the great abolitionist editor.

DANIEL READ ANTHONY was the brother of suffragist Susan B. Anthony; her profile on the one-dollar coin looks startlingly like her brother's. He was a Leavenworth newspaper publisher and a fervent abolitionist. Before the Civil War, when he tried to yank down a Confederate flag at a local store, Dixie sympathizers pulled out their guns. As described in print by Robert C. Satterlee, the publisher of the rival *Kansas Herald*, Anthony ran off like a coward. Anthony hunted Satterlee down in the street and demanded a retraction that he didn't get. When the gunsmoke cleared, Satterlee was dead, and a jury soon set Anthony free. More than a dozen years later, Anthony himself was shot and wounded by another aggrieved Leavenworth newspaper editor. This jury, too, let the shooter walk. "That's just the way with some juries," observed the *Marion County Record*. "They think it no more harm to shoot an editor than a Jack-rabbit." Anthony still waged political war with the locals, got walloped with an umbrella by a reader and horsewhipped by the mayor, and died in his bed at age eighty.

B.H. STONE, editor of the *Talequah Telephone* and a white man married to a Cherokee woman, made some sharp remarks about the editor of the competing *Cherokee Advocate* during an especially nasty Cherokee election in 1887. The other editor, Elias Boudinot Jr., was the son of the pioneering Cherokee publisher who founded the first Native American newspaper in the country. Boudinot stormed over to Stone's office, and when no apology was forthcoming, he shot Stone dead where he sat. The jury believed Boudinot when he said that Stone had gone for his own gun. Boudinot eventually bought the dead man's newspaper.

JAMES KING OF WILLIAM, who added the last bit so as not to be confused with other James Kings, founded the *Evening Bulletin* in post–Gold Rush San Francisco, the Sin City of the West Coast. He used the *Bulletin* like the wrath of God to single out corruption and immorality with a righteous, inky finger. Then that finger alighted on a local supervisor and *Sunday Times* editor, James P. Casey, and revealed that Casey had been a jailbird in New York. On May 14, 1856, Casey stopped King as he left his office and demanded, *Draw and defend yourself!* King fell, fatally wounded, and Casey was swept into the hands of the city's Committee of Vigilance, which

Elijah Pope Lovejoy was reckoned in some quarters to be "the first casualty of the Civil War"—almost twenty-five years before it began. In November 1837, the Presbyterian minister and his abolitionist newspaper were set upon by a pro-slavery mob. Three times before, mobs had trashed his printing press and threatened his life. This time, the building was torched and Lovejoy was shot to death. His murder electrified the anti-slavery movement. Former president John Quincy Adams called him "the first martyr to the freedom of the press, and the freedom of the slave."

hanged him and his accomplice from the committee's storefront on the day of King's funeral. Thousands of King's mourners passed by their dangling bodies.

SAMUEL WALL of the *Tacoma Telegraph* did not like what Herbert Harcourt of the *Tacoma News* had to say about him in print—namely, that Wall "worked secretly in the interest of Seattle" and therefore against Tacoma. This was 1886, and the towns were such venomous rivals that even ministers preached civic Cain vs. Abel from the pulpits. Wall cornered Harcourt in his office. *I've come to kill you!*, he hollered. It was not a scene without comedy, though: a piece of steel in Harcourt's cravat deflected the bullet, and the city editor yanked a roller from a window shade and started swatting Wall with it. Harcourt survived. The local prosecutor didn't try Wall because he didn't think a jury would convict a man who evidently had "something good to say about Seattle."

If it wasn't other newspapermen who were after you, it was some reader, or even someone you'd written about.

WILLIAM BYERS founded Denver's first paper, the *Rocky Mountain News*, by getting his very first issue on the streets twenty minutes ahead of the competition. In 1860, Byers's anti-crime crusades riled up a local vice gang called the Bummers, who ruined Christmas for Denverites one year by stealing the holiday turkeys. The Bummers dragged Byers from his office to a local saloon, but he was able to sneak out the back door. When the Bummers chased him back to the newspaper office, Byers and his friends shot one of the thugs. Before the surviving Bummers finally gave up, Byers had to walk Denver's streets in disguise.

EDWIN E. CROSS edited Arizona's first newspaper, the *Weekly Arizonian*. In 1859, he made fun of a local bigwig, Sylvester Mowry, for spinning tall tales about Arizona to try to get Congress to designate Arizona as a territory. Even though Mowry had gone to West Point, neither man drew blood in their duel, and everyone adjourned to a barrel of whiskey. But a couple of weeks later, Mowry bought the *Arizonian* and moved it to Tucson—without its editor. Cross must have been righteously amused that it didn't take long for Mowry's new paper to fail. The *New York Times* wrote it up as an "affair of honor."

WILLIAM COWPER BRANN, the nationally famous editor of the *Iconoclast*, led the Waco, Texas, newspaper to live up to its name. Brann was ornery in a state

where orneriness could cost you dearly. He hated a lot of groups—women, black people, and especially Baptists. "I have nothing against Baptists," he wrote. "I just believe they were not held under long enough." In 1898, he thundered in print against that Baptist institution of higher learning, Baylor University; Baylor students kidnapped him and dragged him through their campus by a rope. Undeterred, Brann declared that Baylor was a place of lax morals, "a factory for ministers and magdalenes"—meaning prostitutes. That was too much for Tom Davis, whose daughter went to Baylor. Davis shot Brann in the back, right where his suspenders crossed, but before Brann staggered away to die, he shot the loving daddy stone-dead in the doorway of Jake French's cigar store. Brann's tombstone, a large marble "lamp of truth," was shot up two days after it was installed, and the whole thing was stolen from the cemetery in 2009. Baylor Bears have long memories.

CHARLES G. KUSZ was the editor of the *Gringo & Greaser*. Nowadays, if you splashed a moniker like that on a newspaper, you'd be asking for trouble, and Kusz was a man who relished a dust-up. But in Manzano, New Mexico, in 1884, it was the news, not the name, that got Kusz killed. The *Leadville Herald,* a paper in the Colorado mining town where Kusz had once

published another paper, wrote that he "was not the kind of man to be bulldozed and therefore met his death." Cattle rustlers didn't like the paper's law-and-order reporting on their crimes, and it was probably one of them who fired through a window and killed Kusz as he ate dinner in the newspaper office. The *G&G* had been in business for barely seven months. The newspapermen of New Mexico put up a thousand-dollar reward to find the "assassin," declaring that a journalist doing his job "is frequently placed in a position where his life is imperiled," and that's exactly what happened to the "fearless" Kusz.

HENRY TAMMEN AND FREDERICK BONFILS were a couple of rogues who founded the *Denver Post*. The executive office was called the Bucket of Blood for its red walls and for the paper's sensationally scarlet coverage. Tammen was known as the Little Dutchman, a bartender who sold arrowheads of dubious authenticity, and Bonfils was the Napoleon of the Cornfields for his West Point days and his Corsican lineage. In the *Post*, Bon and Tam created what some regarded as a money-making "Coney Island of journalism." Outrage, chicanery, vileness, lies, blackmail, and vituperation were all part of the *Post*'s stylebook. In 1889, the *Post* was crusading against the forty-year manslaughter prison sentence of Alfred Griner "Alferd"

From the 1964 booklet, *The Gringo & Greaser* by Peter Hertzog.

Packer, the Colorado mountain man who had survived by eating and (maybe, or maybe not) killing a snowbound companion. Meeting in the Bucket of Blood, Tam and Bon demanded that Packer's lawyer, W.W. Anderson, relinquish Packer's power of attorney. Words turned to fists, and fists turned to gunfire. Tam and Bon were wounded; Anderson was never convicted, but Tam and Bon were—of trying to tamper with the jury. The winner in this mess was Packer, who was presently freed on the governor's orders. Among Bon and Tam's later adventures: getting horsewhipped by livid readers, publishing a politically corrupt Kansas City newspaper, and, fittingly, running a circus.

CHARLES AND MICHAEL DE YOUNG founded the *San Francisco Chronicle*, and for a time it was the most-read paper in the West. Not all of its readers were happy. Judge Delos Lake felt that justice in general, and his career in particular, had suffered at the hands of the *Chronicle*. He tried to club Charles with his whalebone cane, and when it broke, tried to stab him with the jagged stub.

Five years later, a Baptist minister named Isaac Smith Kalloch was running for mayor; he, too, felt that he had been wronged by the paper, when it brought up some old charges of adultery and some unseemly new ones. Oh yeah? was essentially the candidate's retort. Well, your mother was a whore. He literally said that: that the de Young brothers were "bastard progeny of a whore." So Charles de Young committed a nineteenth-century drive-by. From the window of his carriage, he shot Kalloch twice. But Kalloch lived, got the sympathy vote, and became mayor. Kalloch was still mayor when his son crept into the *Chronicle* offices and killed Charles de Young. As for the surviving brother, Michael: to hate him, wrote the acidulous newspaperman Ambrose Bierce, was "the first and best test of a gentleman." In 1884, Adolph Spreckels, whose brother ran the competing *San Francisco Call*, shot and wounded the surviving de Young brother for writing that the Spreckels sugar company defrauded stockholders and ran its Hawaii plantation like, well, a plantation. The two one-percenter families loathed each other so much that the maître d' at the St. Francis Hotel dining room had to make sure neither was seated anywhere near the other. Michael de Young survived to buy the *San Francisco Call*—and shut it down. Revenge is . . . sugar-sweet.

WE WIN!
BROOKLYN EAGLE
Sports Complete
BAYONETS DRIVE
NAZIS 6 MILES

CHAPTER 4

PASTIMES, FUN TIMES, AND THE FUNNIES

L ike carving up a Thanksgiving turkey, a daily newspaper—and especially the Sunday paper—has always provided something for every member of the family. For the price of pennies, a newspaper in the nineteenth century (and far into the twentieth) was a home entertainment center on paper, with something for dad and mom and the kiddies.

The little ones who splayed out on the floor with their elbows pinning the comics pages to the carpet could turn to the titillations of *Ripley's Believe It or Not!*, learn how to build a radio set or a campfire, and read up on hobbies and crafts like bird-watching or chess. Some newspapers hired chess writers. The little woman—as newspaper publishers imagined "the lady of the house"—could pore over recipes, snip out knitting patterns, and check out the bridge column, even the Ouija-board feature that ran for a time in the *Baltimore Sun*.

TRUTH, JUSTICE, AND THE COMICS.

New York Newsday

In front sections, readers found the vitamin-rich news of important doings—foreign and domestic, government and business, police and military, official and unearthed. It's the kind of information President George Washington and Congress had in mind when they created the postal service in 1792 and set special rates for mailing newspapers, just to make it easier to spread vital information throughout the new nation.

Flip through the pages of local news, the business pages, and finally the fun: sports pages, features, entertainment news, and—party pay-dirt!—the comics, the funnies. It's just as the British publisher Lord Northcliffe once said: "It is hard news that catches readers—features hold them."

Like a '70s mullet haircut, the newspaper was organized for business in the front, party in the back.

Opposite: Jubilation in a Brooklyn tavern as the Brooklyn Dodgers clinch the 1941 National League pennant; the two-word headline in the *Brooklyn Eagle* tells the story. The Dodgers went on to lose the Subway Series to the Yankees.

The *Montana Post*, the territory's first newspaper, started publishing in Virginia City in 1864. The following January, the paper started covering the town's regular series of prizefights; the first went on for 185 rounds.

From a newspaper owner's point of view, the beauty of putting together a paper this way is that even if the only thing people bought the newspaper for is, say, prep sports or the horoscope, they would still have to buy the whole package to get it.

And from the point of view of democracy, even if readers were hunting for just the box scores or the day's prediction for Scorpios, they would glimpse the meatier news headlines as they turned to the back pages. And who knows? Their eyes might be caught by a headline about some event of earth-rattling importance.

SPORTS

The British love of sports like horse racing and fisticuffs survived the American Revolution. It took American newspapers a while to follow those pastimes routinely; the rough-and-tumble of a new nation's politics was sporting interest enough.

One early sports story read more like a police blotter item. A *New York Spectator* account of a July 1823 boxing match with a two-hundred-dollar purse was broken up when the cops swept in and hauled off boxers and fans (and maybe the prize money, too). The editor tut-tutted, "We are grieved to find the pernicious customs which disgrace the populace of Europe creeping among us."

Oh, stuff it, answered other newspapers and their readers. Across the sod-busting homesteads of the prairie, in the gold and silver camps of the West, farmers, ranchers, and miners amused themselves with horse races and boxing matches, and the stories about them.

When Montana was still a territory, its earliest newspaper, the *Montana Post*, splashed big coverage of the "bare-knuckle prize fights" in the gold camps. The January 7, 1865, issue recounted in detail one of the longest such fights in boxing history, with ten-dollar ringside seats to a battle that went on for so many gruesome hours that it was finally called as a draw by a referee before somebody got killed.

The *Montana Post* writer who covered that was Thomas Dimsdale, an Oxford man who gloried in the fancy-pants writing that passed for highfalutin' prose. When a building in town caught fire, locals swore he ran down the street hollering *Conflagration! Conflagration!*

In his account of the fight, Dimsdale struggled just as future generations of sports writers would do for different ways to say *won* and *lost* and *scored*. In Dimsdale-ese, bloody punches were "setting the ruby" flowing and "distilling the vermillion."

A decade earlier, in Hoboken, New Jersey, on a June day in 1855, a baseball game between the Empire Club and the Eagle Club drew the papers' attention for the vast attendance, including, to the reporters' evident surprise, "ladies, who seemed to take a great interest in the game."

The national pastime and the national medium of record were made for each other. During the Civil War, Union teams behind the lines played baseball so devotedly that when an anticipated matchup between the 2nd New Jersey Volunteers and the 77th New York Volunteers didn't happen, newspapers reportedly hammered the 77th for being a spoilsport no-show. Civil War veterans took their love of baseball home from the battlefront, and newspapers soon obliged with separate sports staffs and sections, which in time would

A souvenir glass ashtray from the *Boston Herald* reminded smoking sports fans of who delivered their stories, scores, and stats.

add basketball and even bowling coverage to their bulked-up pages.

The telegraph revolutionized sports reporting the way the shot clock revolutionized basketball. The first telegraphed sports story was anything but gripping prose, but what mattered was that it was first—and it was fast. In February 1849, a *New York Herald* delivery foreman named "Uncle Joe" Elliott was sent to a snowbound field in Maryland to cover a boxing match between "Adonis" Hyer and "Yankee" Sullivan. His is the earliest telegraph account of a big sports story:

"Baltimore, Feb. 8, A.M. The fight took place yesterday about 5 p.m. at Roach's Point, Kent county, Maryland. Hyer won in fifteen rounds. Sullivan is badly punished, but not dangerously. Time occupied, about sixteen minutes." There was a lot more flabby prose, and the *Herald* spread it all over the front page, the novelty of transmission outweighing the news value of the story. From then on, the words *by telegraph* would be a magic carpet to bring the clamor and color of faraway happenings to any

toff or office boy who could buy, borrow, or pinch a paper.

In the vicious wars for circulation, papers realized that they could make a splash by playing up sports coverage, until even the dignified, established papers felt obliged to send a chap or two to write about the old horsehide along with the yachting. (The first Pulitzer for sports writing went to the *New York Herald-Tribune*'s William H. Taylor for his coverage of international yacht races—not exactly *vox populi*.)

Before World War I, the *Philadelphia Record* ran an enormous lighted scoreboard, like an electrified moving ribbon, along the front of its building. It relayed baseball plays, as they happened, to the vast crowds in the street. It was speedy, it was thrilling—and it was a foreshadowing of the Internet Age that cut the ground out from under newspapers.

The tricky part about newspaper sports coverage has always been the final scores. From Abner Doubleday to Mark Zuckerberg, a couple of numbers could easily be hollered across the street, blared out on the radio, or tweeted from the stands. So who needed a newspaper? But a game is much more than the score. Great newspaper sports writing—like any great newspaper writing—delivers something richer than a headline. It gives readers, the fans who already know who won, a virtual trip to the game itself, to keep them on the

What makes a newspaper great?

Back in 1904 the glowering young boxer (left, above) earned $50 by defeating the former world's bantamweight and featherweight champion, Terrible Terry McGovern, in a memorable 6-round bout. He also earned a broken tooth and a stitched lip in same, plus a reputation that brought him further employment in exhibition matches with lightweight champions Joe Gans and Battling Nelson.

In January 1953 the white-haired ring veteran (right, above) earned the James J. Walker Memorial Award for his 50 years of "long and meritorious service to boxing." In the opinion of the assembled greats of the boxing world, it was an honor long overdue the man who is 1953 President of the National Boxing Association, and Chairman of the Minnesota Athletic Commission.

Both pictures, taken nearly a half-century apart, are, in fact of the same man—George Arthur Barton, senior

sports reporter of the Minneapolis Star and Tribune and one of the most sincerely respected boxing authorities in America.

Sportswriter Barton started boxing professionally at the turn of the century to augment his $10-a-week reporter's salary, later became a boxing instructor and referee. He discovered and developed such battlers as Mike Gibbons and Young Jack Redmond. He has been the arbiter in more than 12,000 fights, has raised in victory the hand of nearly every important fighter of our time. As a judge and major figure in the boxing world he helped develop the Golden Gloves tournaments, where hopeful young boxers get a chance to show their stuff in clean, well-organized competition.

Barton's first-hand acquaintance with all phases of boxing is reflected in every story he writes for the sports pages of the Minneapolis Star and Tribune. His ringside reports are

classics of clarity, color and accuracy. His judgments—as referee or scribe—are considered and quoted by fighters, fight fans and officials the country over.

In a region that takes its sports seriously and demands absolute competence from the men who write the sports pages as well as the news pages it reads, George Barton ranks high among the friendly experts whose ability and thorough-going knowledge of their craft helps keep the Minneapolis Star and Tribune the best-read newspapers in America's Upper Midwest.

Minneapolis Star and Tribune
EVENING   MORNING & SUNDAY
620,000 SUNDAY • 485,000 DAILY
JOHN COWLES, President

Left and right, fifty years apart, are photos of boxer-turned-sports reporter George Arthur Barton, who covered boxing for the *Minneapolis Star and Tribune*, which ran this congratulatory ad in 1953.

edge of their seats, teasing out the drama, the tension, all the way to the last out, the last whistle.

Take this pip, from a story about the 1924 Army-Notre Dame football game, with biblical allusions to elevate an afternoon's college pastime to an epic war:

Outlined against a blue, gray October sky, the Four Horsemen rode again. In dramatic lore, they were known as Famine, Pestilence, Destruction, and Death. These are only aliases. Their real names are Stuhldreher, Miller, Crowley, and Layden. They formed the crest of the South Bend cyclone before which another fighting Army team was swept over the precipice of the Polo Grounds this afternoon.

That was the Gettysburg Address of sports writing. The writer was the remarkable Grantland Rice. Stanley Walker, who was Rice's editor at the *New York Herald-Tribune* during the glory days of sports writing, nonetheless regarded the sports section as the newspaper's "toy department."

Playpen was a word that reporters covering the heftier news of finance and government threw at their colleagues who got to go to ball games for a living. But the sports section made money that helped to pay for those "serious" sections, and sports writers like Rice, Ring Lardner, and Damon Runyon raised sports writing to an art, fit for literary anthologies. Over time, sports columnists like these have been among the highest-profile and highest-paid writers at newspapers, with followings just as loyal as athletes'.

Sports is a national Rorschach test, a thermometer of the culture itself. Newspaper stories challenged readers: are athletes heroes

Souvenir pins promoted the *San Diego Union-Tribune*'s staffing of the 2004 summer Olympics in Athens, and the *Fresno Bee*'s reportage of the 2006 winter games in Turin, Italy.

and role models? Do their private lives—sometimes very louche private lives—matter? Is doping in sports a symptom of an entire corrupt culture? Jackie Robinson breaking baseball's color barrier, closeted gay athletes, the moral questions of football concussions—all were raw material for modern sports writers.

Oh, but when it came to women:

A standard pose from the 1960s: the subject of a story shown reading all about himself. Here, the famed Cleveland Browns fullback Jim Brown holds the *New York Daily News* with the account of his 1965 performance against the New York Giants. Brown retired a year later for a film and television career.

Babe Ruth broad-mindedly played barnstorming games against Negro League teams, but when Spokane's *Spokesman-Review* star reporter Margaret Bean showed up to interview Ruth when he came through town, he told her, "I just can't talk to no jane reporter." Boxing champ John L. Sullivan did talk with renowned reporter Nellie Bly of the *New York World* before his big fight in 1889, an interview that had a Barbara Walters celebrity-to-celebrity vibe. "Feel my arm," he said. She did.

Women who cover sports as their beat have paid a high personal price for it. The harassment can be constant, with players and coaches grabbing and groping and propositioning—and threatening. Former *Los Angeles Daily News* sports writer Lisa Saxon has been upfront about what many women sports writers went through in silence. Players threw jockstraps at her, spat at her, called her a bitch, masturbated in front of her.

Security blocked her from the clubhouse so often that Saxon took to holding up her press pass and pointing out, "The credential says, 'Admit Bearer,' not 'Admit Bearer with Penis.'" And, as happens to women reporters on every beat around the world, getting an exclusive story often also meant getting accused of trading sex for inside info.

Inevitably, all sports writers walk a wire suspended between critics who suspect they're all boosters in the bag for the home team, and coaches, players, and fans who are sore that writers are not churning out adulatory copy. The bald fact is, newspaper coverage from the very beginning helped to make big-time sports big. Just by covering it, newspapers implicitly endorsed it. Stories about teams sold tickets; stories about auto racing sold cars.

In the nation's newsrooms, journalists' ethical formula boils down to, "If you're going to cover the circus, don't f— the elephants." For sports reporters, author Jerome Holtzer summed it up with his book title, *No Cheering in the Press Box.* Ethics rules for sports writers were finally codified in the 1970s and '80s to clear up questions about traveling or eating with the team, or the practice—long since ended—of baseball paying some working reporters to keep official game scores.

In 1919, when it came to bigger-picture matters like cheating in sports, most sports reporters turned a deaf ear to rumors that Chicago White Sox players were being paid to throw the World Series. One who didn't was a top-flight sports writer named Hugh Fullerton, of the *Chicago Herald-Examiner.* (Nearly seventy years later, fellow Chicagoan Studs Terkel played him

Jim Cortese, a columnist for the *Memphis Commercial Appeal,* took a sporting vacation in 1959, roller-skating his way from Louisiana to New Mexico, bringing out the umbrella in Dallas, Texas.

in the baseball film *Eight Men Out.*)

Fullerton's own paper wouldn't print his story about the scandal, so it finally ran in the *New York World* on December 12, 1919, with the headline IS BIG LEAGUE BASEBALL BEING RUN FOR GAMBLERS, WITH BALLPLAYERS IN THE DEAL?

That story blew up baseball. Indictments were issued, and a federal judge was appointed to clean up baseball. As for Fullerton, he was a deeply principled man who believed that baseball was "the most serious pleasure ever invented." And baseball had let him down. Years later, he

wrote, "The fact that organized baseball's settled policy for years of 'keeping quiet for the sake of the sport' has been the very thing that made crookedness possible, is overlooked." Today, sports scandals—drugs, athletes' criminal misdeeds—are just another part of the sports writer's beat.

ADVICE AND GOSSIP

Society columns about the celebrities of the day, New York's and London's exalted society, enthralled readers the way reality shows about the rich and profligate do today. Dresses, houses, carriages—no detail was too trivial for scrutiny, and in local papers, too, the weddings and tea parties, the summering and wintering habits of ladies and gentlemen of leisure and means were detailed in long columns of small type.

In time, that enthralled coverage pivoted to movie stars, and the stories managed to be both trivial—a star's wife getting her appendix removed—and monumentally powerful.

Gossip columnists, whose heydays spanned from the 1930s to the 1960s, could make or break careers as easily as any studio chief. Hedda Hopper parlayed a modest movie career into a massive print and radio empire with bullying, flattery, and threats.

Beatrice Fairfax was the first American advice columnist—real name, Marie Manning, a finishing-school girl. She was fed up with the prissy, mincing, hearts-and-flowers stories she was assigned in the Hen Coop section at the *New York Journal*.

The paper was already getting piles of the "please-help" letters that reporters still get today from the desperate. A legendary editor named Arthur Brisbane handed them off to Manning, and once her "Dear Beatrice Fairfax" advice column landed on the *Journal*'s pages on July 20, 1898, the letters flooded in like a plague of Old Testament frogs. There were so many that the post office balked at delivering them, so many that Manning came to shudder at the sight of a mailbag.

Burned out, she left the job after seven years, but others, including men, successively took over as Beatrice Fairfax. Publisher Hearst, wearing his silent movie–producer hat, arranged for a Beatrice Fairfax weekly serial of her derring-do. Beatrice made it into two songs: 1915's "Beatrice Fairfax, Tell Me What to Do," and as a couple of lines—Beatrice Fairfax, don't you dare/Ever tell me she will care—in the Gershwin *frères*' heartrending 1930 song "But Not for Me."

Naturally, other papers and reporters copied the format, none more successfully than Dorothy Dix, a Southern gentlelady who, in the manner of a lady, used a false name in print. Elizabeth Meriwether Gilmer had written for the *New Orleans Picayune*, and then became a New York crime reporter, which prepared her well for doling out advice on the human heart.

At her peak, in 1940, Dorothy Dix reached sixty million readers in more than 250 newspapers worldwide. Her face, like the fictional Carrie Bradshaw's in *Sex and the City*, beamed from billboards and bus ads. Even men of the cloth turned to Dix for help with their own miseries.

The advice she dispensed set the tone for advice columnists thereafter: pithy, level-headed messages on intimate matters of morality, marriage, ethics, home, sex, neighbors, smoking, and drinking. They were just the kind of homilies that people clip out, carry in a wallet, send to relatives, glue in scrapbooks; what we now call a man's midlife crisis, Dix characterized as "last call to the dining car."

In 1955 after Dix died, Eppie Lederer stepped into the vacant byline of the "Ann Landers" advice column at the *Chicago Sun-Times*. A few months later, her twin sister, Pauline, pitched her tough-love "Dear Abby" column to the *San Francisco Chronicle*, creating some sisterly friction—and two of the most-read women in the world.

Advice columns gave us one great piece of American literature: *Miss Lonelyhearts*, the Nathanael West novel about a newspaperman who dispenses homilies under that sappy pseudonym, and how the job eats away at his life and spirit.

WOMEN

After the Civil War, a growing middle class went shopping. In the mercantile boom, newspaper ads reached women, and newspaper stories reached out to keep both ads and readers. Women couldn't vote, but as the family breadwinners made more money in a more sophisticated national economy, it was the women who often opened, or closed, the domestic purse strings.

Sheet music of the popular 1915 song "Beatrice Fairfax Tell Me What to Do" proves the popularity of the first advice to the lovelorn column. One chorus: "Oh Beatrice Fairfax, what shall I do? I want the bare facts, the truth from you."

As the women's movement was gaining power and force, a 1973 cigarette ad used an unidentified woman as a sports reporter covering racing. The reality was much different: women who began covering big-league sports often met with almost as much hostility from male reporters as from male athletes.

Newspapers began covering women. And newspapers grudgingly began hiring women. But for the longest time, the so-called "women's section" was still a pink ghetto, even though, over the twentieth century, it was rebranded with vague code words like Style and Scene. As writer Kay Mills pointed out in her book *A Place in the News*, editors thought it was absolutely fine for women to be out late at night covering charity balls, but not out late covering murders.

The *New York World* gets credit for the first standardized women's page in the 1890s, when such pages were occupied with the domestic doings that the Germans called *kinder, kuche, kirche*—children, kitchen, church.

As the new century percolated along, women's news found itself in a kind of newspaper apartheid. Comparable stories about men wound up in the "real" news sections, a double standard that became even more obvious after women began working in high-profile businesses and political campaigns, and even running for office themselves.

Women writers could scarcely break through the glass front page, unless they covered trials with a woman as the crime victim (plucky or defenseless, pick one), or juicier still, as the murderer herself (stone-hearted gorgon, vengeful divorcee, or cruelly wronged flower avenging her honor). At one such trial, a cynical newspaperman came up with a term to mock them: *sob sisters*, as in sentimental prose gasbags.

Newspapers loved scandals but skittered away from plain language to write about them. Abortions were "illegal operations," and syphilis and gonorrhea were "social diseases," which made them sound like bad breath, not deadly infections. Into the 1960s, a San Francisco-area newspaper decreed that its writers use the word *harmed* as a euphemism for raped, until the day that, as one veteran newsman recalled, the paper found itself reporting that a murdered woman had been "stabbed and strangled but not harmed."

The glass ceiling finally began splintering in the 1960s, '70s, and '80s with women's liberation, women's expanded legal rights, and women's growing place in public life. The women's pages whipped off the apron and picked up the picket

A 1927 magazine ad for the Scripps-Howard newspaper chain extols its appeal to women readers, thanks to its several hundred women reporters, who are "authorities on every subject of feminine interest, from mending a hot water bottle to patching a broken heart."

sign, running forthright stories about civil rights, women's rights, reproductive rights, wife-beating, gay rights—all stories of monumental human importance that were still off the news radar for most white male editors. The fearless columnist Molly Ivins told journalist Kay Mills that at the *Dallas Times-Herald*, bold women writing boldly "got away with murder" because "male editors never bothered to read it."

There was no single moment when "women's stories" started to become just stories about women, when women candidates and women sports heroes began to be covered in the front-section news, not as female oddities. In the 1970s, a newspaper editor in the Southwest pulled a female political reporter off a campaign because both candidates were women, and that, he said, was a conflict of interest. "Have you ever," the reporter demanded, "taken a man off a campaign because both candidates were men?" The editor backed down. But a double standard for who covers what, and how that determines what is important news, persists.

CROSSWORD PUZZLES

Lost in the tar pits of history are the credits many reporters and editors rightly deserve for shaping, molding, and nurturing American culture. But for this one, we know who, we know when. And we defi-

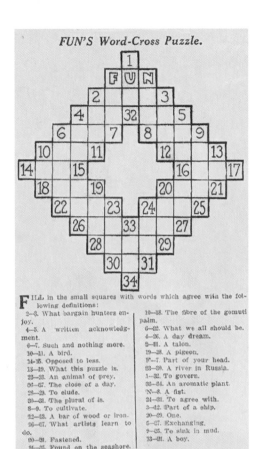

The fantastic appeal of the crossword puzzle has never waned since this, the very first, appeared in the Sunday *New York World* on December 21, 1913.

nitely know what happened thereafter. Next to the Beatles, he is probably the most important Liverpudlian ever to come to America.

Arthur Wynne crossed the Atlantic and worked for the *Pittsburgh Press* before he moved to a desk at the *New York World*, a newspaper that was not reluctant to try out new features in a section called "Fun." Wynne is listed in MIT's database of inventors for this: remembering an English

children's game called Magic Squares, he arranged a diamond-shape grid with clues. His instructions: "Fill in the small squares with words which agree with the following definitions."

The first one ran on December 21, 1913, an early Christmas gift to a world that would go crossword-mad, working them out on trains, on planes, online. Wynne called his puzzle a *word cross*, and however it happened—everyone loves the story of the mixed-up typesetter—it soon turned into *crossword*.

This new cruciverbalism (from *cruci* [cross] + *verbal* [words]) sold millions of copies of newspapers, some of them to people who bought them only for the puzzle. Clubs, parties, tournaments—crosswords became such a craze that the New York Public Library's report for 1921 deplored the fact that "puzzle fans swarm to the dictionaries and encyclopedias so as to drive away . . . legitimate" students and scholars. "As the year closes," it said primly, "there are no signs of abatement."

Nor would there be. Cruciverbalism skipped from feature sections' back pages onto smartphones and tablets, and morphed into numbers-only Sudoku. But for devoted fans like comedian Jon Stewart and President Bill Clinton, the sheer brain-beating frustration of being stymied by 8-Across lasts forever.

An undated snapshot of three kids, the eldest reading the funny papers. From the look on his face, he's the eldest brother assigned to look after the two little ones, and they're interrupting his reading.

THE FUNNIES

He was called *The Yellow Kid*, but what's now credited as the first full-fledged comic strip might just as well have been called the *Golden Kid*, because the Kid, and his thousands of comic-strip "begats," became a gold mine. And newspapers to this day still count on the funny pages as a vein of gold in the red ink.

The Yellow Kid was an odd-looking New York slum child who popped up first as a character in another comic, but by 1895 had his own comic strip franchise. The Kid's speech balloon was not new; it had been part of savage political cartoons since the eighteenth century.

Comic-strip mortality was high, and the Kid was not long for this world. He lasted four years as his own comic strip in two papers. The Kid's "father," Richard F. Outcault, also fathered the more durable and profitable Buster Brown character, but he was never able to copyright either.

Yet these two Kids made a mint as celebrity endorsers. The Yellow Kid sold High Admiral cigarettes, three-cent cigars, gingersnaps, and Florida citrus, and Buster Brown Shoes shod generations of children. Every kid with a *Peanuts* lunchbox, every grown-up with a *Far Side* birthday card, is in the debt of *The Yellow Kid*'s merchandising miracle. (The Yellow Kid's color became shorthand for a kind of paper that practiced "yellow" journalism—titillating, sensational coverage that played fast and loose with the truth and played up everything grotesque and stupefying.)

With his oddball street slang and his sly remarks about current events, the Kid was the first of the wise-beyond-their-years kid comics, from *Nancy* and *Peanuts* to *Calvin & Hobbes*, where trenchant grown-up remarks bubbled out of the mouths of babes.

If a modern-day comic strip gets too topical, it may get yanked from the comics pages altogether. In the presidential election year 1988, the comic *Cathy*, about the perpetual single-girl Baby Boomer, got pulled by some newspapers when one character flat-out endorsed Democrat Michael Dukakis because of his policies on matters like equal pay and daycare. The publisher and owner of two Alabama papers paid from his own pocket for a Bush-for-president ad to replace it.

Gary Trudeau's *Doonesbury* and its cast of Baby Boomers was a sardonic comic-strip forerunner of the *Daily Show*. *Doonesbury* also may be the comic strip most often canceled or exiled to commentary sections when the comic characters

Among the branded memorabilia that newspapers handed out to readers is this umbrella from the *New York Daily News*, featuring the paper's comic strips.

took up subjects like masturbation, or in 2012, a series of strips savaging an intrusive Texas abortion law.

Long before *Doonesbury*, though, a one-time Disney illustrator named Walt Kelly was already a Voltaire of the funny pages. His *Pogo* characters—swamp creatures with Swarthmore vocabularies—ridiculed Senator Joseph McCarthy, Fidel Castro, and J. Edgar Hoover. Kelly ran Pogo

"Johnny Jason, Teen Reporter" was a short-lived comic book. In this spring 1962 issue, Johnny gets a chance to report a story for the *Green City Journal* after his rousing speech to the editors that "Your teen reporter should print only the absolute truth."

the Possum for president and wrote him a campaign song, and NBC liked Kelly's wit enough to hire him as a commentator at the 1956 Democratic National Convention.

What made the vivid funny pages possible were new color-capable printing techniques. Starting with *The Yellow Kid's* canary-colored nightshirt, pages of full-color hilarity enticed children to the fat Sunday supplements. In short order, there were comics for grown-ups, too.

A roll call of comic characters shows their population to be part circus, part census. Pirates and soldiers, soap-opera doctors and meddling landladies (*Rex Morgan, M.D.* and *Mary Worth*), battling married couples and orphans (*Blondie* and *Dondi*), hillbillies and millionaires, cowboys and superheroes, talking dogs and supercilious cats, goofy teenagers and anarchic children (*Archie* and the *Katzenjammers*), and at least two cavemen (*Alley Oop* and *B.C.*).

The democracy of the comics pages quite truly held something for everyone. If the G-rated *Family Circle* was too insipid, there were the wiseacres of *Bloom County*. Underground newspapers created a following for counterculture strips like the legendary Robert Crumb's *Fritz the Cat*. Reporter *Brenda Starr* was a rarity, a comic created by a woman, Dale Messick, who changed her name from Dalia to Dale so

publishers wouldn't know she was a woman and reject her work because of it. She had a point. J.K. Rowling's publishers used her initials on her Harry Potter books, not her first name, because boys might not want to read books written by a woman.

Buoyed by the freedom that real women reporters had carved out for themselves, Brenda chalked up endless implausible scoops. She launched *Brenda Starr* comic

In the summer of 1945, during a seventeen-day strike by New York's newspaper delivery truck drivers, Mayor Fiorello La Guardia read the Sunday funnies aloud on his weekly radio broadcast, with different voices for each character. He then delivered his own homily, like, "Say children, what does it all mean? ... Dirty money always brings sorrow and sadness and misery and disgrace."

The ageless, red-headed scoop-chaser was honored as one of twenty comic characters in an American commemorative stamp series in 1995.

books, dolls, movie and TV spinoffs, and a commemorative stamp. When Brenda married her dashing, one-eyed beau in 1976, First Lady Betty Ford and her husband sent their congratulations.

Brenda changed along with newspapers' fortunes. She took her last bow from the newsroom and the funny pages in 2011, as her beloved *New York Flash* turned into a throwaway freebie with—oh my—bloggers.

President Ronald Reagan told *60 Minutes* in 1989 that he always read the morning paper's funnies first, beginning with *Spiderman*. And during New York's seventeen-day newspaper strike in 1945, Mayor Fiorello LaGuardia used the last minutes of his weekly radio show to give the kids of New York what they were missing: he read them the comics.

HOROSCOPES

Monarchs employed astrologers for centuries, yet it was treasonous for any free-lancers to cast a horoscope for the wearer of the Crown of England. Prophecy was not an amusement; it could shake a throne. On August 24, 1586, two people ratted on a man named Symon Yomans, saying he'd predicted that Queen Elizabeth would die that year. That same day, Yoman underwent "examination"—torture.

Today, anyone can thumb through a newspaper to read that on Her Majesty Queen Elizabeth II's ninetieth birthday, her Taurus horoscope predicted: "This year you could experience a lot of high-voltage surprises, which certainly will keep your life exciting."

Paradoxically, one of the first newspaper horoscopes ever printed was about Princess Margaret, the queen's sister. When she was born, in 1930, the editor of Britain's *Sunday Express* newspaper, uncowed by any Tudor notions of treason, printed the royal baby's horoscope—344 years to the day after the unfortunate Yomans likely met a grisly end for doing much the same thing. (It was foretold that "events of tremendous importance to the Royal Family and the nation will come about near her seventh year," which turned out to be the abdication of her uncle, which made her father the king of England.)

Pretty soon, readers were clamoring for the royal treatment themselves, and the *Express* obliged with a horoscope column.

ROOSEVELT SHOWN BY THE ZODIAC

Mme. Humphreys Casts a Horoscope of the President's Past and Future.

FINDS HIS RADAX RADICAL

And Sagittarius Gave Him a Free, Daring Nature—He Might Have Been Different with Another Birthday.

The *New York Times* interviewed an astrologer, in 1908, who had cast President Teddy Roosevelt's horoscope. Who could have predicted the lasting appeal of astrology?

In 1908, the august *New York Times* ran a story about a Madame Humphreys, who cast President Teddy Roosevelt's horoscope. His "radax," she said, was "radical," and he should be wary of train travel.

On these shores, the *Boston Record* started up an astrology column in 1931, and by the 1980s, about forty men and women—Jeane Dixon, Carroll Righter, and Sydney Omarr at the top of the heap—were writing newspaper astrology columns. They knew that most readers didn't care much about placements of Mars in Leo, and that even though some readers blew off astrology as rank flapdoodle, far more wouldn't dream of starting their days without checking their horoscope, even though it was written for millions, in language vague enough to fit anyone.

If only newspapers could have foretold their own futures.

CHAPTER 5

POPULAR CULTURE AND THE PRESS

"What is that thing?" ... said almost no one, ever, in the history of the republic, and even before the republic was born.

The newspaper—not just the purpose of it, but the actual object, the silhouette, the smell and the heft of it—has been about as familiar to Americans as their own flag. It's as recognizable as the light bulb and the Co-ca-Cola bottle, as the horse in the nineteenth century, and the car in the twentieth.

Even now, with so many newspapers deep in the red, about twenty billion individual newspapers—twenty *billion*—get printed every year in this country. Once, virtually every American old enough to read bought a newspaper every day, or at least scanned

In September 1965, partygoers went crazy posing in hula skirts made from newspapers. Newsprint-as-fabric was such a fad that home-economics teachers assigned students to stitch-up wardrobes from the latest editions, and in 2009, contestants on the fashion reality TV-show *Project Runway* competed to make the best ensemble out of newspaper..

the headlines on someone else's copy on the subway, picked up a discarded one on a bus bench or in a barber shop.

The newspaper was at the common core of public life. People went to different churches and different schools, worked at different jobs and read different books, but high and lowly, man and woman, they usually read the same newspapers.

Any town worth its name had at least one newspaper. In 1790, newborn America published about a hundred different newspapers. By 1867, Cheyenne, Wyoming—population not even a thousand—already had at least four papers. Settlers used to say that "rain follows the plow;" nineteenth-century Americans also believed that civilization—

Opposite: The designer blamed it on the shortage of fabric during World War II, but the reason didn't matter to men: the modern bikini was unveiled, in a manner of speaking, on July 5, 1946, in Paris. Designer Louis Réard chose newspaper-print fabric for his creation and named it "bikini" after the atoll where the U.S. had just begun testing nuclear weapons. The bikini's impact on both fashion and sex: explosive.

The Paper House in Rockport, Massachusetts. Charles Lindbergh's solo trans-Atlantic flight in 1927 generated so much press that the homeowners made an entire desk out of Lindbergh news. His picture hangs above the desk.

people, prosperity, culture, law—followed the printing press. They spread news and commerce as industriously and efficiently as bees spread pollen. A newspaper was "the herald of progress, not the product of it," wrote the historian George H. Douglas.

Wonder whether you should dress your kid in mittens and scarf for school tomorrow? Newspaper weather forecast. Want to find out where to buy your kid mittens and a scarf at a good price? How to find your lost pet? Sell your dining room chairs? Newspaper advertisements. Wonder who's getting married? What caused that car crash on the interstate? What time the game will be on? The newspaper told you.

George Washington read them, and often wished he hadn't: "I have such a number of Gazettes crowded upon me . . . my other avocations will not afford me time to read them oftentimes, and when I do attempt it, find them more troublesome, than profitable."

The satirical newspaper the *Onion* (which went online after a quarter-century as a real newspaper) once carried the headline MAJORITY OF NEWSPAPERS NOW PURCHASED BY KIDNAPPERS TO PROVE DATE, mocking the fact that those oh-so-versatile newspapers were indeed used by kidnappers as "proof of life"—evidence that a victim was alive on the day the paper was published.

After Cuba's leader Fidel Castro had surgery in 2006, he proved he was still alive and kicking by holding up a current issue of Cuba's official Communist party newspaper *Granma* (whose contents probably haven't changed much since the Cuban Revolution).

Similarly, that cartoon Everyman, Homer Simpson, found himself kidnapped by Ukrainian gangsters who forced him to display a newspaper as a time-stamp verification. *What would they do when there are no more newspapers?* Homer asked them. "Perhaps, we'll be living in a world where there'll be no need for kidnappings," they mused. "Way to make me feel obsolete," observes Homer.

You could fill a little lexicon with

Sometimes you are the story, and sometimes you hide behind the story. In this instance, both. Men waiting to be questioned by Philadelphia police in 1944 about an illegal betting scheme try to mask their mugs behind newspapers. —none of them, or so it appears, the *Racing Form*.

words and phrases that newspapers have added to English. From the comics alone, we get "shazam," and "keeping up with the Joneses" (which, in the twenty-first century, was spun into TV's *Keeping Up with the Kardashians*). *Popeye* popularized two real pips that we're still using today—"Jeep" and "goon."

The Oxford English Dictionary hunts down the origins of every word in the language, and it has found that many of them first appeared in newspapers. The *Times of London* is the source for more than sixteen hundred of these, and in the United States, the *Los Angeles Times* gets credited with nearly two hundred, among them "car bomb," "supermarket," and "motel."

The next time you sit down to brunch, clink your mimosa glasses to a *New York Sun* reporter named Frank Ward O'Malley, who leveraged the word "brunch" into our dictionaries about a hundred years ago—not as our swank, Champagne-sodden Sunday repast, but as a newspaperman's grab-and-gulp mid-morning meal. And the San Francisco newspaper columnist Herb Caen mashed together Sputnik, the brand-new Soviet satellite, and Beat culture to give us the 1950s and 1960s proto-hipster character, the beatnik.

Maybe the most famous phrase ever to come out of a newspaper was a writer's answer to an eight-year-old girl's letter to the *New York Sun*. Virginia O'Hanlon said her daddy told her to write in and ask, because "If you see it in the *Sun*, it's so." And *Sun* writer Francis P. Church replied so deftly and so delicately that his signature answer to her—"Yes, Virginia, there is a Santa Claus"—has become a musical, a play, a TV-movie, a cartoon. Church's editorial appeared in print nearly 120 years ago, and it is still the most reprinted newspaper editorial in the world. And "Yes, Virginia" is a two-word assurance of trust and faith even in things unseen.

For versatility, you can't beat a newspaper. It's the Swiss Army knife of modern life.

Rolled up, it does service as a fly swatter. Propped up in front of your face—on a subway, at a breakfast table—it's a perfect wall, a conversation stopper. As a conversation starter—"I read in the paper . . ."—it has launched a million office coffee-pot chats and barroom bets.

Even after it's been read, the newspaper has only started its day. After that, it goes everywhere.

Soldiers have insulated their boots with newspapers, and park-bench vagabonds

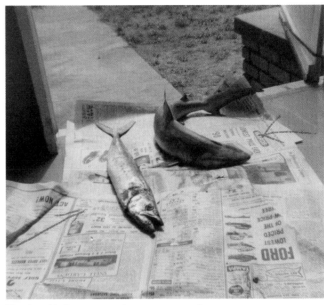

The insult's been tossed contemptuously at newspapers since the 1960s, but one of the myriad uses of newsprint really has been as fishwrap.

nap under them; "Only a hobo," Bob Dylan sang, "but one more is gone/A blanket of newspaper covered his head."

For puppy training, nothing serves better. If Christmas money was tight—or the gift-giver was—the bright Sunday comics did double duty as wrapping paper.

Newsprint has aseptic qualities, and long ago, in poor homes, doctors knew they could deliver babies using newsprint

A 1990s bit of *trompe l'oeil*, a plastic flyswatter made to look like a rolled-up newspaper, the standard weapon in man's war against the pesky *Musca domestica*.

when no sterile towels were on hand. The English doctor Richard Gordon wrote in his 1952 comic novel *Doctor in the House* about an obstetric emergency solved by the *Daily Herald*: "Newspaper, that was it! There was a pile of them in the corner, and I scattered the sheets over the floor and the bed."

Newspapers line chests of drawers and kitchen shelves. You can start a tidy fireplace blaze with one, wedge the sports section under your tires for traction in the snow, clean your car windshield without streaks, pack your breakables when you're moving, and craft a sunhat against the

Four women celebrate July 4, 1908, in Stockton, Iowa, in elegant dresses and bicorne hats made of folded newspapers. The man in the middle didn't get the fashion memo.

For the snowbound, a helpful tip, demonstrated in January 1955: stuff newspapers under the rear wheels to keep your tires from spinning.

fair-weather glare. Tomatoes ripen faster when they're wrapped in newspapers, and seedlings get a head start in a newspaper cradle. Wadded-up newspapers will dry out your rain-soaked shoes.

Get your iPhone to do all of that.

When a French car engineer named Louis Réard constructed the world's smallest swimsuit—a two-piece number he called a "bikini," which a teenaged Parisian showgirl debuted to the world on July 5, 1946—he decided to make it from something that was as recognizable as his bikini would be-

come: a newspaper-print fabric.

Then Twiggy, the matchstick model of 1960s chic, posed in a newspaper-print dress in 1967, and the black-and-white gold rush was on. Newspaper fabric has never been out of print. Nineteen-sixties paper dresses made the point that fashion, like a newspaper, was an of-the-moment disposable thing. But the pattern is hardly reserved for throwaways. From French designer John Galliano's boxer shorts to Chinese-made down-market knockoffs, all it takes is a bolt of fabric, a large-lettered masthead in Old English type, and long columns of text in a solemn serif font.

A magazine ad for new rayon-fabric underwear exploits both sex and the "Extra! Extra!" motif, which has also come in handy for peddling Chevrolets, pears, Scotch, and diapers.

In a pet-toy think tank one day, some genius thought, "If dogs are supposed to fetch newspapers, what about a dog-toy newspaper?" In the jaws of a pup, the squeaker in the toy wheezes like a moth-eaten accordion.

New York designer Kate Spade turned out a clutch handbag looking like a real, rolled-up newspaper, but where a bona fide newspaper cost about a buck, the Spade bag set you back more than three hundred dollars.

The newspaper reporter, caricatured

Nun-brellas! In 1962, nuns at a Catholic college's horse show in Fond du Lac, Wisconsin, make expert use of newspaper pages, fashioning newspaper wimples to ward off the August sun.

and cartooned, was right up there with secret agents and cowboys. Kids played quick-witted reporters in swashbuckling board games like Five Star Final, and Scoop, and Front Page—and, before them all, Around the World with Nellie Bly, an early "product placement" item capitalizing on the real, globe-circling adventures of that daring "girl reporter." Mickey Mouse mashed a fedora down over his ears and roared off to the story as a roving reporter in a Wheaties comic, and then presumably wrote up his story on the *Mickey Mouse Club*'s official cub reporter tin typewriter.

Amusement parks and tourist attractions printed up novelty newspapers with anyone's headline news bannered across the top—in this case, Mel Johnson's getting hitched in Ocean City, New Jersey. That's Mel, left, in the carefree sandals, and the new missus, right, in the striped trousers.

Newspaper journalists as glamorous characters generated board games with all the thrill of reporting without the inkstains. The 1956 Parker Brothers game Scoop! The winner was whoever managed "to possess the best and the financially strongest newspaper." Shades of Monopoly. Five Star Final was a 1937 game piggybacking on the sinister 1931 movie of the same name.

Newspapers may not survive the twenty-first century as anything recognizable, but games that are played on screens, not on boards—games like Pokemon and Monsterpocalypse—still use newspapers and reporters as plot devices.

Well past the mid-century mark of the twentieth, the newspaper still showed up on the doorstep right alongside milk bottles, so it was only natural that newspapers showed up in songwriters' repertoires. You could fill a jukebox with newspaper-themed tunes. (Note to Millennials: a jukebox is a very large, gaudily lighted pay-to-play iPod.)

Before World War I, the era of big, brassy military marches, only one newspaper march tune went platinum: John Philip Sousa's *The Washington Post* march, which is still performed today in patriotic medleys. In 1889, the newspaper asked Sousa to compose a little something to accompany an essay-awards ceremony. Whoever won has been forgotten, while *The Washington Post* march goes on and on.

Other newspaper marches were stirring but unmemorable. Who today whistles *The Indianapolis News* march or *The Seattle Post-Intelligencer* march? (The *Indianapolis News* closed in 1999, after being in print for 130 years, from the day Jesse James robbed his first bank to the day ac-

tor Zach Galifianakis turned thirty.)

Jazzman Louis Armstrong delivered the best version of the mournful, lonely-hearts ballad "I Guess I'll Get the Papers and Go Home," when he crooned "I get some consolation when I read/of someone else's lonely heart."

Yankees and Dixie raced to the bottom of bathos to weep over the poor little newsboy. Here's Tin Pan Alley's "Rags," about a downtrodden New York lad: "On a busy corner, while other kiddies play, there's a little hero, selling papers each day . . ."—versus the country-western lament over the equally downtrodden "Jimmie Brown the Newsboy," selling the *Morning Star*, hatless, shoeless, fatherless, and

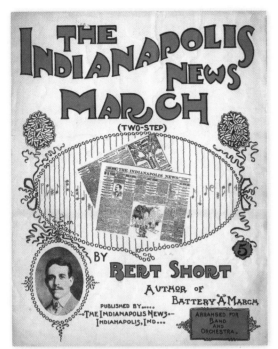

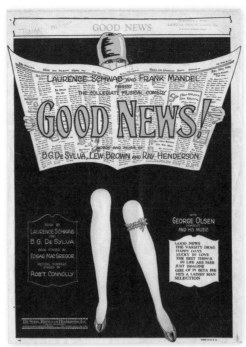

In 1862, Johann Strauss was commissioned to write the first newspaper-themed music, "The Morning Papers" waltz, for an Austrian journalists' association. In this country, John Philip Sousa's "Washington Post March" has been a hit since it was first performed in 1889. Other newspapers had less memorable music dedicated to them, like the *Indianapolis News* March," left. Center, "Good News!" was a 1927 hit Broadway musical that had nothing to do with newspapers. Right, the "plucky little newsboy" appears on the cover of the sheet music for "Rags."

destined (it's a country-western song, after all) for "a place in heaven sir to sell the Gospel News."

A newspaperman named Vern Partlow wrote "Newspapermen Meet Such Interesting People," a song that Pete Seeger recorded. It was a good match of politics and popular music, because Partlow really meant the song to entice his fellow reporters into joining the newspaper union, writing lyrics like, "Oh, publishers are such interesting people; It could be press-titution, I don't know."

The R&B girl-group Honey Cone sold a million copies of its number-one song, "Want Ads:" "Extra, extra, read all about it—wanted: young man single and free. Ex-

perience in love preferred but will accept a young trainee."

Starting in the topsy-turvy 1960s, songwriters were reading newspapers with a more cynical eye, and writing songs to match. The sentiment in Tom Paxton's "Daily News" in 1964 ("Seven little pennies in the newsboy's hand / And you ride right along to never-never land") would have resonated with Chuck D, the Public Enemy rapper, who furiously railed in "Letter to the *New York Post*" about the Big Apple's raw, shameless tabloid as "America's oldest continually published daily piece of bullshit."

It took a little indie band called Yo La Tengo to get the same kick out of tabloid

headlines that readers do, with an album of songs inspired by outlandish headlines: OHIO TOWN SAVED FROM KILLER BEES BY HUNGRY VAMPIRE BATS; RETIRED GROCER CONSTRUCTS TINY MOUNT RUSHMORE ENTIRELY OF CHEESE.

And leave it to the Rolling Stones to compare an ex-girlfriend to a pile of back-issue papers: "Who wants yesterday's papers? Who wants yesterday's girl? Nobody in the world." That was 1967, the same year the Beatles, in "A Day in the Life," sang more pensively, "I read the news today, oh boy . . ."

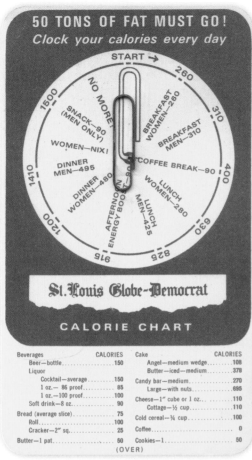

Easy to pin up on a kitchen cabinet, a "calorie clock" for subscribers showed the *St. Louis Globe-Democrat* to be a full-service newspaper, helping readers to mind every mouthful.

Before TV mock-news comedy shows, newspaper parodies appeared now and then, like this one, when the stumble-tongued, spud-misspelling Indiana senator Dan Quayle became vice president in 1989. Creating and printing up a bogus newspaper is a tricky, pricey undertaking. The best was *Not the New York Times*, a subtly written satire—by actual writers such as Nora Ephron and Jerzy Kosinski. It lived for only one edition, on October 23, 1978, during a strike that stopped the presses at the real *Times*. Among its features, "The Newest Antique," and "Insulating with Pate: Winter Warmth With Good Taste."

Nobody makes fun of a nobody. Comedy punches up, and if there's any more proof needed that newspapers have been monumentally important in the national life, it's that they're the butt of jokes.

Jerry Seinfeld, in his gee-whiz fashion, marveled: "It's amazing that the amount of news that happens in the world every day always just exactly fits the newspaper."

As for what was actually in those pages, the cowboy humorist Will Rogers, beloved for his aw-shucks truth-to-power style, went onstage, a-twirlin' his lasso, and regularly opening up his monologue with, "Well, what shall I talk about? I ain't got anything funny to say. All I know is what I read in the papers." (The fact that he knew what was *in* the newspapers because his column appeared in hundreds of them didn't make the line any less appealing.)

A few decades later, stand-up comedian Mort Sahl made the newspaper his comedy partner, too. He walked onstage with the day's paper, wielding it like a rapier and riffing on the state of the world with a sardonic improv that rechanneled comedy from the placid riverbed of scripted schtick into edgy, deflating political satire.

The *National Lampoon*'s cockeyed idea of a Sunday newspaper, the *Dacron Republican Democrat*, mocked hyperlocal reporting—editors desperate to find a local angle on a huge international story—with a story about a devastating Japanese volcanic eruption that began, "Possible tragedy has marred the vacation plans of Miss Frances Bundle and her mother Olive as volcanoes destroyed Japan early today."

The *Onion* headlines like ONLINE UNIVERSITY CRACKS DOWN ON ROWDY ONLINE FRATERNITY and PRICE OF NUCLEAR SE-CRETS PLUMMETING were only a double-take away from reality. The *Onion* has been so effective in mocking the bizarre nature of news that writers from even sober-sided publications have started stories about astonishing actual events with the caution, "It's not from the *Onion*—it really happened."

Presidents especially love to enlist newspapers as their straight men. At the hot-ticket 2015 White House Correspondents' Association dinner—in Washington, they call it the "nerd prom"—Pres-ident Barack Obama, teas-ing newspaper reporters

Whenever someone struck a match on this wall-mounted "striker," the flame lit up the name of the paper.

Left, a 1956 young-lit biography of pioneering reporter Nellie Bly, and one in a series of adventure books for the Hanna-Barbera character Huckleberry Hound. "I never heard of a dog reporter before!" he says, before heading off to ask for a job at the *Daily Bugle*.

about their beleaguered trade, described the 2015 Oscar-winning film *Spotlight* as "a movie about investigative journalists with resources and autonomy to chase down the truth. Best fantasy film since *Star Wars*."

Maybe the oldest newspaper joke known to man is the schoolyard riddle, "What's black and white and read [red] all over?" The answer had always been "the newspaper." Until 2012, when comedian Jimmy Kimmel posed the puzzler at that year's correspondents' dinner, and an-swered it himself:

"Nothing, anymore."

A newspaper "collectible," a tin wind-up dog-newsboy ringing a bell and peddling an "Extra!"

LADIES AND GENTLEMEN OF THE CINEMATIC PRESS

Cary Grant. Gregory Peck. Tom Hanks. Humphrey Bogart. Robert Redford. Warren Beatty. Denzel Washington. Clark Gable. Jimmy Stewart. Jack Lemmon. Mel Gibson. Clint Eastwood. Ronald Reagan. Don Knotts. Dustin Hoffman.

There is one role, and only one role, that every one of these movie stars has played: Newspaperman.

The movies love scripts about newspaper reporters and editors because journalists can play heroes or scoundrels, charming scamps and scapegraces. Directors can drop newspaper reporters into almost any plot, because on film, reporters' jobs can take them everywhere, from exotic and dangerous places—like Mel Gibson and Joel McCrea in *The Year of Living Dangerously* and *Foreign Correspondent*—to sleazy city streets, like Broderick Crawford in *Scandal Sheet*. From the offices of the *Daily Planet*, Clark Kent could keep watch on the world—and the girl—he is trying to save. Marvel Comics has "published" the *Daily Bugle* for decades, just so its heroes, like news photographer Peter Parker, can show up anytime, anywhere, without raising suspicions. (It has not gone unremarked about that neither Clark Kent nor Peter Parker ever covers a regular story, like a

city council meeting or a car-theft ring, only stories that are about superheroes.)

In fact, responsible newspapering is not a cinematically compelling line of work. Reporters make phone calls. They interview people. They research records, they fact-check, and they type. They type a lot. If there's a chase scene in a newspaper reporter's life, it's probably a paper chase, and the payoff is the kick from tracking down some smoking-gun document that can send a crooked politician to prison. They do this without gunplay or undercover antics, without romancing sources, and—except for foreign correspondents and combat reporters—usually without anything more hazardous to life and limb than the mysterious crud at the bottom of the newsroom coffee pot. But these are movies we're talking about, not documentaries.

The first known film that got all this celluloid rolling was a 1900 Biograph short called *Horsewhipping an Editor*, a four-minute tale about a livid reader who shows up at a newspaper office, where a cleaning lady and a copy boy get the better of him.

By 2015, the newspaper film *Spotlight* won an Oscar for best picture, and another true-to-life newspaper story followed it, *The Post* (2017), about the *Washington Post*'s

Brenda Starr, Reporter is a 1945 episode of a long-running serial beginning with "Hot News," and based loosely on the adventures of the russet-haired cartoon glamor girl, the real-life likes of whom has probably never been seen in any American city room.

struggle to print the Pentagon Papers.

More than a century between these offered dozens of newspaper movies—heroic, sardonic, comical. *Cimarron*, the first western to win a best-picture Oscar, was a historical epic based on an Oklahoma frontier power couple who also published a newspaper.

It Happened One Night, in 1934, was the Oscars' first "grand slam" film—best film, director, actor, actress, screenplay—a rom-com tale of a scamp of a reporter (Clark Gable) who chases down the story of a runaway heiress (Claudette Colbert).

Filmmakers from Alfred Hitchcock to Billy Wilder and Orson Welles haven't exactly been hung up on journalistic authenticity or ethics. And so generations of American moviegoers have come to believe that reporters are louche drunkards who gleefully skate on thin moral ice and rejoice in crafting big stories out of human misery, even as they delight in deflating the pompous and powerful.

In most newspaper films, authenticity stops with the word *newspaper*. Judging by movie posters for noir films like *Chicago Deadline* and *Night Editor*, reporters prefer Smith & Wessons to Smith Corona typewriters. Movie journalists can talk their way into, or out of, anything. They leap into danger's path, sleuth around like detectives, shoot it out with bad guys, go undercover to pretend to be other people—in short, commit a dozen firing offenses in the space of ninety exciting-but-implausible minutes.

Just consider this 1971 film, *The Cat O' Nine Tails*. The reporter (James Franciscus) manages to escape being poisoned; gets into a fistfight, a knife fight, and a police chase; and is locked in a crypt.

Ronald Reagan was cast as a comically frenetic reporter in the 1941 *Nine Lives Are Not Enough*, the kind of movie where, as Reagan himself said, the future U.S. president played "a jet-propelled newspaperman who solved more crimes than a lie

Still in costume as Julius Caesar, actor John Gavin gets a break from filming the 1960 movie *Spartacus* to read the *Wall Street Journal* as his wife knits. President Ronald Reagan appointed Gavin, his fellow former actor, to be the U.S. ambassador to Mexico.

detector." (*Variety* gave Reagan's film a cautionary review: "There's a bushel of newspaper stuff of the sort audiences love and although it's exaggerated beyond belief it's nearly all funny.")

In 1939, Reagan's first wife, Jane Wyman, starred in the last of a series of films about the snappy blonde newspaperwoman, Torchy Blane, the newsgal who, as Wyman described her years later, stormed the city desk insisting, "Stop the presses! I've got a story that will break this town wide open!"

Heartbreaking but true: nobody yells *stop the presses!* But it's such a beloved mov-

ie cliché that Ron Howard made it work in his rowdy 1994 film, *The Paper*, about a big-city tabloid. City editor Michael Keaton—who also starred as a more heroic editor in *Spotlight*—wants to redo the front page with evidence that two accused killers didn't do it. Randy Quaid, playing a columnist who's always carrying a hangover and a handgun, eggs him on: "How many times in your life are you gonna get to say it?"

One critic of *Hold That Girl* (1934) conceded that "the newspaper office and the city editor are not so afar as usual," and the following year, another review grudgingly credited *Front Page Woman* with "a faint

Actress Marilyn Monroe reads the paper alongside a rack of newspapers carrying the September 1952 headlines that Charlie Chaplin had been banned from returning to the United States for his supposed "radical" sympathies.

smattering of truth to coat the implausibilities." Each of those movies starred a future Oscar winner, Claire Trevor and Bette Davis, as a plucky newspaperwoman.

In an era when most working women were usually laboring in a classroom or a diner or a front office, a "newsgal" and her notebook got to go just about everywhere a man went. And a daring career girl in distress made an even better plotline than the derring-do of a newspaperman.

Newsgals could play it heroic or helpless, although the plot almost always demanded that they finally thaw out for Mr. Right. In *Hold That Girl*, Trevor escaped the clutches of a madman by writing *help* in lipstick on her panties and dropping them out the window. Davis managed to stay clothed as she competed toe-to-toe with a rival who believed women make "rotten" newspapermen.

Being sexual tricksters juiced up newspaperwomen's characters, too. Katie Holmes's character used sex to get quotes from a tobacco lobbyist in 2005's *Thank You for Smoking*.

Sally Field, in *Absence of Malice* (1981), played a Miami newspaper reporter with a trifecta of failings: she is tricked by some fake federal documents into writing a bogus story; she breaks a confidentiality pledge to a source who then commits suicide; and she sleeps with another source. In the real newspaper world, she'd be lucky to end up delivering newspapers, much less writing for one.

The movies' most engaging newspaperwoman—though far from the most ethical—has to be Rosalind Russell in *His Girl Friday* (1940). It's a remake of the 1931 classic *The Front Page*, except here, the Hildy Johnson character is a woman, not a man. She, too, schemes to get out of newspapers and into a little country cottage. Her fiancé is a dreary, doting fellow compared to the bull-slinging charm of Hildy's ex, editor Walter Burns, played by Cary Grant. The dialogue is faster than an electric typewriter, and every modern newspapering rule is broken, every principle violated—but it's all forgiven because, as often happens in newspaper films, no matter how shady the reporting, good stories take down bad men.

That was in 1940. A year later, the country was at war, and movies, like the nation and the newspaper business, sobered up. In the 1945 "good war" film *The Story of G.I. Joe*, Burgess Meredith plays Ernie Pyle, the revered World War II correspondent. The movie came out just before Pyle was killed on the job in the Pacific.

Then, in the 1960s and beyond, as public trust in institutions dimmed, moviegoers could choose to watch two kinds of war correspondents, just as they were choosing sides about the war in Southeast Asia. In John Wayne's gung-ho Vietnam movie *The Green Berets* (1968), the cynical reporter, played by David Janssen, comes around from skeptic to cheering section. In the nuanced, fog-of-war 1984 film *The Killing Fields,* about the same conflict, Sam Waterston plays Pulitzer Prize–winning *New York Times* reporter Sydney Schanberg in the true account of covering the Cambodian genocide with photojournalist and interpreter Dith Pran.

Screenwriters who needed a villain in the newsroom realized that "reporters and editors were too busy trying to capture the crook or expose corruption," wrote author and journalism scholar Joe Saltzman. And so "greedy, hypocritical, amoral publishers were crowding the conscientious publishers off the screen."

In 1952's *Park Row*, the publisher is a relentless woman. The poster's come-on: *She had blood in her veins . . . he had ink . . . and guts!* As a bloody newspaper war blazes, she proposes a merger with her upstart competitor, but he's only interested in merging their lips. She turns him down. Then his paper is bombed in retaliation for its gutsy stories, and she kills off her own paper so that his—and they—can succeed. (*Park Row*'s most reality-based moment is the editor's crusade to raise money to install the Statue of Liberty—something the *New York World* actually accomplished.)

Some casting notes for reporters in movies and on television:

THE GOOD GUYS

- Jimmy Stewart, in the true-story 1948 film *Call Northside 777*, is as skeptical as they come, but once he ferrets out the facts, his stories get an innocent man sprung from prison.
- Gregory Peck is a newspaper correspondent in *Roman Holiday* (1953) when princess-on-the-run Audrey Hepburn falls

into his lap, and he falls for her. Peck's scruples overcome his eagerness for a scoop and a rich payoff, and he lets Princess Charming have a few days of anonymous fun and a bittersweet romance to remember for a regal lifetime.

- Ed Asner, in the TV series *Lou Grant*, is the gold standard of editors—gruff, sensitive, principled, wise, and wisecracking. He guides the young staff of the *Los Angeles Tribune* through daily deadlines and life quandaries, and made reporters look at their own editors and wonder why they couldn't be more like Lou.
- Editor Humphrey Bogart, in the climax of 1952's *Deadline—U.S.A.*, is standing next to the printing presses as they run off a story naming a mob thug as a killer. The thug is on the phone with Bogart. "What's that racket?" he asks. "That's the press, baby, the press!" says Bogie. The last scene is a lingering nighttime shot of the newspaper building, to the strains of "The Battle Hymn of the Republic."
- Denzel Washington is a *Washington Herald* reporter in *The Pelican Brief* (1993), investigating and finally writing Julia Roberts's story of political assassination but keeping her identity secret, as he promised.
- Katharine Hepburn is the *Woman of the Year* (1942), a famous international affairs correspondent, and Spencer Tracy is a sports columnist. Despite Hepburn's

high-minded career—based on the hugely influential newspaperwoman Dorothy Thompson—the usual job-vs.-wifehood struggle follows, and in the end, Hepburn changes her ways and her byline to save her marriage.

- The cast of 2015's *Spotlight,* each portraying a *Boston Globe* journalist in the movie story of the newspaper stories that won a Pulitzer.
- Jack Webb, as a wooden editor in *-30-,* the 1959 film that tells the story of a dramatic day at a Los Angeles newspaper during a downpour in L.A.—as if—that washes a little girl down a storm drain. The tense hunt is drawn from a real 1947 heroic effort to save a little girl who fell down a well. Editor Webb's big page-one headline—CHILDREN STAY OUT OF THESE—is almost as stiff as he is.
- Mary Tyler Moore—our Mary—after her hat-flinging TV-news job in Minneapolis, went on to play briefly a look-out-for-the-little-guy consumer columnist at a Chicago tabloid. *Mary* the show didn't last long on the air; MTM has become legend.

CORNER-CUTTERS AND CHARMING ROGUES

- Chevy Chase is *Fletch,* the kind of reporter other reporters hate, and he does all the things that can get you fired—going undercover and pretending to be a dope addict, a doctor, an insurance man; in-

vestigating crimes, committing a few himself—all to nail the bad guy, and all a 1985 vehicle for Chase being Chase.

- Barbara Stanwyck is fired from her newspaper job in *Meet John Doe* (1941), and for her farewell column (which proves she deserved to be fired) she fakes a letter from a suicidal man. When it becomes a cause célèbre, she finds a patsy—Gary Cooper—to play Doe, falls in love with him, repents, and figures a way out for everyone.
- Gary Cooper repeats his patsy role with reporter Jean Arthur in *Mr. Deeds Goes to Town* (1936). She tricks his country-boy-turned-millionaire into believing she's a poor hard-working girl so she can get his story. Another unscrupulous newspaper siren redeemed by a good man's love—and an apron.
- Darren McGavin, in his white suit and porkpie hat, lasted only a season on *Kolchak, the Night Stalker,* from 1974 to 1975. The reporter who went out to investigate supernatural occurrences, only to have his evidence somehow vanish, still has a cult fan following.
- Clint Eastwood in the 1999 film *True Crime* is a caddish, alcoholic reporter (what, another one?) who nonetheless saves a man from being wrongly executed with only a minimum of legal and ethical rule-breaking, because what's a little breaking and entering when a man's life

is on the line? As in far too many newspaper movies, he is a reporter who does not take notes.

- Burgess Meredith is the printer's devil in the *Twilight Zone* episode of the same name, a sinister typesetter and reporter who saves a small-town paper with scoops on crimes that turn out to be . . . his own.

ROTTEN APPLES

- James Cagney is a bottom-feeding picture snatcher whose ghoulish tabloid newspaper job is getting photographs of crime victims, even if it means pulling them off the bedroom walls. Picture stealing was a real and really despicable line of work in early-twentieth-century newspapers. *Picture Snatcher* (1933) has a "torn from the headlines" moment: Cagney's character lying his way into covering a prison execution, and strapping a hidden camera to his ankle to take a picture of the woman in the electric chair. This was only five years after a New York tabloid actually pulled that stunt at the 1928 execution of murderer Ruth Snyder. Cagney gets the promotion and the girl.
- Edward G. Robinson is a tabloid editor in *Five Star Final* (1931) who rakes up a decades-old scandal with stories that push two newlyweds to commit suicide. Boris Karloff—a few months before he starred in *Frankenstein*—is Robinson's monster, a

lowlife reporter who poses as a minister and then prints a confidential confession.

- Kirk Douglas is one of the sleazier movie reporters in Billy Wilder's *Ace in the Hole*. Douglas is a bad newspaperman and a bad human being, fired from every paper where he's worked. He makes himself into a hero with his interviews of a man trapped in a cave, but he deliberately slows up rescuers. The 1951 film was inspired by an incident in 1925, when a Kentuckian named Floyd Collins was trapped in a cave. As rescuers dug away, a wiry little reporter named Skeet Miller wiggled in to give Collins food and prayers. Douglas's character was stabbed to death by the victim's wife; the high-minded Miller went on to create NBC radio's live-events coverage.

- The most famous newspaper movie of all, and by some rankings the best movie ever made, is *Citizen Kane*. It was Orson Welles's cinematic nose-tweak of the newspaper mogul William Randolph Hearst. The groundbreaking 1941 movie showed Kane as a manipulative, monstrous genius—which is often how newspaper films have portrayed publishers. The resemblance was close enough for Hearst to ban its ads from his papers.

STARRING THE NEWS

Woe betide the movies if real newspapers ever disappear from the public's mental landscape.

Movies rely on newspapers to nudge the narrative. A twirling edition comes to a full stop, full screen, to reveal a blazing headline about a big plot development. A newsboy hurls a paper onto a lawn, a delivery man drops a bundle of papers at the curb, and you can read all about it. As a prop, the newspaper gives an actor a bit of business to fiddle with. Paul McCartney hid behind one in *A Hard Day's Night* (1964). Tommy Lee Jones, as the sheriff in 2007's *No Country for Old Men*, sits in a diner scanning a paper, and reads a story about a bizarre crime to his deputy. "You can't make up such a thing as that," he reflects. "I dare you to even try."

As Agent K in *Men in Black* (1997), Jones scoops up an armload of supermarket tabloids. "Best investigative reporting on the planet," he tells his partner. "Go ahead, read the *New York Times* if you want—they get lucky sometimes."

Once in a while, newspapers on TV and in movies are the real deal. Tony Soprano was a loyal subscriber to the *Newark Star-Ledger*. *Back to the Future: Part II* splashed Martin McFly on the front page of the October 22, 2015, issue of *USA Today* (price six dollars)—along with a story of "Queen Diana's Visit" to Washington, D.C.

Making fake newspapers is cheaper than buying the rights to use a real one, but the same prop paper sometimes pops up in different films or TV shows, to the delight of people who suss out movie goofs.

Actor Tim Robbins spills the beans on prison corruption to the imaginary *Portland Daily Bugle* in *The Shawshank Redemption* (1994). The *Bugle* does take the wind out of its front-page scoop when it misspells *indictments*.

Most prop papers take their names from a mashup formula that looks like: city name (Las Vegas, Boston, Los Angeles, Smallville) + generic newspaper name (*Tribune, Telegram, Banner*) = instant paper. A goodly number of these are made by a business in Los Angeles called Earl Hays Press, which crafts authentic-looking newspapers from the 1880s to the future. It's been in business since 1915—which means it's outlasted a number of newspapers it's imitated.

A made-up front page that looks like a real newspaper becomes a useful plot-exposition device in *The Godfather* (1972) and then, inevitably, a refrigerator magnet.

CHAPTER 6

ONCE A WEEK, WITH FEELING

The big papers break the big stories, get their correspondents on the big network shows, and get the bigger bucks. And yet just about the hardest job in newspapers may be at the local newspapers, the small-town dailies, and the weekly newspapers that laid the foundation for American newspapering, and which, to this day, still shoulder a hefty part of that work.

In the abstract, all newspaper reporters and editors have to deal with what their sources and their readers think of their work. But how much trickier is that when a man busted for embezzling from the church turns out to be the editor's neighbor? When the mayor, whose foolish remarks about the police chief are quoted by the paper's city hall reporter, also happens to teach the reporter's fifth-grader? Or when unflinchingly covering an outbreak of salmonella in eggs could hurt business for the local egg company, which is the town's biggest employer and one of the newspaper's biggest advertisers?

Such are the ethical and practical quandaries that small news-papers have to manage all the time.

Local newspapers are the base of the pyramid for actual information about every part of this country. It's on-the-ground accounts from these weeklies, like those in the small local daily newspapers, that catch the attention of bigger dailies and in time reach national papers.

Small papers are also farm teams for journalists, and many renowned bylines climbed the career ladder from that first rung. Turner Catledge, the future *New York Times* executive editor, began working at Mississippi weeklies; newspapering, he wrote decades later, was "a lot easier than plowing a field in Mississippi." At the *Tunica Times*, in 1922, Catledge was hired by the publisher to do interviews and sell subscriptions, and when the paper printed publisher Clayton Rand's bold series against the Ku Klux Klan, the KKK retaliated by torching the newspaper building, whose owner was Jewish.

Great newspaper men and women came out of those papers,

Opposite: In The Dalles, Oregon, the *Mountaineer* opened for business in 1859 as *The Dalles Journal*, which merged with the *Times Weekly* about 1882. Before the paper closed up shop in 1904, it published a woman's edition, edited by and for women—perhaps including the two women pictured here.

and great ones still work there.

Twice a week, Iowa's *Storm Lake Times* is filled with the doings of a small town—a firecracker ban, prep sports scores. Its story about a blind World War II veteran bowling a perfect game swiftly went national, a charming account of the man who prayed in the tenth frame, "Lord, let me throw three more good balls."

But in 2017, the paper owned and run by the Cullen family won the Pulitzer for its muscular editorials that stood up to Big Ag, challenging a secretly backed defense fund in an agribusiness lawsuit. The paper split most of the prize money between a local refugee resettlement charity and Iowa's Freedom of Information Council.

In 1979, the same brave and spirited local journalism won the Pulitzer Prizes' highest honor, the public service gold medal, for a tiny California weekly, the *Point Reyes Light*. Four years after Dave and Cathy Mitchell bought the paper, their series exposed how a drug rehab program called Synanon, which was headquartered nearby, had become a cult that abused its tax-exempt status and threatened its

Since 1925, the family-run *Louisiana Weekly* has covered local and national issues of social justice and racism of importance to African Americans; only Hurricane Katrina, in 2005, disrupted its publication. As the genealogical website *creolegen.org* noted, the paper also covered the church and business and social doings at a time when big daily papers "ignored us as a people and the rich community from whence we came."

critics. Synanon sued the paper for libel and lost, in a case that strengthened press rights in California.

Small rural newspapers have their own versions of the Pulitzers. The Gish Award is given by the Institute for Journalism and Community Issues at the University of Kentucky. It honors the Gishes, Tom and Pat, who spent about a half-century publishing the *Mountain Eagle* in a small town in eastern Kentucky.

They made more enemies than money. Tom Gish had worked for United Press International, and Pat Gish had been a reporter at a Lexington paper. Together, they made the mom-and-pop paper a force. They opened the doors of secret school board meetings and exposed dirty and

unsafe mining practices. The Gishes' lives were threatened. Businesses canceled their ads. And in 1974, someone torched the paper's offices. A local cop was convicted of paying a couple of men to do the job, and a local judge sentenced him to probation. "No great surprise," Tom Gish wrote caustically.

When the Gishes took over in 1956, they changed the paper's motto from "A Friendly Non-Partisan Weekly Newspaper Published Every Thursday" to "It Screams." A week after the arson fire, it changed the motto again, this time to "It Still Screams."

During the watershed civil rights year of 1964, the *Neshoba Democrat*, a Mississippi weekly where Turner Catledge had once set type, editorialized about the "outsiders" who were trying to "stir up trouble." Two months after that editorial, three civil rights workers were murdered in Neshoba County.

Then, in 1966, a man named Stan Dearman bought the *Democrat* and made the paper into a civil rights megaphone. Eventually, his crusade to rehabilitate the town's race relations and to get Mississippi to pursue what happened to those three civil rights workers helped to convict a KKK organizer of the killings, forty-one years after they happened. The paper's crusade earned Dearman the hostility of some local readers—and, in 2008, the Gish Award.

Through it all, for each week's paper for thirty-four years, Dearman had gone on "covering everything from the city council to the sheriff's department to the zoning board," marveled the *Jackson Clarion-Ledger*. "Each week, he read through wedding announcements and obituaries to make sure all the names were spelled right."

That's a neat resume of life on small newspapers. It can be a precarious kind of journalism, more vulnerable than city dailies to the choler of readers, the fortunes of a company town, a single bad harvest, or the costs of ink and paper. *Publisher* and *Editor* are grand titles, but at a weekly, those jobs can also mean being sweeper of floors, seller of ads, and taker of angry phone calls canceling subscriptions when a story didn't go down well with the locals.

The technology of writing and printing has changed; the work, not so much. In the Oscar-nominated film *Nebraska*, the small town's weekly newspaper, the *Hawthorne Republican*, is in real life the office of the *Plainview News*. And every particular is right on target: the paper's archives are kept not on-line but in huge binders, decades of back copies—the town's history in pulp and ink.

Births and deaths, weddings and engagements, the city council meeting and the police blotter—

Swift Lathers, the sturdy, take-no-guff founder and editor of the *Mears Newz* in Mears, Michigan, ran his weekly newspaper from 1914 until he died in 1970.

they're bread and butter for weeklies and small papers. So, too, are the lucrative legal notices, all the official business and notices governments are required to publish. When Montana's *Fallon County Times* marked its centennial in 2016, its onetime owner, Jim Anderson, recalled the days when "it was a really good living," when the old saying was that "owning a paper in a small town was like having a license to steal." And "the people were so nice."

The Internet has altered weeklies and small dailies profoundly, even as the need grows for solid local coverage that hit-and-miss blog posts can't accomplish. Some of these papers have died. Some have tried to keep up with costs and technology by going online.

Constellations of local papers have been agglomerated under a single owner, hoping for economies of scale. Many have survived by adopting hyper-local coverage for readers who can always find stories about Washington, D.C., online or on TV, but little about their own schools and city halls.

Every place has its share of eccentrics. Maybe they're just more noticeable in small towns, and especially when they run the local paper.

In Mears, Michigan, *Mears Newz* was operated for fifty-six years by the splendidly named Swift Lathers, who set his own type and printed copies on a press that operated, like a vintage sewing machine, by foot treadle. The *News* was only four pages, and every issue bore a headline proclaiming that something—asparagus, woolen undershirts, sleds—was "ripe in the land of Mears."

Mary Cain, "Hacksaw Mary," the publisher of the Mississippi weekly the *Summit Sun*, crusaded in its pages against integration and New Deal federal programs. The feds padlocked the paper in 1952 when she didn't pay her $42 Social Security tax, and she cut off the lock.

Size didn't matter in Mears, where Lathers and his little paper punched up, high up. Lathers took on topics like school taxes and press freedom. He took up the cause of Mexican migrant workers, chastising churches and employers that gave them short shrift. *Time* magazine once put him in the top ranks of weekly newspaper editors. For one of Lathers's critics, canceling a subscription wasn't protest enough. The result: a fistfight that left Lathers with the haphazard dental work of a failed middleweight.

Summit, Mississippi, had the *Summit Sun* and Mary Cain, one of that species of publisher-politician—a two-time candidate for governor and a committed segregationist in a part of Mississippi that witnessed some of the worst violence in the civil rights movement. In March 1962, the front page of her *Sun* unapologetically ran a schedule of events to mark White Monday in Mississippi.

She picked fights with the feds that had nothing to do with race. The New Deal was "diabolical," and Social Security was "unconstitutional, immoral, and un-American." That's why she didn't pay $42.87 for her own Social Security taxes.

But as she was publicly daring the feds to "pop your whip" for the Social Security money, she sold the paper to her niece for one dollar to try to dodge the consequences.

The feds *did* crack the whip. In 1952, the IRS padlocked the *Sun*. Cain sawed the lock off and mailed chain and lock back to the IRS. She lost at the Supreme Court, but she never paid that tax bill, and ever after carried the nickname Hacksaw Mary.

Characters like Lathers and Cain make for great barroom tales, but the fact is, the work of local papers and professional local journalists is a relentless task of monitoring every day what's going on in the planning department and the police department, where everything looks like the same-ol', same-ol', until the day it doesn't.

These community papers have been going belly-up so often and so fast that they should have their own "extinction clock," counting down to zero. David Simon, the *Baltimore Sun* reporter who created the HBO show *The Wire*, warned the U.S. Senate in 2009 that without the local newspapers surviving to put their backyard institutions under dogged, regular scrutiny, "The next ten or fifteen years in this country are going to be a halcyon era for state and local political corruption."

Within days of the news in early 2018 that West Virginia's biggest newspaper, the *Charleston Gazette-Mail*, was filing for bankruptcy, an attorney for a big coal company gleefully showed off to a coal-industry gathering a fake pink slip, to mock the newspaper's dogged and fearless coal-industry reporter, Ken Ward Jr. In a bankruptcy-related document, Ward was one of several *Gazette-Mail* journalists named as "the heart and soul of the *Charleston Gazette-Mail*'s newsroom."

PAPERS PEOPLE CALL THEIR OWN

Everybody wants a newspaper to call his own. Harry Potter's wizarding world had one. American labor unions had newspapers, and so did big businesses. At one time, two circus newspapers were covering the big news about the Big Top. World War II defense plants published chatty, upbeat papers like the *Twin Cities Ordnance News* in Minnesota, and the first professional photos ever taken of Marilyn Monroe were shot for an Army newspaper, back when the teenaged Norma Jeane Dougherty was assembling drones in a Van Nuys, California defense plant.

Just as there's now a website for every taste and passion, available to anyone with a computer or phone, cheaper printing technology once made anyone a publisher. Carrie A. Nation, the American anti-liquor crusader, published the *Smasher's Mail*, and for those who couldn't read, she illustrated it with an image of herself gripping the hatchet she used to bust booze bottles to smithereens.

With the endorsement (and supervision) of the U.S. government, the Japanese Americans incarcerated in World War II camps published newspapers, the most famous of them California's *Manzanar Free Press*. It was published for three and a half years, and although its staff covered camp doings, the paper was anything but "free." Its chipper tone and content never touched on the internees' living conditions or political thinking, and for three weeks at the end of 1942, the paper was shut down altogether because of rioting in the camp.

Ansel Adams photographed three men reading the *Los Angeles Times* outside the office of the *Free Press* in the Manzanar internment camp in California during World War II. The *Free Press* was the best-known of papers published in the camps, but it was not free to publish everything going on.

The weekly *Desert Trail* newspaper in Twentynine Palms, California. Bill Underhill opened the paper in 1935 with the pledge "Watch Twentynine Palms Grow!" He and his wife, Prudie, are memorialized in a town mural depicting the paper's masthead and Underhill sitting at a Linotype machine.

THE B-B-BLIZZARD.

KINSLEY, KANSAS, SATURDAY, JAN., 23, 1886.

The four-page, one-edition newspaper crafted by and for several hundred train passengers stuck in the town of Kinsley, Kansas by the epochal blizzard of 1886.

It's beyond question that our newspapers, as the novelist and devoted newspaper preserver Nicholson Baker told the *New York Times*, are "lovely, successive snapshots of our history." Even the most ephemeral of them is a selfie on paper. The *B-B-Blizzard* newspaper printed one issue only, written by the passengers aboard snowbound trains stuck in Kinsley, Kansas, in January 1886. Union soldiers handwrote the *Old Flag* newspaper in their Confederate prison camp in Tyler, Texas. Subscriptions could be bought with "segars" or a pallid caffeine substitute they called "Lincoln coffee."

Every newspaper is a mirror to our well-meant selves, and our savage selves. *Lucifer the Lightbearer* was a late-nineteenth-century, ahead-of-its-time anarchist and feminist weekly. When it printed a letter about marital rape at a time when writing about the subject was against the law, the editor was thrown in prison, where he spent six of the twenty-four years of the paper's life.

Americans also published—and read—anti-Masonic and anti-Catholic newspapers. Car maker Henry Ford used his *Dearborn Independent* to spread his anti-Semitic venom with headlines like THE PERIL OF BASEBALL—TOO MUCH JEW. Before World War I, in a flyspeck town in southwestern Missouri, the *Menace* printed anti-Catholic screeds that became so popular that the railroad had to lay on extra tracks to handle the rolls of newsprint coming in and the bundles of weekly newspapers going out to a million and a half subscribers.

The 1960s revolution in cheap printing processes coincided with a revolution in American culture, and so it was that "alternative newspapers" arrived—forebears of the tabloid-sized weeklies you can still find stacked up in hip and near-hip hangouts. These counterculture—"underground"—publications of the 1960s and 1970s put on the record a generation's anti-war political fury, the marginalized energies of young people and minorities,

and, of course, sex, drugs, and rock 'n' roll.

Most of these papers were chaotically crafted, and read as if they were written on drugs (as occasionally they were). They were sometimes as short-lived as a Zig-Zag rolling paper. Indecorous, funny, fulminating about the draft, the law, women's and gay liberation, minority power, drugs, and corporate America, they gave the fantods to police and to federal law enforcement, which set out to hobble them.

The reach of the *Black Panther*, the Black Panther Party's newspaper, was international. "Circulate to educate," it told its readers, and gave them stories about policing in black neighborhoods, prison reform, and the party's programs and politics.

More than other radical papers, the *Panther* wound up in the crosshairs of fed-

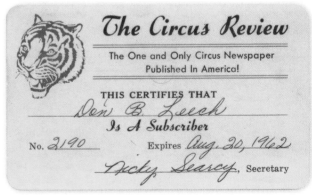

The Circus Review

The One and Only Circus Newspaper Published In America!

THIS CERTIFIES THAT

Dan B. Leech

Is A Subscriber

No. 2190   Expires Aug. 20, 1962

Dicky Searcy, Secretary

Yes, there are specialty newspapers for everything—including those who run away to write about the circus for people eager to read about it. This is a 1962 card identifying the bearer as a reader of *The Circus Review*.

In 1870, waves of fellow Irish immigrants inspired Patrick Ford to publish the weekly *Irish World*—later the *Irish World and American Industrial Liberator*. The paper sold in the tens of thousands nationwide. This vendor is in Seattle, where, as the sender of this 1907-postmarked card noted, "any one that has been to Seattle knows the *Irish World.*"

eral counterintelligence attacks trying to dent its reputation.

Elsewhere, lawmen used the pretext of drug searches, and "ransacked equipment and files," as Geoffrey Rips wrote in his book *Unamerican Activities,* about the crusade against the underground press. Many of these papers folded, because the same seat-of-the-pants operation that let them get away with printing shock comics and explicit language also meant

they didn't have mainstream papers' deep power or deeper pockets to defend themselves.

In 1965, the *Berkeley Barb* became the *New York Times* of San Francisco Bay's revolutionary music and radical politics. Like the *Barb*, the *Los Angeles Free Press*—the *Freep*—wasn't free; thousands of people paid to read pieces by Charles Bukowski or about Timothy Leary.

The paper was also the flagship of a news syndicate that shared content among underground newspapers, just as mainstream newspaper chains do. In the 1968 dope comedy *I Love You, Alice B. Toklas,* actor Peter Sellers, kitted out in an ankh amulet necklace and hippie hair, peddles the *Freep* out on a sidewalk. The paper's headline: HAS THE FREEP GONE ESTABLISHMENT?

In all, those glory days lasted about a decade. The underground papers left a survivor's legacy: the free big-city weeklies, and smaller-town monthlies, that still cover politics and entertainment with an edgy verve. *Rolling Stone* and the *Village Voice* are the most enduring and evolving of those 1960s papers. In 2000, the *Voice* won the Pulitzer for its foreign reporting—the first alternative newspaper to do so. Would the ghosts of 1960s editors rejoice, or reject it?

From before the American revolution until World War I, German was the second-most-common language in the United States, and German newspapers served an enormous readership. This rather fanciful illustration shows the Germania building in Milwaukee, the flagship of a newspaper publishing empire throughout the Midwest until 1918. The historic building has been converted to apartments.

To millions of Americans, their newspapers were not alternative. They were a landline and a lifeline between their old countries and their new one. Hundreds of newspapers in dozens of languages kept immigrants in touch with one another, with the ways of their new homeland and the news of their old one. They wrote deeply about immigration and foreign politics, matters that may have received only glancing notice in English-

The *Soho Weekly News* (1973–1982) was a hyper-hip weekly operating in a former ice cream parlor in a still-affordable neighborhood. Its founder pledged to "run as many community bulletins as possible," and soon the paper was covering politics and music. A 1974 headline—YOU DON"T KNOW HIM, BUT YOU WILL—alerted readers to a Jersey rocker named Bruce Springsteen.

language papers.

Until World War I sent German Americans underground, the most common foreign tongue in the United States was German, with scores of German-language newspapers, one of them briefly published by Ben Franklin. Emigres from northern Europe read the news in their own languages.

In New York, one Yiddish-language newspaper rolled wobbly off the presses in 1870. By the end of the decade, there were at least a half-dozen, and more to come. The first and most enduring of Jewish American newspapers remains the *American Israelite*, a weekly founded in 1854 in Cincinnati, Ohio, the heart of reform Judaism.

Newspapers were "old news" to Spanish speakers. Latin America's first newspaper appeared in Mexico in 1772. In the course of two centuries, more than three hundred Spanish-language papers started their print runs in Texas alone.

Newspapers were big players in the politics of the Texas republic, and of Mexico and Spain. In the turmoil around Mexico's 1912 revolution, opposition journalists headed north to safety, where they published papers whose stories reverberated south of the border. Nothing survives of New Mexico's first newspaper in 1834—it printed only a handful of issues—but its name promised grandeur: *El Crepúsculo de la Libertad*, the *Dawn of Liberty*.

In 1851, Los Angeles's first newspaper, *La Estrella de Los Angeles* (the *Los Angeles Star*), began printing four bilingual pages. As Anglo power marginalized Los Angeles's Mexicans, the paper killed off its Spanish pages. So a teenaged employee named Francisco P. Ramirez quit to start up his own Spanish-language paper. *El Clamor Público* (the *Public Outcry*) covered Latinos and crusaded for their rights and

Native American women in the Southwest share the Sunday paper with everyone including the baby in this undated photo.

the rights of black Americans. "Is it fair," Ramirez wanted to know, "that they are punished for committing the crime of not being born white?"

Today, although Spanish-language television news has cut into newspapers' reach, Spanish-language newspapers still can prosper, and new ones have followed immigrants to places as far from Latin America as Iowa and Virginia. In Compton, California—the small city set in the wide plain of Los Angeles—the weekly

After the Yankees took over California from Mexico, *El Clamor Público* became, in 1855, the first Spanish-language newspaper in the state. Its teenaged editor, Francisco P. Ramirez, did indeed clamor for rights for increasingly marginalized Latinos, African Americans, and women.

Compton Herald acknowledged the city's new 60-percent Latino demographic in 2017 with a Spanish-language edition, *El Heraldo de Compton*.

Newspapers in dozens more languages are still printed for immigrant communities. You can find a Hmong paper in Minnesota, and a bilingual Arabic one in Dearborn, Michigan.

Asian-language newspapers, too, popped up wherever immigrants arrived. Chinese railroad workers read the country's first Chinese-language paper, San Francisco's *Golden Hills' News*, in 1854. In English, on the front page, the publisher welcomed "the astonishing flight of the hitherto immobile Chinamen across the Pacific Ocean to seek refuge and liberty in the bosom of 'The Golden Hills.'" And it asked businessmen to "come forward as friends, not as scorners of the Chinese."

Los Angeles's influential Japanese-language newspaper the *Rafu Shimpo* was

Its first issue, in Georgia in February 1828, made the *Cherokee Phoenix* the first Native American newspaper. It was printed in the newly codified Cherokee alphabet and in English. The *Phoenix's* voice became louder as Andrew Jackson's presidency persecuted the Cherokee nation, and it ended its run in May 1834 after the government reneged on pledges to support the paper. The next year, a Georgia guard unit carted away the press and stomped the Cherokee-alphabet type into unrecognizability. Phoenix-like, the paper's name has been revived as a monthly paper and news website.

founded in 1903 by a trio of University of Southern California students with a copying machine. After World War II, it was able to start printing again only because the publisher had managed to conceal the Japanese-language lead type under the office floorboards before he was shipped off to an internment camp.

The first Americans' first newspaper was born in 1828, in the Cherokee nation in present-day Georgia. The *Cherokee Phoenix* used the Cherokee alphabet that had been created not quite twenty years earlier. The federal government inevitably objected to the paper's forceful advocacy, and it shut down. The paper's name was revived in this century as a print and online publication. As its founder predicted, the *Phoenix* did, indeed, rise again.

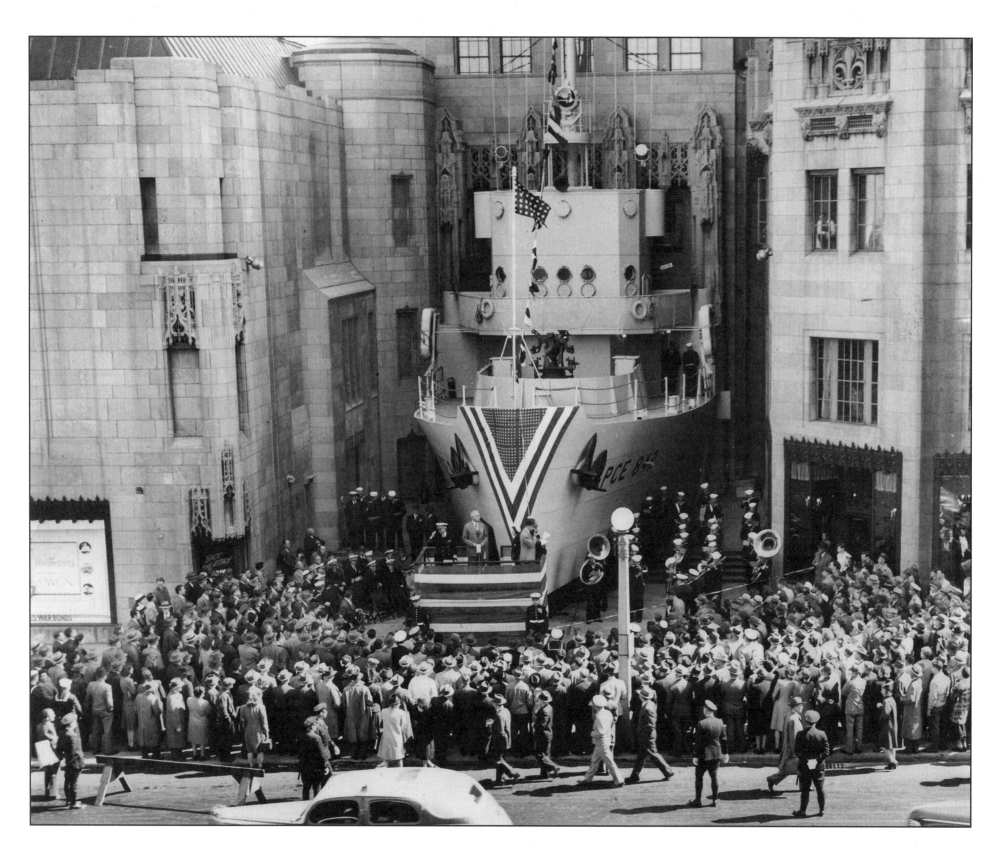

CHAPTER 7

MOTTOES AND MISSIONS

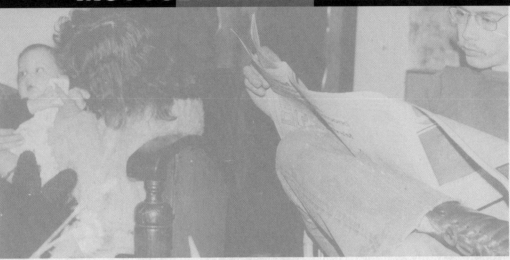

A newspaper has to perform a high-wire balancing act to make the Flying Wallendas quaver: making enough money to stay in business, and playing a civic role in the daily doings of democracy. As publisher Hosea Paddock set forth in 1883, when he bought the first of several Illinois newspapers, the paper's job was "to fear God, tell the truth, and make money."

Papers begin their lives setting forth grand mission statements, mottoes that are both a bit of chest-thumping self-promotion and a covenant with readers.

Most of them opt for brevity. The *New York Times* has its celebrated "All the News That's Fit to Print." It began when Adolph Ochs bought the newspaper in 1896. He wanted to mark it out, he declared, as something apart from New York's sex-

Through his newspapers, William Randolph Hearst underwrote summer outings for poor kids, charity drives, and sporting events like this 1943 *Detroit Times* rifle competition.

and-murder "yellow" press—something "clean, dignified, trustworthy, and impartial."

Ochs splashed his "all the news" saying in red lights at Madison Square. And he dangled one hundred dollars in prize money to the winner of a competition to replace it. The chosen entry was "All the World's News, But Not a School for Scandal," but Ochs stuck with his original, which appears on the front page to this day. (Anyone who's ever partied to the New Year's Eve ball drop in Times Square can thank Ochs for the tradition. For December 31, 1907, he ordered a huge ball, ablaze with 25-watt light bulbs, to slide down a flagpole. It's mesmerized New Yorkers ever since. You're welcome.)

Until 2017, the closest thing the *Washington Post* had to a motto was the informal advertising slogan, "If you don't get it, you don't

Opposite: Outside the *Chicago Tribune*'s massive tower, this wooden replica of the bridge and bow of a naval patrol escort carrier, the USS *Bond Quota*, launched a new World War II bond drive in September 1943. Newspapers lent their voices to the war effort, just not always in such a spectacular fashion.

get it." But at about the same time President Donald Trump was declaring the press to be the "enemy of the people," the *Post* launched its new mission statement, the First Amendment warning siren that "Democracy Dies in Darkness."

The *Tampa Times* used the sprightly, modern "Life. Printed Daily" until it stopped printing altogether, in 2016. The *Chicago Tribune*, which strutted through the Midwest as the "World's Greatest Newspaper," also featured for years on its front page the blustery slogan "An American Paper for Americans."

The slogan of the *Big Tree Bulletin and Murphy's Advertiser* was longer than its lifespan. The paper in California's gold country proclaimed it was "Independent in all things, neutral in none." In 1858, it published all of sixteen issues, running them off on a press assembled on the stump of a giant sequoia tree, before the editor called it quits.

Scripps-Howard, the chain of newspapers in small- and mid-sized American cities, chose for its logo a lighthouse with a shining beacon and, for its credo, a rewrite job on Dante, "Give light, and the people will find their own way."

Even though the founding publisher of the *Los Angeles Times*, Harrison Gray Otis, had once belonged to the typographers' union, when it came to the paper he owned—and by extension the city he all but controlled—unions were the devil's spawn, and all the more so after union-

An early and farsighted 1971 recycling campaign by the *Hawk-Eye*, a Burlington, Iowa, newspaper which began in 1838 as the *Iowa Patriot*. The paper set up this recycling trailer outside its offices, and sent off the old newspapers to be converted into wallboard.

Newspapers didn't mind shaking the tin cup for readers' contributions to good causes, especially when the papers could add their own brands. The *Chicago Herald-American* sold this customized deck of cards for its relief fund, or gave it away as a premium to readers who donated money.

ists bombed the *Times* building in 1910. Through the 1960s, long after Otis was dead, the paper signaled its anti-union sentiment with the masthead motto "Liberty under law, true industrial freedom."

The American South must have the upper hand when it comes to droll mottoes. The Pulitzer Prize–winning *Atlanta Journal-Constitution* once promised that it "Covers Dixie Like the Dew," and the website for a pair of Louisiana papers, the *Morgan City News* and *Franklin Banner-Review*, today boasts that it's "Covering St. Mary Parish Like Gravy on Rice."

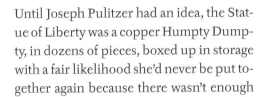

Until Joseph Pulitzer had an idea, the Statue of Liberty was a copper Humpty Dumpty, in dozens of pieces, boxed up in storage with a fair likelihood she'd never be put together again because there wasn't enough money.

So in 1885, the publisher of the *New York World* set his paper on a six-month crusade to raise the last hundred thousand dollars needed to set Miss Liberty on her feet, on a granite pedestal in New York Harbor. Pulitzer had already taken rich people to the woodshed for not making up that difference; now the ordinary people made it happen—a few pennies from children, a day's wages from immigrant workmen, more than one hundred thousand people all told.

Local spelling bees gave remembrances to contestants, like this handsome 1934 medal from the *Boston Herald*. The national bee was originally sponsored by a group of newspapers as a way to promote literacy.

It was a public-spirited campaign and a shrewd public relations move. In 1900, a Galveston hurricane killed as many as twelve thousand people, the worst natural disaster in American history. Pulitzer's publishing rival, William Randolph Hearst, sent three trains of relief supplies. Pulitzer sent his own trains, and on board one of them was the legendary founder of the American Red Cross, Clara Barton—another front-page coup.

Most newspapers' philanthropic campaigns are locally benevolent. The *New York Times* began a Fresh Air Fund to get city kids into the country during the summer, printing the names of contributors, however small the donation. Over a forty-year lifespan, Los Angeles's Times Mirror Foundation gave out more than eighty million dollars in grants of the newspaper chain's

money, a lot of it to the arts. In 2018, the *Houston Chronicle* devoted part of the money from its book about Hurricane Harvey to hurricane relief funds. The *Dallas Morning News* raises money for homeless and poor children's services. The *Denver Post* supervises a community foundation for the needy and the arts. In 1949, the daughter of the *Fort Wayne News-Sentinel*'s former publisher donated an outdoor amphitheater to the city that's still used today.

It was charity-by-extortion, but the Hearst Foundation and family gave away millions of dollars' worth of food to the San Francisco Bay Area's poor in 1974 to meet the demand of the terrorist group that had kidnapped newspaper heiress Patricia Hearst. On their own terms, newspapers have promoted community blood drives, bond drives, student writing contests, neighborhood cleanups, and piano competitions.

For the magnitude of its impact, one campaign can hardly be surpassed: at the turn of the twentieth century, birds by the millions were slaughtered and tortured toward extinction for their feathers, to adorn women's hats. Then, almost with one voice, dozens of influential newspapers shamed the feather trade, editorializing ferociously for bird protections, which the government, by slow steps, endorsed. The *Indianapolis News* argued more practically than sentimentally that "a live bird is worth

The publisher of The Meridian Tribune has offered to give to the Meridian Training School a Large Astronomical Telescope mounted on a stand if we will secure 100 new subscribers to the Tribune at $1 per year. We need only a few subscribers to complete the number. *Won't you assist us by sending your name, together with one dollar, to our Treasurer, Prof. Walter Stuart, Meridian, Texas?* Read the "Message" on the other side. Send at once.

B 3210 Meridian Training School, Meridian, Tex.

Texas's *Meridian Tribune,* which ran a regular "training school column," pledged to buy the school a telescope if 100 new subscribers signed up. With it, anyone who wished could see "the canals of the planet Mars, nebulas, and a thousand other wonderful and mysterious things."

more to the agriculturist than a dead one to a woman's hat."

These days, some newspapers are on the receiving end of philanthropy. The *St. Petersburg Times* was a ferocious newspaper that made its journalism felt in Washington as well as Florida. But its many Pulitzer Prizes couldn't keep it profitable, and now, as the *Tampa Bay Times*, it's owned by the nonprofit journalism-focused Poynter Institute. The *Philadelphia Inquirer*, that city's biggest paper, along with the *Philadelphia Daily News* and the philly.com website, were all donated to a journalism nonprofit in order to keep them up and running.

Not-for-profit newspapering may turn out to be the salvation and operating template for twenty-first-century journalism.

Muscular journalism takes more than Superman spandex. It takes a lot of ink, and a lot of thinking. It's one of the most powerful services a newspaper can do: expose to the public civic malfeasance, lawlessness, and plain old chicanery. But it has to be in the public's interest, not just the publisher's private one. In 1922, a trade paper called the *Fourth Estate* quoted a *New York Evening Post* columnist nicknamed the Shop Talker. A newspaper crusade, he concluded, is "an occasional duty not to be

shirked ... on behalf of some public cause." But he sagely warned against newspapers that "are constantly crusading on matters which have more to do with their owners' pocketbooks or idiosyncrasies."

As for idiosyncrasies, Horace Greeley pioneered modern journalism with his *New York Tribune,* but also insisted that his reporters use the word *news* as a plural, as in, "No news are good news."

❦

Newspapers' reporting has helped to change child labor and workplace safety laws, clean up politics from bottom to top, free the innocent from prison, and promote safe food and drug reform. Newspapers have put themselves at risk by taking on vested interests. In Columbus, Georgia, the *Clarion-Ledger*'s 1926 battle against the revived Ku Klux Klan won the Pulitzer, and so did the *Anchorage Daily News* series in 1976 about the Teamsters' influence on the state's politics and economy.

Owner/publishers did pursue their own personal causes, both on and beyond the editorial page. R.C. Hoiles used his two-dozen-plus Freedom Newspapers to endorse his libertarian free-markets philosophy. He believed that government schools had handicapped his education, so in print, his newspapers regularly referred to public schools as "taxpayer-supported schools." Yet Hoiles's voice bellowed loud and lonely against the incarceration of Japanese Americans in World War II as "a result of emotion and fright rather than being in harmony with the Constitution and the inherent rights that belong to all citizens."

Tennessee's crusading editor Edward J. Meeman editorialized passionately for the Tennessee Valley Authority project that brought electricity to rural Tennessee, against the poll tax that disenfranchised black voters, and against both Nazism and Communism. When he died, the cigar maker's son who had started his career as a four-dollar-a-week cub reporter in Indiana left a multimillion-dollar fortune to promote environmental science and science journalism.

William Randolph Hearst adored animals—his miniature dachshund Helen had the run of Hearst Castle in San Simeon, California—and he used the thundering power of his papers to denounce vivisection, the experimentation on live animals. "Dog torturers," he called vivisectionists. His voice powered the present-day movement against cruel cosmetic and medical tests.

Before movies came along to show Americans how other people behaved and believed, it was newspapers that did that job, both by advertisements and by their stories, sending out cues like:

The picture side of this July 1912 subscription card to the *Cedar Rapids Republican and Times* shows readers what their subscriptions pay for—not only a newspaper, but a day of fun for plucky little newsboys.

- *Look what the folks upstate are wearing to church this spring.*
- *Don't commit the social sin of halitosis.*
- *Here are some tasty new recipes that your new icebox lets you whip up ahead of time to serve to your friends.*
- *The Elks chapter is spending the weekends raising money for an old folks' home.*
- *Women have started drinking cocktails!*

For the kids, there were wholesome advice and wholesome activities. *Etta Kett* began as a small 1920s comic strip dispensing humor and modeling good manners to teenagers, and soon turned into a club with a loyal membership.

The *Detroit News* enlisted tens of thousands of kids in its Fair and Square Club.

It grew out of serial mystery stories in the *Cincinnati Enquirer* about a riverfront boys club with a secretary—"Sekatary Hawkins"—who recorded his friends' adventures. Among its members was writer Harper Lee, who gave a cameo to a Sekatary Hawkins novel in her novel *To Kill a Mockingbird*. The club's pledge was "A quitter never wins and a winner never quits," and it laid down rules like, "Always leave word with your mother where you are going."

A lapel button identified members in good standing of "Etta Kett," a popular newspaper-based children's good-conduct club.

HEADLINES

The comics are just for fun. The obituaries are *schadenfreude*. The editorials are like a high-fiber diet—good for you.

But witty, playful headlines—especially the rollicking, raunchy tabloid headlines—are sheer guilty pleasure.

Pity the newspaper readers of two hundred years ago. Pages were composed of long single columns of ads interspersed with news dispatches, and headlines were vague and curt, FROM WASHINGTON or LATE NEWS FROM THE FRONT. Over the years, as technology allowed and competition demanded, headlines got bigger, and, in the racier newspapers, they no longer spoke—they hollered.

A good many legends about newspaper headlines happen to be true, but here are some that definitely aren't:

NEWSPAPERS PRINT SOME HEADLINES "JUST TO SELL PAPERS." Almost every newspaper today is sold in advance by subscription, although readers still pick up tempting tabloids in airports and subway stations. Mainstream newspapers print who-what-where headlines, not teasers:

WAR ENDS

TRUMP WINS

FEDS RAISE INTEREST RATES

Jacqueline Kennedy met the press on July 14, 1960, the day after her husband, Massachusetts senator John F. Kennedy, won the Democratic nomination for president a continent away in Los Angeles. For the occasion, the hometown *Boston Globe* brought out what is called the "Second Coming"-size type for its headline.

The tabloid headline like AXIS OF WEASEL—raging against Germany and France for sitting out the U.S. war against Iraq—means readers can expect a jingoistic whack at American allies.

The most enthralling headlines might not be completely fair, and vice versa.

Editor and writer Michael Kinsley once launched a competition for the dreariest newspaper headline ever, inspired by this one from 1986 in the *New York Times*: WORTHWHILE CANADIAN INITIATIVE. (That worthwhile initiative actually turned out to be the incendiary trade deal

In Lincoln, Nebraska, a newsboy sells the *Sunday Journal and Star* with the grave news of September 3, 1939 that Great Britain declared war against Nazi Germany. He's the very image of a newsboy, right down to the cowlick in his hair and the news vendor apron slung over his shoulders.

called NAFTA.) The winner of Kinsley's contest was DEBATE GOES ON OVER THE NATURE OF REALITY.

REPORTERS WRITE THEIR OWN HEADLINES. At most papers, designated editors do that, squeezing information and style into a few words, which is far harder than it looks. It's why there are awards for headline writing. Newspaper headline writers of yore built up their own weird, abbreviated glossary of words that fit small spaces. As a result, you used to read *solon* for legislator, from an ancient Greek statesman's name; *mull* for consider; *nab* for arrest, and *tot* for child. Has anyone actually ever said, "Did you see that solons are mulling new laws to nab tot-nappers?" The mini-words exist, like some crossword puzzle clues, almost exclusively in dictionaries—and in headlines.

Headline writers practice the rule that "A dirty mind makes a clean newspaper," alert for some innocent-looking phrase that carries a wicked double entendre. *Washington Post* writer Gene Weingarten remembered one about home food canning with the exuberant but accidentally R-rated headline

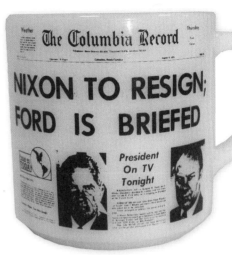

Newspapers commemorated historic headlines on souvenir mugs, usually from stories about elections, the moon landing, or Watergate. This one is from the front page of South Carolina's *Columbia Record* in August 1974, as Richard Nixon resigned and Gerald Ford became president. Like most newspapers published in the afternoon, the *Record* was overtaken by TV news and closed in 1988.

YOU CAN PUT PICKLES UP YOURSELF.

The tabloid *New York Post* deliberately went full-out vulgar in 1999. After the U.S. Senate refused to convict President Bill Clinton of perjury and obstruction of justice in the Monica Lewinsky scandal, which included an episode with a stogie, the *Post*'s headline: CLOSE BUT NO CIGAR. And Bernie Beck, the revered copy desk chief at the *San Francisco Chronicle*, recalled that a very proper society writer at the *Los Angeles Daily News* guilelessly wrote a raunchy headline on her own column about a debutantes' gala: DEBS TO BALL UNDER TENT.

Headline bloopers happen when deadlines got close, and someone didn't take a second look before the presses rolled. Newspeople and readers collect the niftiest of them, like the Ohio newspaper's headline WOMAN KICKED BY HORSE UPGRADED TO STABLE, and, for the papal election of Polish-born John Paul II, Florida's *Hollywood Sun-Tattler*'s geo-theological confusion VATICAN ELECTS FIRST NON-CATHOLIC POPE.

Newspaper language is the language of the here and now. Slang changes so fast that a headline that had our grandparents in stitches is now as puzzling as string theory. In 1936, when an American woman named Wallis Simpson divorced her second husband to clear the decks to marry the king of England, Edward VIII, one American newspaper headlined it KING'S MOLL RENO'ED IN WOLSEY'S HOME TOWN. A brilliant headline then, a mystery to decipher now: *moll* is snarky slang for a girlfriend, usually a mobster's; *Reno'ed* means divorced, because in the 1930s, Reno was just about the only place in the United States to get a quick split; *Wolsey* was Cardinal Wolsey, King Henry VIII's right-hand man; and Wolsey's hometown was Ipswich, where Simpson got her divorce decree.

The year before, the show-business newspaper *Variety* had scored an all-time hit headline with STICKS NIX HICK PIX. It meant that rural America (the *sticks*)

Atomic bombers criticize Enola homosexual exhibit

The ASSOCIATED PRESS

CHICAGO — They dropped the atomic bombs that destroyed two cities and ended World War II. Forty-nine years later, they're fighting another battle – this time over how they'll be remembered.

Survivors of the top-secret 509th Composite Group, which was formed to drop the new weapons on Japan, say an exhibit on the bombings of Hiroshima and Nagasaki at the Smithsonian Institution will be too apologetic.

"It's slanted more in sympathy to the Japanese than it is to us," said Fred Olivi, copilot of the B-29 that dropped an atomic bomb on Nagasaki on Aug. 9, 1945.

"They say nothing about Pearl Harbor, the Bataan Death March, China and Singapore," he said Saturday.

About 100 of the top-secret unit's survivors concluded their semiannual four-day reunion Sunday. And many were critical of the exhibit, which is scheduled to open in May.

Some veterans haven't read the detailed, 559-page script of the exhibit, but they don't like what little they have seen.

"I happened to glance to an open page at random, and the heading of that page said 'Did They All Go Crazy?'" said Ted "Dutch" Van Kirk, who navigated the Enola Gay on its run to bomb Hiroshima.

"They focused on the problems of one man," he said. "It's just an example of the types of things in there. That's a perfect example."

The Smithsonian exhibit landed in hot water shortly the script was circulated among veterans groups. The display at first was only to concentrate on the last few months of the war.

Veterans complained that left out the Japanese aggression that brought the United States into the global conflict.

The plane that dropped the first atomic bomb was named "Enola Gay," but Illinois' *Northwest Herald* evidently was on autopilot when it followed its 1994 style and usage rule, and replaced the word "gay" with "homosexual."

doesn't want to watch (*nix*) movies about farmers and rustics (*hick pix*). That one, as they say in Hollywood, has legs. Versions of it showed up on *Sesame Street* and *The Simpsons*, and the *New York Times* couldn't resist using its wordplay in a 2002 editorial headline about nuclear inspections: HICKS NIX BLIX FIX. The enchantingly named Hans Blix was the head of the International Atomic Energy Agency, and "hicks" was a merry reference to the "cowboys" in the Bush administration opposing the inspection deal.

The most famous headlines aren't just on top of stories—they have backstories:.

● ATOMIC BOMBERS CRITICIZE ENOLA HOMOSEXUAL EXHIBIT.

The story in Illinois's *Northwest Herald* was about World War II veterans angry over a Smithsonian exhibition about the dropping of the atomic bomb.

The lead B-29 bomber was the *Enola Gay*, named for the pilot's mother. But the style at that newspaper in 1994—as it was at other newspapers then—required that the word *gay* be replaced by *homosexual*. Someone wasn't paying attention to the context, or to history.

● JERKED TO JESUS ran in the *Chicago Times* in about 1875, over a story about four condemned men who repented on the gallows. It was apparently the handiwork of Horatio Seymour, who got a bonus and a promotion from his delighted editor, Wilbur Storey. Storey was a misanthropic, racist scorpion of a man whose journalism philosophy was "raise hell and sell newspapers." (The same headline supposedly ran a half-dozen years later in a paper in a Colorado mining town where a railroad worker was hanged for killing a teamster over a five-buck bet in a card game.)

● FORD TO CITY: DROP DEAD was not exactly what President Gerald Ford said, but the *New York Daily News* interpreted it that way for its headline the day before Halloween in 1975. Ford refused to

Senator Lyndon B. Johnson studies newspaper coverage of his battle to pull delegates away from Senator John F. Kennedy and win the Democratic presidential nomination at the July 1960 convention in Los Angeles. In short order, the headlines would be about him accepting Kennedy's invitation to be JFK's running mate.

● KILLED SWEETHEART, SLEPT WITH BODY was the 1937 headline that provoked the pioneering Marvel Jackson Cooke to quit her job. New York's *Amsterdam News* was founded in 1909 by a black man named James H. Anderson, who began it with only ten bucks, six pieces of paper, and a pencil or two to his name.

Cooke said years afterwards that she understood the pressures of circulation for black newspapers that forced them to go for "the murders, the offbeat social conditions," but insisted she had to resign in protest. Cooke then went to work at the *Compass*, as the first African American woman reporter at a major white-owned daily paper. The *Amsterdam News* is still one of the most important African American publications in the nation.

A definite runner-up for the best American newspaper headline of all time: the December 13, 2017 *New York Daily News* announcing Alabama Senate candidate Roy Moore's loss with a photo of him on horseback and the up-yours headline SCREW YOU & HORSE YOU RODE IN ON.

Still, connoisseurs prefer the *New York Post*'s 1983 headline for the ages,

A woman eats up the news from January 1954 about movie star Marilyn Monroe and baseball hero Joe DiMaggio getting hitched. The headline assumed, rightly, that everyone would know who "Marilyn" and "Joe" were; the "Frisco" name for San Francisco may have played in New York, but it's spoiling for a fight in the city by the bay.

HEADLESS BODY IN TOPLESS BAR, about a decapitation murder in a strip joint. But we came close to not seeing it.

Managing editor Vincent Musetto wrote it in a moment's inspiration, but sweated it out while a reporter went to the crime scene to make sure that it really was a topless joint. The place was locked, but she hoisted herself up to a window and saw a "Topless Dancing" sign. The *New York Times*'s decorous headline for its story of the same crime? OWNER OF A BAR SHOT TO DEATH; SUSPECT IS HELD.

bail out the Big Apple, and his decision, and that headline, may have cost him the White House, because he lost New York State to Jimmy Carter the next year. The *Daily News* struck that New Yawk tone again in 1995.

On the late-night David Letterman show, New York's mayor, Rudy Giuliani, jokily chose "We Can Kick Your City's Ass" as a fitting city slogan.

The *Daily News* gleefully offered buttons, bumper stickers, and magnets with a mockup of a might-have-been front-page headline.

Yep, it's snow, all right. In an undated snapshot, likely from the 1950s, a couple of bundled-up women show off the local paper to prove that it was indeed a record snowfall.

It was never actually a tabloid headline, but a souvenir pin from the *New York Daily News* splashed a 1995 joke Big Apple slogan from David Letterman's show onto a mockup front page.

In April 1945, two jubilant GIs—one with a bottle of suds—decide to pose with two different papers that chose the same two-word headline to commemorate the biggest news in years. Even in the age of the iPhone, Americans buy up newspapers headlining world-altering events—the tangible, un-Photoshopped proof of what happened when.

SUNDAY 1/14/18

STARADVERTISER.COM >> *$2.25 Oahu, $3.25 neighbor islands* >> *Mostly sunny and pleasant. High 83, low 69* >> *B4*

The Pulse of Paradise

Star ★ Advertiser

OOPS!

'Wrong button' sends out false missile alert

The chest-thumping exchanges between President Donald Trump and North Korean leader Kim Jong-Un about their nuclear missile launch buttons had already been jangling nerves in Hawaii. Then, on Saturday morning, January 13, 2018, an emergency worker "pushed the wrong button," as Governor David Ige put it, and alerted the whole state—incorrectly—that a ballistic missile was headed its way. "Seek immediate shelter. This is not a drill." The message triggered a statewide panic until the stand-down correction alert thirty-eight minutes later. It also triggered a modern classic of newspaper headline writing and design in the next day's Honolulu *Star-Advertiser*.

● **False alarm triggers mass panic; officials worried tourism could take a hit**
PAGE A13

● **Outraged citizens could take it out on Gov. Ige in the upcoming election**
PAGE A14

● **From panic to anger to relief, tweets and Facebook posts are emotionally charged**
PAGE A15

● **We all make mistakes. But somebody needs to get fired for this one!**
LEE CATALUNA B1

CHAPTER 8

UNHEARD VOICES, UNSEEN FACES

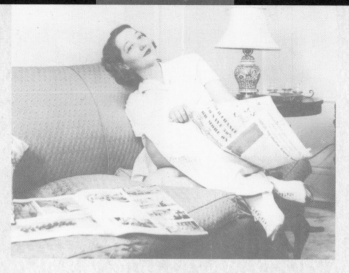

For about half of the history of the republic, more than half of Americans were not fully American. They had virtually no legal rights. They could not vote. They could not own most property. Intellectually, morally, legally, they were not regarded as full people, or full adults.

It's hardly a surprise, then, that women, African Americans, and other legally "invisible" Americans were virtually absent from early newspapers except—in the case of black Americans—when they were advertised for sale. Later, they showed up in mainstream papers, all right—usually in the sports pages, and in lurid crime stories, and about their gruesome murders at the hands of lynch mobs.

Women, themselves denied the vote and other rights, were at their newsworthy best when they were fallen women, maidenly victims of crimes, or, for the well-bred on the society pages, when they were born, married, and died—bred, wed, and dead.

Into the twentieth century, you could still find some American newspapers using the *n*-word as a sneering synonym for a black person. Genteel papers preferred *negro*. The *New York Times* announced in 1930 that it would thereafter capitalize *Negro*, "in recognition of racial respect for those who have been generations in the 'lower case.'"

Is it any wonder that women and minorities had to find recognition and regard by publishing their own newspapers? And that those papers made no bones about campaigning for their readers' full rights as Americans?

They were forceful about social and legal injustices many decades before those topics became front-page, mainstream news. They stood for civil rights, economic rights, voting rights, and children's rights, and against wife-beating, gambling, and drunkenness. They wrote about, and for, the people the mainstream news media of the day rarely did: the legally disempowered.

Opposite: Three women run the print shop at an unidentified newspaper. ca.1920.

A mid-twentieth-century tourist postcard of a man reading *Ka Hoku o Hawaii*, one of a number of Hawaiian-language newspapers—some of them started by Hawaii's last king—that managed to serve as a conduit and a home for local language, heritage, and even political opposition to American control.

GOOD WOMEN'S REVOLT

Not one woman signed the Declaration of Independence, but in early 1777, when the Continental Congress printed that document with all the signatories' names, the job was done by a Baltimore publisher. M.K. Goddard ran the *Maryland Journal* with her brother. This time, she boldly put her full name, and hers alone, at the bottom of the Declaration: Mary Katherine Goddard.

In the decade spanning the Civil War, the free-thinking Sara Parton Willis was pulling down a stupefying one hundred dollars a week as a columnist, writing sardonically about women and men for the *New York Ledger*. She used the pen name Fanny Fern so as not to disgrace her family more than her divorce had already done. (For her third marriage, to a younger man, she insisted on a prenup to keep her own money.)

The first woman to collect a *New York Times* paycheck also used a pseudonym. As Grace Greenwood, Sara Jane Lippincott relished "pricking with my pen" the crooked pols she observed in Congress.

Those female pen-pricks drew blood; in 1889, Congress changed its press admissions rules to effectively exclude Grace Greenwood and her news sisterhood.

The end of the Civil War opened up not only the West, but also opportunities for newspaperwomen. In Portland, Oregon, Abigail Scott Duniway's *New Northwest* crusaded for women's suffrage every week for fifteen years, in the same town where her brother opposed it just as mightily as editor of the powerful *Oregonian*. (After he died, she won.)

The first woman editor of a daily American mainstream newspaper was, so far as it can be certain, Laura de Force Gordon, who ran California's *Stockton Daily Leader* for about a year in 1873 and 1874. She died in 1907, but her public image was reborn in 1979, after a hundred-year-old time capsule was dug up in San Francisco. The lead box held oddments like railroad timetables, dentistry pamphlets, and Gordon's brief book on California geysers. But what she wrote on the flyleaf was the grabber. "If this little book should see the light after its hundred years of entombment, I would like its readers to know that the author was a lover of her own sex and devoted the best years of her life in striving for the political equality and social and moral

The weekly *Lynchburg Sentinel* in Tennessee had been gutted by an 1883 fire that razed half the town, but by the next year, Katie Frost, a member of the Frost family that published the paper, was on the letterhead as "editress and proprietress."

Behind her proper Victorian costume and her pen name "Fanny Fern," Sara Willis Parton was at one time the highest-paid columnist in the country.

Laura de Force Gordon was the first woman to edit an American daily newspaper, the Stockton *Leader,* beginning in September 1873. She was praised in an 1880 history of Stockton as a woman "of manly ambition."

Carrie Ingalls, the sister of Laura Ingalls Wilder, the author of the *Little House on the Prairie* books, was the *compleat* newspaperwoman, working at three different small-town South Dakota newspapers and managing two of them. Adept at every facet of the job, she could melt down lead to make into type.

In 1880, 288 American women were professional journalists, out of 12,308 journalists nationwide. The men sneered at "women's news" as frivolous. But men were even more caustic when a woman's writing outshone their own. The best backhanded compliment a woman reporter could get was that she wrote "just like a man"—and she did it at a fraction of his salary.

When stories by women made it to the front page, they ran to the "dames in danger" sensations, "stunt girls" who delivered a frisson of sex and peril by rising in hot-air balloons, plunging under the sea, venturing into gambling dens, fending off men who took them for prostitutes—and writing about it.

Other papers had been quick to imitate once they saw the circulation leap when the *New York World* sent the enterprising Nellie Bly around the world in eighty days, dispatched her to bust the chops of lobbyists, get hypnotized, and prance onstage as a barely clad Amazon.

Whether or not editors intended them to be simply one more brand of titillation, the first-person stories by "girl reporters" assigned to go undercover into sweatshops and asylums and hospitals and jails—to pretend to be destitute immigrants, or

women looking for abortions—were, in fact, important early exposés of the underside of politics and capitalism, and of the price women paid for it.

Stunts or sensationalism, the mere presence of newspaperwomen's names and deeds out in the world of men "shaped new public spaces for women within the physical pages of the newspaper, while also writing into being a far-flung new public world of women," wrote Alice Fahs in *Out on Assignment: Newspaper Women and the Making of Modern Public Space.* Girls who dreamed of being reporters were actually dreaming of life in a world made bigger by women's presence in it.

Wars always change society. As women pushed oh-so-gradually into covering wars, they found themselves whipsawed between male gallantry and male jealousy.

elevation of women." From the grave, so the speculation ran, Gordon might have been telling the future San Francisco that she was a lesbian.

Mortality and necessity turned many women into editors and publishers, in jobs they inherited from fathers or spouses, or at least shared the duties. Elva Ferguson and her husband drove a wagonload of printing equipment into the Oklahoma Territory in 1892 and started the *Watonga Republican.* She kept publishing when her husband was appointed governor and after he died. Sound familiar? Edna Ferber made a novel out of it; Hollywood made a movie out of that. *Cimarron* won the best-picture Oscar in 1931.

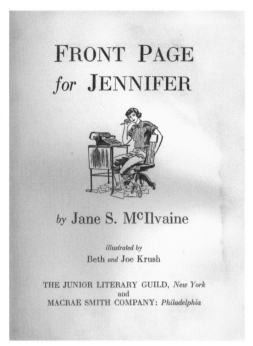

In this 1950 novel, one in a series of *Jennifer* career-girl adventure books for teens, the college girl and newspaper cub reporter Jennifer Collings lands the story, and the boy, naturally.

Two women at work at the *Madelia Times-Messenger*, a weekly newspaper created out of two papers in 1903 in Madelia, Minnesota, where it still publishes. This photo card was sent to a friend by Elvina Jacobson, left. 1912.

The military brass wasn't always happy to honor their press credentials, and getting a great exclusive story could smear a woman with whispers that she'd traded sex for a scoop. Any unsolicited benefit her sex gave her could cost at least twice as many disadvantages.

Women weren't frontline correspondents during the Civil War, but Mary Shaw Leader made her own newspaper history in November 1863. She walked fourteen miles from Hanover, Pennsylvania, to Gettysburg, where Abraham Lincoln was dedicating a military cemetery. She took down his speech word for word and walked back home, where the Gettysburg Address ran in the *Hanover Spectator*, a paper published by her widowed mother.

To Peggy Hull goes the honor—with battle stars—of being the first woman the U.S. military ever formally credentialed as a war correspondent, and that required a battle of her own. In 1916, working for the *El Paso Morning Times*, she covered General John Pershing's border war with Mexico. A couple of years later, Hull set off to cover the world war, and the American forces sent in to keep order in eastern Russia as revolution broke out. Kerrie Logan Holihan noted in *Reporting Under Fire: 16 Daring Women War Correspondents and Photojournalists* that Hull was turned back by U.S. military brass. She came storming back brandishing a note from a general that

ordered, "If your only reason for refusing Miss Peggy Hull credentials is because she is a woman, issue them at once."

The first woman journalist to win a Pulitzer Prize was also the first woman on the *New York Times* editorial board. As a foreign correspondent in a Europe rolling toward World War II, Anne O'Hare McCormick interviewed the grand slam of prewar leaders: Hitler, Stalin, Mussolini, Churchill, and FDR. More than a hundred women correspondents in World War II earned that coveted C-for-correspondent armband, sometimes facing fire like the men but just as often facing down hostile officers and rules that kept sidelining them to hospitals and camps far from the front. Some resorted to subterfuge to get to the war. Magazine writer Martha Gellhorn hid in the bathroom of a hospital ship to accompany the Allies to their landing on D-Day. Four days after that, the *Boston Globe*'s Iris Carpenter slipped her "handlers" and got to Cherbourg, where she interviewed First Army soldiers who took part in the landing. As tanks rolled

out of a landing ship and onto the shore, they told her, their drivers "cried and vomited as they had to drive over the bodies of their buddies."

No one beat the *New York Herald Tribune*'s Marguerite Higgins to the story if she could help it. The hard-charging Higgins got to the war very late, but she was there when the U.S. Army liberated Dachau. Covering the Korean War, she was ordered

stateside by an exasperated general who likely didn't care for the prospect of having the first dead woman combat reporter on his watch. General Douglas MacArthur intervened to keep her on the job, and her stories won a Pulitzer. (MacArthur could hardly have done otherwise; *Life* magazine

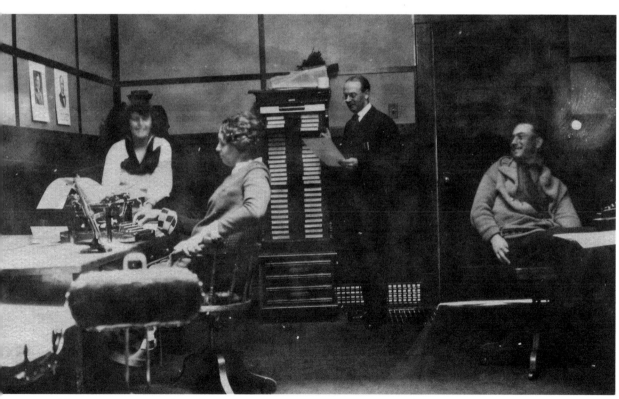

The men and women of the *Owyhee Avalanche* having a laugh, in a pre-World War II photograph. In the American West, the shortage of manpower made womanpower possible. The Idaho newspaper started up its presses a few months after the end of the Civil War, changed names, changed cities, and eventually brought back the "Avalanche" masthead in 1984. It still publishes weekly.

Thérèse Bonney once said she went to war with a gun, all right—a flashgun, the one on her camera, as recounted in Catherine Gourley's book *War, Women, and the News*. Bonney ran her own European photo news service, and made a point of coming back to the U.S. during the World War II to share her photos of civilians, mostly children. As she wrote in the *Los Angeles Times*, their devastated lives—"little tots on refugee-packed, strafed roads, wild children who snatched my food from a café terrace"— were the stories she wanted her pictures to tell.

The legendary Agness Underwood, the first woman city editor of a major American paper, ruled the city room of Los Angeles' *Herald-Express* with all the vigor the job demands—and the outsized baseball bat that she said she kept on hand to keep Hollywood PR people in line.

had just featured Higgins as a "girl war correspondent," and preposterously noted that she "still manages to look attractive.")

Higgins wrote for *Newsday* about the early years of the Vietnam War. That's where she contracted the parasitic disease that killed her in 1966.

Nearly three hundred other American women—a number of them freelancers—also covered Vietnam, where journalists could, for the first time, get military credentials easily, and travel freely out in the field with the troops. Reporter Jurate Kazickas won five hundred dollars on the TV game show *Password* and spent it on a one-way ticket to Saigon. Gloria Emerson had been in Vietnam in 1956 and, as one of the few reporters with real knowledge of the

country, returned in 1970 to write with a critical eye for the *New York Times*.

Dickey Chapelle's death proved the common risks of war reporting. She had photographed Marines on Iwo Jima and survived two months in a Hungarian prison in 1956. She was killed in Vietnam in 1965 when shrapnel from a land mine slashed her throat. The first American woman journalist to die covering a war, she'd once said, "When I die, I want it to be on patrol with the United States Marines." The Marines gave her a Corps burial.

On the home front, the newsprint ceiling could be as unyielding as the glass ceiling, and women who broke through had to be tough and stubborn. Aggie Underwood began working as a switchboard operator in 1926 at a small Los Angeles paper. In 1947, she was promoted to be the first woman city editor of a big-city daily, the *Herald-Express*.

In that era, a half-dozen daily papers ran through a half-dozen editions a day, and Underwood fought—and sometimes fought dirty—with them all. Reporting on the murder of a waitress, she dropped a white carnation on the corpse just so she could call it the White Carnation Murder.

All this was happening in a hats-and-glove postwar culture that exalted the Mrs. and the mom. (The *New York Times* didn't adopt "Ms." until 1986.) As a ferocious political columnist, Mary McGrory was a headliner at the *Washington Star*. Then the *New York*

Peggy Hull was the only U.S. "girl correspondent" officially credentialed to cover World War I, on the Western Front and with American military forces in Siberia. She also went to the Pacific in World War II. Here, in 1918, she wears a uniform of her own design, with a "correspondent" armband and a military-style ID bracelet.

Strictly ornamental: the Newspaper Reporters Association of New York City annually crowned a beauty queen, "Miss Byline." In 1958 it was Doris Bourgeois, posing at a typewriter. Her measurements were obligingly listed as 35-23-35.

Times Washington bureau chief offered to hire her—on the condition that she also run the office switchboard part-time. The year McGrory did the work that won her a Pulitzer, 1974, was the year that women at the *Times* sued the newspaper for sex discrimination, part of the "good girls revolt" at newspapers, magazines, and TV newsrooms across the country.

Some of the most hidebound holdouts against newspaperwomen were their fellow newspapermen. As first lady, Eleanor Roosevelt insisted that newspapers send women to cover her press conferences. But women were barred from joining the National Press Club.

The *New York Times*'s Nan Robertson described that struggle in *The Girls in the Balcony*—the hot, cramped balcony whence they were sometimes allowed to watch an important speaker but not to ask questions. In 1959, women reporters persuaded Soviet premier Nikita Khrushchev not to speak at the club unless women reporters could be there, too. The top Commie was tickled to stick it to the Beltway boys, and women were allowed in—for that event only.

In *Reporting from Washington: The History of the Washington Press Corps*, Donald A. Ritchie found that in 1963, the *Washington Post* pulled reporter Susanna McBee off a civil rights story because she couldn't get into the press club to cover an important speaker. Black male reporters had been admitted since 1955, but in 1963, when women reporters asked Martin Luther King Jr. to boycott the press club on their behalf, he went ahead and spoke there anyway.

The gentlemen of the Washington press—some of whom spent their workdays writing about civil rights and injus-

Margaret Lyons began her newspaper career as advice columnist Pegge Parker, and kept the name as she wrote about World War II. This 1943 cigarette ad, she wrote later, was done under frankly false pretenses, "earning a dishonest dollar advertising cigarettes I have never smoked!" The venerated wartime columnist Ernie Pyle, who did smoke, posed for a similar ad for Chesterfield cigarettes. Doing ads and product endorsements is today strictly off-limits to real journalists.

tice—saw no unfairness in shutting out their women colleagues. The mossbacks held out until 1971. On the February day that two dozen women joined the National Press Club's ranks, the club's band played *Thank Heaven for Little Girls*.

NEWFOUND FREEDOM TO PUBLISH FREELY

In the American South, a slave who learned to read—and, especially, to write—could have a finger chopped off, be whipped, or even killed for it. Literacy was power, and power in black hands—and black brains—was dangerous.

Yet within twenty years of their emancipation, free black Americans were writing and publishing their own newspapers, using once-forbidden ink and paper to give powerful voice to civil rights. Like black churches, these newspapers were influential and relentless. And also like black churches, they were targets. In the Wilmington, North Carolina, white riot of 1898, the state's only black newspaper, the *Daily Record*, was torched. The armed mob then posed for a picture in front of its ruins.

To read how black papers covered the same stories white papers did is to fall through the looking glass. The people who were scarcely visible on one side were central figures on the other. Author Lee Finke summed up black newspapers' impact, and their mission: "When a white man reads a Negro paper for the first time, it hits him like a bucket of cold water in the face."

The first newspaper run entirely by black Americans was the short-lived weekly *Freedom's Journal*, founded in New York in 1827 to "plead our own cause." Co-editor John B. Russwurm was a free, mixed-race man who soon followed his own editorial

advice and moved to Africa.

Frederick Douglass, on the other hand, was an escaped slave, and before the Civil War, he became the face and voice for abolition and suffrage for black and female Americans alike. He founded his newspaper, the *North Star*, in 1847, under the motto, "Right is of no sex—Truth is of no color—God is the Father of us all, and we are brethren." It circulated to readers black and white, and Douglass kept on publishing, under different names, until the paper shuttered in 1874.

By then, black-owned newspapers were about to reach African Americans across the country. In Richmond, Virginia, once the capital of the Confederacy, a baker's dozen of former slaves opened the *Richmond Planet* in 1882. The *Planet* was unsparing in its campaign for black rights.

From the age of twenty-one until he died on the job forty-five years later, the *Planet*'s uncompromising editor was John Mitchell Jr. In the face of death threats for his stories about a Virginia lynching, he answered with Shakespeare—"There is no terror, Cassius, in your threats"—and carried a brace of pistols with him to cover the crime. The *New York World* took notice of him as "a man who would walk into the jaws of death to serve his race." That line is chiseled on his grave marker.

Two twentieth-century black newspapers in the North lighted the way for the

The slave-born Frederick Douglass, featured in a 1995 Civil War-series postage stamp, amplified his powerful voice through his abolitionist newspapers.

Great Migration. So massive was their influence that they were suppressed, even banned, in parts of the South. Black railroad workers—porters and waiters—smuggled them into Southern towns where they were passed from hand to hand and read from front to back.

The *Chicago Defender* had a name grander than its beginning, on the dining room table of Robert Sengstacke Abbott's landlord. Abbott sold his first issue—all four pages of it—door-to-door in May 1905. For fifty years of its long life, the *Defender* was a daily newspaper printing stories the white press didn't usually cover, like one from March 1, 1930: PROTEST SEGREGATION OF GOLD STAR MOTHERS. Abbott's

A MAINE MYSTERY

This astonishing photograph, ca. 1890s, shows four people, white and black, male and female. A bit of sleuthing found they may very well be members of the staff of the Waterville, Maine newspaper, the *Democrat*. On the front is written, "The Democrat Force"—force, as in workforce. On the back are the names of the foursome; the white woman, Etta Pomerleau, the two white men, F.V. Brown and Lennie V. Clark—and the black woman, Alice Osborne.

And there too, mysteriously, even ominously, the written command to "hide this picture out of sight (per order) Frederick James Ward." Was a racially mixed newspaper staff too daring even for Maine, where slavery had been outlawed since the revolution?

Alice Osborne's family history is remarkable: her grandfather was captured in Africa and brought to America on a slave ship. Her father, Samuel, was born a slave on a Virginia plantation around 1833. He came to Maine right after the end of the Civil War, with the help of a colonel of a Maine infantry regiment.

Sam Osborne spent thirty-seven years as the janitor of Colby College, in Waterville. The Osborne family sometimes hosted Colby students at Thanksgiving dinners, and Sam put up with their occasionally racist pranks and jokes.

In 2017, Colby renamed the president's house for Sam Osborne. He and his wife, Maria, had six daughters and one son.

Alice, born in 1871, graduated from the local high school and her sister Marion, younger by several years, became the first African American woman graduate of Colby.

(Another Colby alum was Elijah Parish Lovejoy, an abolitionist newspaper editor murdered in 1837 by a pro-slavery mob in Illinois.)

Alice was still alive for the 1940 census, living with her brother and the widowed Marion in the old family home. The census record shows that she was still working, but at what, the census-taker didn't ask.

A picture postcard of the home of the nation's first abolitionist newspaper, the *Emancipator*, founded and funded by a Quaker named Elihu Embree, to "hasten an even balance of equal rights to the now neglected sons of Africa." From April until October 1820, it published in Jonesborough, in east Tennessee, an area with some anti-slavery sentiment. (In the 1905 novel *The Clansman*, the book behind the incendiary 1916 film *The Birth of a Nation*, the hero and future KKK leader Ben Cameron argues that the *Emancipator* proves the South is really not all bad when it came to slavery.)

motto for the *Defender* was simply "American race prejudice must be destroyed."

The paper demanded cabinet posts for African Americans, and the integration of schools, police departments, government jobs, and unions. With its reach and power, it told Southern readers how to move North, printing railroad timetables and advice on how to live and work in the Windy City. The Underground Railroad had gone above ground.

The other nationally influential paper was the *Pittsburgh Courier*. About a month after Pearl Harbor, a *Courier* reader named James Thompson, who worked in the cafeteria of a Kansas aircraft plant, wrote a letter to the editor proposing a Double V campaign—victory over fascism abroad and racism at home. "Certainly," the *Courier* editorialized, "we should be strong enough to whip both of them."

The *Courier*'s Double V crusade found supporters in Humphrey Bogart and Ingrid Bergman and former Republican presidential candidates Wendell Willkie and Thomas Dewey. Lionel Hampton, the old *Defender* newsboy, performed the Double V crusade's song, "Yankee Doodle Tan," on a national radio show.

But to FBI Director J. Edgar Hoover, stories in the *Courier* and other black newspapers about the hypocrisy of fighting for democracy and freedom while American blacks lived under Jim Crow were a divisive threat, even anti-war sedition. He wanted them all locked up.

Cabinet members met with black editors and publishers, and by 1943 the Double V campaign had faded. Yet *Courier* star reporter Frank Bolden said the paper wasn't scared off. Patrick S. Washburn, author of *The African American Newspaper: Voice of Freedom*, quoted Bolden: "Hell, no, the government pressure didn't cause us to back off. We welcomed it. It helped sell more papers when we wrote about it. We wanted Roosevelt to arrest one [black] publisher for sedition and shut his paper down. But he was too smart to do that."

On the far side of the country, the *California Owl* was already rolling its presses. In 1879, a teenager named John Neimore started up a paper for black Americans who saw in California a blank slate on which to write their own histories.

When Neimore died in 1912, a disconsolate woman who used to go door-to-door to collect the money for his subscriptions

The *Richmond Planet* was not the first African American newspaper in the American South, but it gained a national voice from its founding in 1883 until its end in 1938, reporting on matters like "Negro Exodus to the North" and the systematic disenfranchisement of black citizens.

watched as the paper went up for auction. She could not keep her deathbed promise to Neimore to take over for him, until a neighbor offered to buy it for her for fifty dollars. That's how Charlotta Bass became the first black woman to run her own newspaper, by then named the *California Eagle*.

In 1915 Hollywood, she protested boldly against D.W. Griffith's *The Birth of a Nation*. In the 1920s, she won a libel suit with the local KKK. After World War II, the *Eagle* joined forces with Los Angeles's other black newspaper, the *Sentinel*, for a Don't Buy Where You Can't Work campaign, boycotting stores that took black shoppers' money but wouldn't hire them. For the paper's seventieth anniversary, in 1949, more than eleven thousand people celebrated at a Los Angeles baseball stadi-um. Bass sold the paper in 1951 to devote her time to politics, and in 1964—the year before the Watts riots—it closed.

A number of black newspapers are still vigorous, like the *Kansas City Call*, and Minnesota's *Spokesman-Recorder*, founded more than eighty years ago by a man who had to moonlight as a bellhop to pay the bills. Cecil Newman's newspapers became a potent political voice in the Twin Cities, and one of his photographers, Gordon Parks, went on to renown.

The dilemma that many black newspapers have found themselves in, though, is this: The rule of thumb is that the more readers a paper has, the more it can charge for advertising. But white businesses were leery of advertising to a black readership, and black entrepreneurs had a hard time getting capital to open businesses at all. As good as the news stories and editorials were, the money wasn't always there, and many papers were forced to stop their presses.

That did not keep black reporters from reporting, nor black editors from editing. Even in the Civil War South, two free New Orleans black men, Louis Charles Roudanez and Paul Trevigne, founded and edited first *L'Union*, in 1862, and, in 1864, *La Tribune de la Nouvelle-Orleans*, which was printed in English and French. When their lives and livelihoods were threatened, the men redirected the paper's abolitionist fires into subtler critiques drawn in the style of French satirists.

Far to the north, Thomas Morris Chester's wartime writing reached readers of the mainstream daily, the *Philadelphia Press*. Its editor sent the free-born Chester to the front as a special correspondent for the last ten months of the Civil War—a first for a mainstream American paper. Under the pen name Rollin, Chester wrote ardently about the valor of black Union troops and the sufferings of black slaves.

In one of the most moving pieces of reportage of the entire war, after the fall of Richmond, Virginia, in the spring of 1865, Chester walked into what had been the

The *Chicago Defender's* Ethel L. Payne—called the "first lady of the black press"—interviews a soldier in Vietnam. As one of a handful of African American reporters accredited to the White House in the 1950s, she asked probing questions about racial discrimination—so probing that, by several accounts, the Eisenhower White House tried to find grounds to revoke her credentials. In the 1970s, CBS made her a national radio and TV commentator.

Confederate Senate, sat down at the desk of Jefferson Davis, and there wrote to his readers that he was "seated at the Speaker's chair, so long dedicated to treason, but in the future to be consecrated to loyalty."

Through newsprint and ink, black women often spoke more forcefully than their sisters on white papers could. Nearly eight decades before Rosa Parks refused to move to the back of the bus, a primly dressed black woman named Ida B. Wells boarded a Memphis train with the first-class ticket she always bought for the trip.

This time, the conductor ignored her ticket. To the applause of some white passengers, he yanked her out of her seat when she indignantly refused to move to the filthy "smoking" car. After she won a round in her lawsuit against the railroad, the *Memphis Daily Appeal* wrote about the "darky damsel" winning a "verdict for $500."

Soon Wells was writing fiercely against lynching and segregationist laws as co-editor and owner of the *Free Speech and Headlight* newspaper. A white mob trashed the newspaper's building after the paper ran her article about the myths of inter-racial sex that lay behind many lynchings. That, and threats to her life, impelled her to move to Chicago, where she wrote about the same topics for the important black newspaper the *New York Age.*

Marvel Cooke, two generations younger, grew up in a politically engaged household, and got her first job at the NAACP's magazine. Her prose and her politics took her to her groundbreaking job as the first black woman on the staff of a white newspaper, New York's liberal *Daily Compass.* For her 1950 "Bronx Slave Market" series, she hired herself out as a day-laborer cleaning woman. "I was the slave traded for two truck horses on a Memphis street corner in 1849," she wrote. "I was a slave trading my brawn for a pittance on a Bronx street corner in 1949."

Civil rights protests and the riots of the 1960s showed mainstream newspaper editors how inadequate to the job their newsrooms were. As the 1965 Watts riots roiled L.A., a black *Los Angeles Times* advertising messenger named Robert Richardson dropped into the all-white newsroom to let the editors know what he was seeing in his neighborhood. They sent him out to bring back more. He gave them first-person accounts of getting knocked down and handcuffed by cops, of how his press card got him out of custody, and of hearing the black men still in the police station lockup chanting, *Burn, baby, burn!*

Richardson was speedily hired on the *Times* news staff and assigned to the night police beat. But he got no training, no guidance—and within a year he was

A woman and child look through the window of the *Pittsburgh Courier*'s Chicago office, one of the many regional editions of the influential African American newspaper.

Five U.S. postage stamps were issued in 2008 to honor journalists who put their lives on the line covering seminal events of the twentieth century. Los Angeles newsman Ruben Salazar was killed in 1970 as he covered the city's Chicano anti-war protests.

out. A *Times* reporter ran into him years later and heard his story. What happened to him, she wrote, was sink-or-swim, and he sank.

Nor were American Latinos in evidence in bigger newsrooms until well into the twentieth century. The national black-white construct of race relations ran so deep that an expanding Latino population, with its complexities of demography and geography—as citizens, immigrants, and refugees—got blurred or obliterated in news coverage.

ONE VOICE IN TWO LANGUAGES

Latinos had Spanish-language newspapers, radios, and even television. It took the cultural shakeouts of the 1960s and '70s to bring more Latinos onto mainstream newspaper payrolls. In 1984, Latino journalists at the *Los Angeles Times* won a gold-medal Pulitzer for their monumental series about Latino L.A.

In *Below the Fold*, a 2007 documentary about their reporting, *Times* journalist Virginia Escalante remembered working at the *Stockton Record* and looking for its clipping files on Latinos, Mexican Americans, Chicanos, and coming up empty-handed. The librarian directed her to the "Ws"—for "wetbacks."

In 2008, a postage stamp honored the groundbreaking *Times* columnist Ruben Salazar, who was killed by a tear gas projectile as he covered the city's 1970 Latino anti-war marches. Almost fifty years later, newspapers are still trying to get Spanish-language names and words right. It matters; the word *año* means "year." Without the little tilde over the "n," the same word means "anus."

Newspapers learned the hard way that racial blind spots were costing them goodwill and good coverage. They were missing minority stories, but falling short on bigger-picture journalism without the news judgment of fellow journalists with different lives and experiences.

Eventually, the ranks of African American reporters were joined by Latino and Asian journalists whose bilingual skills and cultural knowledge meant some absent American voices would be absent no more. And at last, America's newsrooms were beginning to look like the Americans they covered.

CHAPTER 9

TAKING ON TECH

It may not look that way now, but newspapers don't always resist new technology; they thrive on it. Sometimes they may not see it coming—the Internet hurtled their way like an uncharted meteorite—but when it comes to "early adopters," newspapers have been at the front of the line.

The telegraph, the typewriter, the telephone, newfangled types of printing presses, the photo transmitter, the fax—they all gave eager newspapers the power to report more news faster than ever before.

These "eureka" breakthroughs were revolutionary. Over time, newspapers could be printed on both sides of the page at once,

January 1967 marked the end of the dot and dash news that began during the Civil War—the last time that the United Press International's domestic news service sent a news story via a clickety-tick Morse code key. Thereafter, bulky teletype machines noisily churned out line after line of stories, and a system of bells alerted editors to the importance of the story, from "urgent" to "bulletin" to "flash." The few words breaking the news of the assassination of President John F. Kennedy merited a "flash"—ten bells. (The old ban on whistling in a newsroom may have originated with the notion that it masked the sound of an incoming "bell.")

could deliver color comics, could roll off hundreds of thousands of copies in a few hours on rolls of paper standing three feet tall and weighing nearly a half-ton each.

Not much changed between Gutenberg's first movable type and the mid-nineteenth century. Newspapers were usually set in type by hand, by pressmen who selected metal-cast letters of different sizes and fonts from wooden type cases, then assembled them one letter at a time into words, sentences, paragraphs, stories. That's one reason early newspapers weren't thick—it took too much time to put together more than a few pages each day.

But the appearance of the Linotype machine—an unwieldy

Opposite: The composing room and printing press of the *Iron Herald* in Negaunee, Michigan, showing how the press is won. ca. 1900

Men operating a row of Linotype machines before World War I at the *Philadelphia Record*, assembling the lead-type letters that made up each story and advertisement. In its seventy years, the crusading newspaper won a readership far beyond the city.

The switchboard operator at the *Morning Call* newspaper in Allentown, Pennsylvania, takes and places calls to and from journalists, advertisers, and subscribers.

cross between a clattering pipe organ and a six-foot-tall typewriter that put words in lead instead of on paper—allowed one man sitting at a keyboard to bang out hundreds of metal "lines o' type" at a dazzling thirty words a minute. This technological long-jump made it possible to put together more stories, and more lines of advertising, to run in ever-bigger and ever-more-profitable newspapers. (By 2016, Colorado's weekly *Saguache Crescent* was still being crafted on a 1921 Linotype machine, probably the last paper in the nation to do so. That's like using a reel-to-reel tape recorder in a world of iPhones.)

The idea of the "next new thing" in printing always held such promise that newspaperman Mark Twain dropped the equivalent of at least four million dollars on the invention of the Paige Compositor, to make typesetting easier and faster. The only thing it ever achieved was to drain Twain's fortune and force him back out on the lecture circuit to try to recoup his losses. Only one of the machines survives.

Richard March Hoe's 1847 rotary press meant newspapers could print from one single continuous roll of paper; Thomas Bullock's 1863 improved version printed on both sides, then folded and cut the papers. (Bullock died of gangrene after his leg was mangled by his own invention while he was setting up a new press for Philadelphia's *Public Ledger*.)

Every day's stories were written and edited in the newsroom, assembled in the composing room, and printed in the pressroom. Stories were set by hand into long, vertical columns called galleys, and galleys were wedged (sometimes with the ungentle help of a special hammer) into a page-sized frame called a chase, which was rolled around the pressroom on a sturdy trolley called a turtle. All this equipment had to be heavy-duty, because spilling a whole page of type ruined hours of a craftsman's work. It's called "pieing the type," and it was also saboteurs' way of attacking newspapers.

Like an image in a mirror, or a photo negative, stories had to be typeset in reverse to be legible when they were printed. One page at a time was "inked up" so one copy could be made and proofread before

Massive Hoe presses, like these running at the *Los Angeles Times*, made it possible to print color in a daily newspaper, and could turn out more than 200,000 32-page newspapers in a single hour.

Ingenuity made the wheels turn. In Quilcene, Washington, the weekly *Megaphone* powered its printing press via a water wheel turned by a mountain stream above Quilcene Bay.

the chase was carried off to the presses.

If a story wasn't quite long enough to fill a galley, typesetters plugged the gap with a filler, some pre-set tidbit or factoid kept on hand just for that purpose. Connoisseurs of these fillers once collected them with delight; who wouldn't want to know that "There are eight hundred purple grackles for every Congressman in Washington"?

Pressmen were indispensable to newspapers, and in the years after the Revolution, joined forces from time to time to demand more money. In 1852, typographers formed the first enduring national union. On four square miles of land in Tennessee, from 1911 until 1967, pressmen had their own combination union

headquarters, retirement home, and training center. Unusually, the union welcomed women members. In 1994, at the Union Printers Home in Colorado Springs—a fanciful prairie castle of red sandstone—an eighty-six-year-old retired *Chicago Tribune* typesetter named Lucy Zylkowski told the Denver weekly *Westword* that when she was a little girl in Neenah, Wisconsin, she glimpsed a Linotype through the window of the newspaper office and decided on the spot to become a typesetter.

A Wisconsin newspaperman named Roland Gelatt became publisher of the *La Crosse Tribune* in 1917, a man who so loved the steampunk beauty of metal type that, as the paper later wrote, he "would actually pet a new case when it was unpacked."

Not everyone was so besotted with the romance of type, however. California's first newspaper, the *Californian*, along with its slightly younger competitor, the *California Star*, stopped publishing after gold was discovered in 1848, because the pressmen ran off to go prospecting. (No great loss, maybe; as the state's special collections librarian Gary Kurutz told *Monterey County Weekly*, the *Californian* was known to misspell the word "California.")

Newspapers' transition from composing papers by hot type into cold type and then to computers eclipsed typesetters' craft, but papers themselves boomed as they found they could deliver the news faster and more cheaply with fewer craftsmen and more technology. These days,

A 1908 report to the International Typographical Union noted the "notoriously unhealthy occupations" of printing and typesetting—severe lung problems, probably from breathing droplets of chemical ink in close spaces. Beginning in 1892, ailing members could retire to the union's massive red-and-white stone "castle" in the high, dry air of Colorado Springs, seen here in a tinted postcard.

The *Scranton Times* erected a radio transmission tower taller than its newspaper building after it bought radio station WQAN in 1923. It was an inadvertent symbol of how broadcast news would dominate print's audience—but still depend on print for a lot of the news it broadcasts.

many broadsheets—the opposite of tabloid-sized papers—have shrunk in width to save paper, and money.

Technology beyond the pressroom altered the newspaper landscape, too. In the 1920s, newspapers saw a good thing in the new game of radio, and by 1923, the *Memphis Commercial Appeal* newspaper had already bought its own radio station, WMC. The *Scranton Times* raised a massive radio tower with the call letters of its radio station, WQAN, atop its building. The paper still decorates the tower with lights at Christmastime and makes a great

ceremony of flipping the switch. The *Detroit News* broadcast the 1920 presidential election results on the station that became radio and then TV station WWJ. By 1975, so many newspapers owned radio and TV properties that the Federal Communications Commission ordered their breakup, although rules were relaxed more than thirty years later.

Newspaper technology wasn't up to printing photographs until 1880, and then, in 1899, the earliest photo was sent remotely via the Telediagraph, invented by a Minnesota watchmaker to send fax-like photo images via telegraph lines. The first picture ever transmitted was sent from the

New York Herald to newspaper offices as far away as Chicago. It showed the first gun fired at the 1899 Battle of Manila, and it took nearly a half-hour to arrive.

By 1929, that time was cut to one minute. The Associated Press's Wirephoto became an industry standard. A half-century later, newspapers finally entered the computer age that had transformed other large enterprises and upended many of their processes, protocols, and traditions.

Newspapers were "early adopters" in a way most people don't realize. Portland's influential *Oregonian* newspaper operated radio station KGW beginning in 1922, and took the operation on the road.

LOS ANGELES
TYPOGRAPHICAL
UNION NO. 174

OFFICE OF THE SECRETARY
446 - 447 I. W. HELLMAN BUILDING
411 S. Main St.   TUcker 4225

WORKING CARD
No. 75898

Thomas A. Gilbertson

IN ACCOUNT WITH
LOS ANGELES TYPOGRAPHICAL UNION
For the Year Ending May 31, 1925

Dues must be paid not later than the 10th of each month
Union meets last Sunday of the month in the Union
Labor Temple at 1:30 p. m.
Office Hours 9 to 12:30; 1:30 to 5:30; Saturdays 9 to 1

A rare 1925 membership card from the Los Angeles Typographical Union.

Western Union International, Inc.

PRESS

A form in use through the 1970s allowed reporters to file stories via Western Union, flagging the message as an urgent press story.

Newspaper photographers were drawn into the computerized workflow. With the images from new digital cameras eliminating the darkroom and negatives and all the intermediate steps of photo processing, they were sending off digital photos in a matter of seconds, just as their reporter counterparts could do by hitting the "send" button on stories.

Coin-operated newspaper vending machines first popped up in 1947, nudging old-fashioned newsstands to the sidelines, and in 1988, the machines got their own Supreme Court ruling: a city didn't have "unbridled discretion" over rules about setting up these machines, lest it use that authority to muzzle newspapers the city didn't like.

Whatever rocks—and rolls—their new newspaper world, every editor and reporter and photographer still knows the thrill of that daily moment when a button deep in the building gets pushed, and they feel that seismic rumble as the presses create the newspaper all over again.

Adios, newsboy, hello, newsbox. This prototype of the "robot newsstand" debuted in 1962, designed to handle "publications that vary greatly in size, thickness and flexibility."

THE REAL "NEWSIES"

The reporters have typed their last -30- mark for the day, the editors have hooked their last paragraphs, the ink has set on the last edition.

Now what?

Now the newspapers have to get to their readers.

Long, long ago, people came to the news, not the other way around. An ancient forerunner of newspapers was Rome's Acta Diurna, "daily acts," official doings posted around the Eternal City. In nineteenth-century El Paso, Texas, the central plaza's "newspaper tree"—a plank

Two little street vendors, in an undated vintage picture, doing what newsboys did—look eager and winning to help sell their papers.

Aviation pioneer Glenn Martin in his biplane with a stack of newspapers on the wing, waiting to fly them from Fresno to Madera, California, to promote flying's manifold uses.

nailed to an ash tree—was good enough for sharing public information until a real newspaper came along, printed on pulp made from other trees. (In 1941, the city replaced the felled original with a replica tree, and in 2003, a local online nonprofit news site named itself Newspaper Tree.)

Not until the great age of newspapers in New York, though, did one of journalism's most legendary figures arise: the newsboy.

The plucky newspaper boy was a Central Casting urchin in knee pants and a raggedy sweater, standing on a street corner, out-hollering the boy on the opposite corner selling the competition's paper. Or he was that nice boy from down the street,

Left, just like the post office, neither snow nor more snow kept Ricky Smith from delivering the *Fairbanks Daily News-Miner* in January 1954, a half-hour route by dogsled. *Right,* when the canine can't fetch the paper, maybe the bovine can. Suzy brings in the *Cleveland Press* at the Raymond Balogh family farm in Grafton, Ohio, in 1956.

nonchalantly steering his bike through sedate neighborhoods with one hand and hurling a neat roll of newsprint onto porch after porch with the other.

Before some great men ever made headlines, they delivered them: Martin Luther King Jr. with the *Atlanta Journal*; Walt Disney in Kansas City—on a bobsled, if the weather required it; Jackie Robinson in the Pasadena, California, sunshine; and nearby in Glendale, Marion Morrison (with his big Airedale) got the nickname "Duke" from firemen, and John Wayne used it ever after. In 1955, a newsboys' organization presented its one-time colleague President Dwight Eisenhower with a thirty-inch trophy honoring "yesterday's

newspaper boy—tomorrow's leader." The paperboy took on the Norman Rockwell contours of the virtues of American boyhood: sturdiness, reliability, ambition, and a modest profit motive.

The earliest newsboys were not by any stretch Eisenhowers or Disneys. They were New York tenement boys, and they were the cheapest way for the city's dozens of newspapers to battle for circulation—rumbustious little human vending machines, shouting out enticingly flamboyant come-ons for the latest *Extra!* edition. Theirs was

A sorrowful stunt: a trained and chained chimpanzee peddling the *Miami Herald* on a Miami street in 1946. The animal came from a Dania, Florida, "chimp farm," where they were raised for scientific research.

A *Sunday Register and Leader* newsboy, ca. 1915. Iowa's *Des Moines Register* has been the state's dominant paper for more than 150 years and has won sixteen Pulitzer Prizes.

A little newspaper boy does the bicycle delivery bit one better with a skateboard on his delivery route in 1979.

a knife-edge survival. Newsboys first had to buy the newspapers they sold, and eat the cost of the ones they didn't, which explains their sales tactics.

Anyone who's seen *Newsies*, the 1992 movie or the Broadway musical, knows that a simmering series of small strikes broke into labor warfare in 1899 when the Hearst and Pulitzer papers began charging newsboys more for their papers. The boys went on strike. They blocked the distribution of the offending papers. Scabs refused to take the boys' places. Their leader was a one-eyed fourteen-year-old Napoleon

with the tabloid-perfect nickname Kid Blink. He roused his troops with stirring speeches like the Shakespeare-goes-to-Brooklyn line, "Dis is a time which tries de hearts of men."

In the end, the two moguls backed partway down; they'd buy back the papers the newsboys didn't sell. Newsboys in other cities were inspired to flex their muscles. Papers at last began to look out for newsboys' welfare, organizing outings and picnics. The California Newspaper-boy Foundation offered scholarships to promising lads. Eventually, child labor laws extended their protections, and dailies began being delivered by grown-ups in cars, leaving weeklies to kids on bikes.

Chicago outdid them all, in its ".38 caliber circulation drive" that began in 1910, when the Hearst paper enlisted gangs of goons who took guns and brass knuckles into street fights over circulation. One newsstand was shot up to "persuade" its owner to sell the shooters' paper, and tons of newspapers were commandeered and dumped into the river. Two other papers joined the fray, but, as the *Chicago Tribune* reported decades later, most readers didn't know about it. The papers and authorities kept it all quiet, and only the *Chicago Socialist* chronicled the violence.

In more decorous places, readers could pick up the tonier morning papers from newsstands on their way to work,

A vendor's apron for New Jersey editions of the *New York Daily News*.

and the blue-collar afternoon papers on their way home. "Whaddya read, whaddya read?" the news vendors called out. They knew their regular customers' preferences in newspapers the way Starbucks baristas know what to start brewing for frequent quaffers.

With the suburbanization of America, newspapers bought fleets of trucks to carry their editions to homes farther and farther from the printing plants. And what could be more natural in an aviation-mad nation but that the *St. Petersburg Times* became, in 1914, the first newspaper to deliver the day's edition by air? They went to Tampa, a distance of maybe twenty miles.

Right out of a *noir* film, a onetime chorus girl named Bunny Duchaine works at a Chicago newsstand, hawking the hometown papers in August 1952.

GUTENBERG'S OFFSPRING

You can take the word *press*—as in "ladies and gentlemen of the press"—literally. Because to make a printed document, a sheet of paper or vellum and a bed of type had to be pressed together, with ink in between.

One of America's earliest printing press models was called the Washington. The machine bore an image of George Washington and could turn out one sheet at a time, at a pretty fast clip. It was on a Washington press, in 1833, that Mormons in Independence, Missouri, were printing their newspaper when an anti-Mormon mob trashed the newspaper office and tossed the Washington printing press into the Missouri River. It was salvaged and began its travels via covered wagon to Colorado, soon getting carted from mining settlement to town, printing short-lived newspapers and moving on.

In 1867, men from Boulder, Colorado, who coveted the press in nearby Valmont simply pinched it. They apparently got the editor likkered up and stole the whole works from under his nose, hauled it back to Boulder, and started their own paper. The press moved to New Mexico, where it disappeared from the record in 1870.

In the East, printing presses were easier to come by, but in the West, they were

The *Detroit News* printed up postcards that bragged of having "the world's greatest newspaper plant," with gleaming presses which could print, cut, fold, and count 360,000 48-page newspapers in an hour.

almost as scarce and as coveted as the gold that men came searching for. The printer and provisional governor of Mexican California, Agustín Zamorano, opened a print shop in 1834 with a Boston-made Ramage press—its price, a reported $460. He printed books, pamphlets, and manifestos, but the Ramage press began turning out news-

papers only after Americans took over the state. With paper almost as hard to come by as printing presses, the *Monterey Californian* was published on cigarette paper.

Ingenuity drove the presses for some papers. A mountain stream running down to Quilcene Bay in the state of Washington turned the water wheel that powered the presses at the *Quilcene Megaphone*. Before the Civil War, Charlie, an old blind horse, walked a treadmill to print the weekly *Galveston News* in Texas, and in the 1860s, steam made the presses roll at the *Portland Oregonian*.

Like that printing press that rose from the mud of the Missouri River to make the trek to Colorado, South Dakota's first printing press wandered from its Cincinnati foundry to Iowa, to Wisconsin, and in 1858, to Sioux Falls, to print the *Dakota Democrat*. Settlers abandoned the whole town—including the printing press—

Rolls of newsprint are ready for the presses at the *Philadelphia Record*. The paper was a forthright crusader, investigating among other civic outrages, crooked contractors and the abuses of patients at mental hospitals. The *Record* supported labor, but paradoxically, in 1947, it closed after strikes by some of its workers.

during the 1862 Indian wars. Native Americans destroyed the printing press but salvaged the lead type for ornamental inlay for ceremonial pipes, some of which they sold to the new settlers.

Cincinnati also produced Arizona's first printing press, another Washington model that was shipped downriver to New Orleans, across Panama, and hauled via the Jackass Mail mule team to Tubac, Arizona, population four hundred, where the state's first newspaper, the *Weekly Arizonian*, debuted on March 3, 1859.

The paper closed within a few months, and the printing press journeyed to Tucson, where it printed two local papers, and was briefly held captive by the Union Army. It moved to Tombstone, where it published two newspapers, including the renowned *Epitaph*. Now it rests in a Tubac museum, and turns out souvenir copies of its first issue.

The printing press of the *Cimarron News and Press* in New Mexico had already published New Mexico's very first newspaper, in Taos, in 1834. It was then shuffled around the territory until January 19, 1876, when Clay Allison, a Texas gunslinger who once rode through a Texas town

The Daily Gate City letterhead and note:

Daily, established sixty-one years
Official paper of city and county
Leading Home Paper of this section

Daily average circulation 3728
January to June, 1907

Chicago Office: 750 Marquette Bldg.
Payne & Young, Representatives
New York Office: 140 Nassau St.
LaCoste & Maxwell, Representatives

THE DAILY GATE CITY
BY THE GATE CITY COMPANY
C. F. SKIRVIN, Publisher

Keokuk, Iowa, 7/17/07.

Dear Ed:

I send you under separate cover copy of the Gate City containing photograph—electro—of the new Goss I am going to out in here this coming October. She is a peach. When I get 'er in want you to come down and help christen it. Best wishes to you.

A new printing press was a thing of beauty. This note from the *Daily Gate City* newspaper in Keokuk, Iowa, fairly purred with anticipation about a new printing press. "She is a peach."

wearing nothing but his gun belt, led his cowboy gang charging into the newspaper offices.

They smashed the place up, hammered the press to bits, and dumped the bits in the Cimarron River, says the *Encyclopedia of Lawmen, Outlaws, and Gunfighters*. Allison scooped up the week's half-printed issue, scrawled "Clay Allison's Edition" on the blank side, and rode around Cimarron handing them out—or extorting one dollar a copy, as some tell it. A day later, he went back to the newspaper with two hundred dollars in contrition money, but by then, New Mexico's first printing press was already scattered to the water and the dust.

A scaled-down metal nameplate for a Goss Headliner printing press at the onetime *San Diego Union and Evening Tribune*. The two papers merged in 1992.

Columbia University

School of Journalism

School of Business

CHAPTER 10

THE IVY LEAGUE FOR INK-STAINED WRETCHES

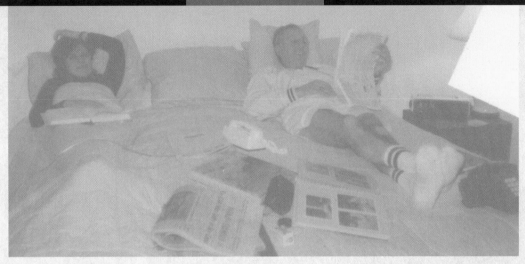

A school for training reporters and editors may have been dreamed up on a front porch in Lexington, Virginia, not long after the Civil War. Here's how the journalism weekly *Editor & Publisher* told it about a half-century later, in 1916:

A bearded old warhorse, the subject of thousands of newspaper stories himself, was on his porch, talking with a New York newspaperman. Finally, said the old man, "War is over, but the South has a still greater conflict before her. We must do something to train her new recruits to fight her battles, not with the sword, but with the pen."

The old gentleman was the most famous man in the Confederacy, the ex-General Robert E. Lee. He meant that the South needed more professional reporters to tell its stories. Lee was by then president of Washington College, and there, his support helped to create the country's first journalism school.

Lee recommended to the college board of trustees "the direct and indirect influence for good of a body of men educated to the culture and tone proposed for our students, distributed among the newspaper offices of the United States, and by their example and aims, elevating the standards of journalism." Washington College soon offered fifty scholarships of printing and journalism; in the 1860s, the two skills were still intertwined.

That scholarship program pretty much died with Lee, but scores of journalism classes and journalism schools still pack 'em in to take up the career of "ink-stained wretch," as the old description of reporters goes, even as newspapers are struggling to keep publishing.

The Missouri School of Journalism has been a going concern since 1908. The best known, Columbia University's graduate journalism school in New York, which administers the Pulitzer Prizes, opened four years later, thanks to the then-stupendous sum of two million dollars provided by publisher Joseph Pulitzer, who wanted to "raise journalism to the rank of a learned profession" from its origins as a job for knockabouts and opportunists.

Opposite: Founded in 1912, Columbia University's journalism school sat alongside the university's business school, founded in 1916.

Tom Wicker, the Washington bureau chief for the *New York Times*, wrote deeply about the 1971 Attica, New York prison riots, and evidently thought enough of prison rehabilitation programs to hand out certificates to seven graduates of a prison journalism course in March 1977.

One of journalism's great debates had begun. Is a degree better than learning on the job? Can a classroom educate reporters and editors as well as a newsroom can? There were doctors and lawyers practicing long before there were medical or law schools, weren't there?

The same 1916 article that spun the story of Robert E. Lee's front-porch musings quoted a *New York Herald* editor named Frederic Hudson: "The only place where one can learn to be a journalist is in a great newspaper office."

Unlike law or medicine, though, there's no exam, no license to prove that a reporter is a reporter. Instead, journalists re-qualify for their jobs every time they put their names—or faces, or voices—on their stories, certifying that their work is as full, factual, fair, and forthright as it can be, on deadline. It's not possible to license journalists the way doctors or lawyers are—but not for the reasons you might think.

Certainly, it irks professional reporters when people who've never so much as covered a city council meeting on deadline call themselves "journalists." Yet licensing and certifying reporters would be incalculably dangerous for democracy. It would mean that the government sets standards for who is and isn't a journalist, and that

wouldn't even begin to pass the First Amendment smell test. Good, competitive journalism itself should make good journalists. The way that reporter and author Jonathan Alter put it, "Because we shouldn't be accountable to government, we have no choice but to be accountable to each other."

So what can a journalism school teach? No "j-school" graduate is ever going to interview someone about the history of the Linotype machine. Apart from teaching the vital mechanics of reporting fully and writing coherently, journalism schools create critical thinkers and generalists. Journalists need to report deeply and substantively, and also to know about politics, history, science, business, civics, art, technology, human culture. Reporters aren't mere stenographers. They have to distill and discern, to deliver background, context, and content. Yes, this is today's news story—but "today" doesn't ever exist in a vacuum.

As journalism became more professionalized, j-schools helped to standardize codes of conduct and ethics for reporters and editors to practice, helping newspapers to rise out of the ethical muck of their own creation.

At college and high school papers, journalism students practice what they learn, sometimes with fiery results. High school newspapers have defiantly printed unflinching stories about drugs, bullying, and sexual harassment on campus. After a Virginia school superintendent killed a story about a dangerous new marijuana trend, the young editor took the story to the local newspaper—which ran it online.

Fledgling journalists in Missouri took their school to court after their teen pregnancy stories were censored from their high school newspaper. Ultimately, the Supreme Court ruled that most public high school papers don't have the same First Amendment protections as professional newspapers. Yet administrations' outright censorship hasn't killed off nearly as many school papers as budget cuts have. Student newspapers—especially in poor school districts—have become "luxuries" that at least half the nation's public high schools can't afford any more.

The last words on the matter go to Joseph Pulitzer. In 1951, a bronze plaque was put on the wall of the journalism school he paid to start:

> Our republic and its press will rise or fall together. An able, disinterested, public-spirited press, with trained intelligence to know the right and courage to do it, can preserve that public virtue without which popular government is a sham and a mockery. A cynical, mercenary, demagogic press will produce in time a people as base as itself. The power to mold the future of the Republic will be in the hands of the journalists of future generations.

And Pulitzer's words ring true, whether those hands are holding newsprint or smartphones.

Dorothy Anne Hobson was nine years old in 1937, and she decided her tiny lumber town of Valsetz, Oregon, needed a newspaper. She started putting out the monthly *Valsetz Star* with a card table and a mimeograph machine. The story of the doughty little editor added readers like Shirley Temple to her subscriber list. Here, in 1940, a year before her last issue, she poses in bed with a "-30-" sign: in newspapering, that's the end of the story, and the end of a news-packed day for her.

CHAPTER 11
NEWSPAPER PALACES

When you could set up a printing press and assemble a dozen desks just about anywhere, why did some newspaper offices become large, lavish newspaper palaces?

Because as papers got bigger and more influential, publishers wanted to convey the power and might of the press in general—and themselves in particular. And especially if it hollered "my edifice is bigger than your edifice" to the competition.

So New York wound up with Newspaper Row, a palisade of

The very opposite of marbled newspaper palaces: past a white picket fence, under a trellis arch, and through a garden was the entrance to the Parkersburg, West Virginia, News and Sentinel Building, circa 1973. The two papers, one morning, one afternoon, merged in 2009.

newspaper palaces along Park Row. Boston had its own newspaper row, and San Francisco's version, Newspaper Angle, stood downtown. The fires from the 1906 earthquake took down the San Francisco Call Building, where Mark Twain once worked, and William Randolph Hearst's Examiner Building, too. The bones of the surviving San Francisco Chronicle Building are now a Ritz-Carlton hotel.

That kind of grandeur is the exception. When newspapers were growing up in early America and then growing out into new

Opposite: Since its final paper edition in 2009, the *Seattle Post-Intelligencer* has existed only online, but its 1946 neon globe, with a ribbon at the equator reading "It's in the P-I," is an official city landmark and belongs to the city's history museum.

The frontier storefront *Buffalo Voice* was one of two weekly newspapers in the Wyoming town. They helped "to encourage moral and social progress," said a 1918 survey of Wyoming towns by the regional phone company. In an early nod to customer parking, the *Voice* put a hitching rail out front.

The 1925 neo-Gothic Tribune Tower in Chicago is ornamented outside with fragments of stone brought back by reporters from the Taj Mahal, the Alamo, Lincoln's original tomb, the Great Pyramid. The building was sold in 2016 to become condominiums.

American territory, a storefront on Main Street sufficed; after all, newspapers often bloomed and withered right along with the boom-and-bust towns themselves.

As the *Gary Tribune* was putting itself on the Indiana map before World War I, it spread a sheet over a shoebox building and splashed the paper's name and new address across the front. Big-city newspapers would come to fret about where patrons could park; the *Buffalo Voice* in Wyoming set up a long hitching rail out front.

More than a few newspaper palaces went phallically vertical. The soaring neo-Gothic tower of the *Chicago Tribune* (the self-proclaimed World's Greatest Newspaper) and the fanciful tower of the *Miami News* still stand, both listed in the National Register of Historic Places, as are dozens of other newspaper buildings. The 1925 cupola-topped News Building became a center for Cuban refugees, and then a museum and art space. The Tribune Tower is destined to become that mash-up of commercial, shops, and condos so recently beloved of downtown revitalizers.

Any number of newspaper buildings installed clocks atop their towers or rooftops. Remember, in an age when a working man couldn't always afford a watch of his own, a glance at the newspaper clock could hurry him to work on time—and remind him that it was the newspaper helping him be prompt. South Carolina's *Greenville News* and its sister evening paper the *Greenville Piedmont* shared a downtown building with a spectacular neon clock that could be seen for blocks. Its time ran out when the place was torn down in the late 1960s. In Portland, Oregon, the dueling newspapers had dueling clocks—the *Journal* and the *Oregonian*. The *Oregonian's* was torn down in 1950; the *Journal's* is still a civic landmark.

The clock on the twenty-two-story Oakland Tribune Tower in San Francisco's

The enormous, distinctive double-faced clock marked the hours above the *News-Piedmont* newspaper building in Greenville, South Carolina; its sands ran out when the place was torn down in 1968. The *Greenville News*, as it has been called since 1985, lives on, in print and online.

In Gary, Indiana, the *Tribune* became a daily newspaper in 1908, when this photo postcard was taken, and it made sure readers could find its new premises. "This town is a marvel for Ind.," wrote the sender of the postcard. The *Tribune* merged with the *Gary Post* in 1921 and in 1966 it dropped the name of the beleaguered steel town name from the newspaper's name altogether.

East Bay still shares the skyline with the fanciful, verdigris-copper topper on its Italianate campanile. In 1923, the paper marked the boffo opening of its tower with magician Harry Houdini dangling upside-down from the ninth floor like a butterfly in a chrysalis. Above a street full of people, he emerged from his straitjacket and handcuffs, the paper wrote, "as easily as a boy takes off a sweater."

Next to clocks, newspapers loved globes, a subtle message that "we deliver the world's news." The *Los Angeles Times* opened its round marble lobby in 1934, with a massive rotating globe in the center. In Seattle, the globe stood on the outside, above the doors to the wonderfully named *Post-Intelligencer*'s offices, and although the paper has moved on, the globe stayed put.

As the 1920s roared, newspapers raised up brick-and-mortar and marble-and-bronze monuments to themselves in works of surprising beauty.

In the industrial colossus of Detroit, the *Detroit Free Press*—the newspaper "older than the state of Michigan"—orna-mented its headquarters with statuary, stained glass, and bas-relief sculptures of goddesses and heroes of communication. The newspaper has moved away, but the inscriptions remain to remind visitors that newspapers cast themselves as the lash of the unrighteous: "Scourge of Evil Doers," "Exposer of Secret Iniquities," and "Unrelenting Foe of Privilege and Corruption." Bracing lines like these could invigorate any newsroom today.

A Press Room Café opened in the Detroit Free Press Building, and in Shepherdstown, West Virginia, a restaurateur put the quarters of the old *Independent* newspaper to new purpose with the Press Room restaurant.

The *Miami Herald's* sleek Biscayne Bay office building, with the paper's name in distinctive red neon letters, and below it, *El Nuevo Herald*, for its Spanish-language edition, was sold to a Malaysian casino company in 2011. The paper's staff moved to a suburb and the building was bulldozed in 2014.

In the lobby of the vanished *Washington Evening Star*, a series of seven half-moon murals once lauded human intelligence and progress. In one of them, called *News Gathering*, oddly classically clad (and un-clad) figures appear to be releasing carrier pigeons as messengers.

On the façade of the Dallas Morning News Building, chiseled in vast letters, is a statement by a long-gone publisher beginning, "Build the news upon the rock of truth and righteousness." The quote became the building's identity, and people came to call the place—sometimes in mockery—the Rock of Truth.

It would be impossibly expensive to build such magnificent edifices again, which is why many are getting new leases on life, like Tacoma's Perkins Building, once the headquarters of the *Tacoma Ledger*, now a condo building. Three thousand miles to the east, the boutique Press Hotel makes the most of its history as the building that once housed Maine's *Portland Press-Herald*. An eyeshade-era newspaperman would recognize the typewriters, the *Front Page*–era desks and headline fonts.

Perhaps older, grander newspaper buildings have a better lease on survival because they're singular and even historic buildings; smaller newspaper buildings, not so much. In 1938, in La Crosse, Wisconsin, the *Tribune* put up a dazzling Streamline Moderne building, all curves and glass block—so different from the

EGYPT'S
GREATEST
DAILY

EMBLEM OF POWER

SACRED BEETLE

EXTERIOR VIEW

CROWNING PTOLEMY IX

ENTRANCE

INTERIOR VIEW

Home
of the
SENTINEL
———
CENTRALIA, ILL.

PRIVATE OFFICE

The gloriously eccentric ornamentation of the *Centralia Sentinel* combined southern Illinois's nickname as "Egypt" with the King Tut craze of the 1920s, with adornments like "Crowning Ptolemy IX" and "sacred beetle."

paper's old building that the pressroom employees printed a message of thanks to the publisher for the "Modern, Sanitary, Air-Conditioned, and Daylight" plant. But when the paper left, the distinctive glass was covered up, and the building lost its chic as it was turned into first a beer concern and then the site of Bimbo Bakeries, producing croutons and stuffing.

Size didn't save the riverfront Chicago Daily News and Sun-Times Building; it was torn down, and a Trump hotel was built on the site. In Miami, hurricanes couldn't take down The Mothership, the *Miami Herald*'s mid-century waterfront building, but in 2015, wrecking crews from the new owner, a casino company, did. From the immense "The Miami Herald" name beaming in neon from the front of the building, the paper reported that it had salvaged and stashed the letters "M" and "H."

The most exuberant, exotic, and charming newspaper building of them all still survives in Centralia, Illinois, and is listed in the National Register of Historic Places. The Sentinel Building was remodeled in the 1920s as the world went "Tut-nuts."

After the 1923 opening of King Tutankhamun's tomb, the *Sentinel*—which covers the part of southern Illinois known as Little Egypt—installed a soaring Egyptian panel in its lobby, and a pharaonic bust and Nile-themed terra cotta friezes outside. Beneath lotuses and papyrus ornaments, it chiseled the newspapering ideal: "Here shall the press the people's right maintain/Unawed by influence/Unbribed by gain."

CHAPTER 12

THE AMERICAN PRESS: AN EPILOGUE?

L et's say that someday, the *paper* part of newspaper disappears. But the *news* part of newspaper, like the need for it—not rumor, not social-media gossip, not paid spin, but real, reported news—never vanishes. It is more durable and more enduring than the forces trying to besmirch the institution—the press—that meets that need.

The third president of the United States of America, Thomas Jefferson, proclaimed that "Our liberty depends on the freedom of the press, and that cannot be limited without being lost." The forty-fifth president of the United States of America,

In 1981, well before the Internet started wiping newspapers off the map, the *Washington Star*, like many afternoon papers, was done in by production costs, changing news tastes, and afternoon TV newscasts. (The *Washington Post* bought the bankrupt *Star*, lock, stock, and printing presses.)

Donald Trump, has called journalists "the enemy of the people."

That's the vocabulary of autocrats. Snapping *fake news!* is a tactic of intimidation. It's been picked up by politicians around the world and here at home. The sorry trope no more disproves a well-reported story than saying "fake arithmetic" proves that two plus two does not equal four. David M. Shribman, the executive editor of the *Pittsburgh Post-Gazette*, wrote in the *New York Times* that his staff is hearing Trump's "fake news" line more and more. The "most prominent public-relations officer in Pittsburgh told us that a

Opposite: The *Columbus Citizen-Journal* traced its beginnings to the year Abe Lincoln was born,1809. It took its final bow on New Year's Eve 1985 with an irresistible headline.

159

Skater's bodyguard arrested in Kerrigan attack — A10

THE UNION

FRI/SAT
January 14-15, 1994

FINAL-46¢
©1993 The Sacramento Union 143rd Year Vol. 286

SERVING SACRAMENTO SINCE 1851

We're history

City's longtime alternative voice finally falls silent

By PAMELA MARTINEAU
UNION STAFF WRITER

Like a weary elder statesman who's spent too many years on life support, The Sacramento Union will gasp its final breath today, ending a 143-year tenure in California's capital.

Buffeted by a continuing decline in advertising revenue and subscribers, Union Publisher Ralph Daniel Jr. announced Wednesday that the paper his family bought in 1992 will cease publication with today's issue.

■ A historical perspective of The Union. **Special section.**

Union's lobby at 301 Capitol Mall.

The Daniel family bought the newspaper from developers Danny Benvenuti Jr. and David Kassis in October 1992. The sale culminated three years of financial losses for Benvenuti, as well as a succession of owners who preceded the Sacramento developer.

The paper was founded in 1851 by a group of compositors from

The *Sacramento Union*, the oldest daily newspaper west of the Mississippi, began publishing in 1851. Late in the next century it lost its way, becoming at one point a cranky right-wing tabloid. It couldn't compete with the more robust *Sacramento Bee*, and folded in 1994. Mark Twain's 1866 dispatches to the *Union* were sent from Hawaii, not penned in Sacramento, but in 1993, newspaper archivist Dave Astor heard Bay Area columnist Herb Caen recall that during Caen's short stint at the *Union*, whenever the paper needed some cash, it would sell off the "Mark Twain desk" for $200—and it sold "dozens" of them.

perfectly benign, and completely accurate report on his institution's activities was another example of 'fake news.' Our police reporter repeatedly gets emails accusing her of producing 'fake news.'"

When a president of the United States calls reporters "scum" and "horrible people," and goads his supporters to jeer and scream at journalists, he does more than attack them and smear their work. He attacks a foundational principle of democracy. Some far-right conservatives have picked up a Nazi word, *Lügenpresse*—lying press—to insult reporters.

The ex-sheriff David A. Clarke Jr., a passionate Trump booster, tweeted that the "ANTIDOTE" to the "lying LIB MEDIA" is to "Punch them in the nose & MAKE THEM TASTE THEIR OWN BLOOD." On the eve of being elected to Congress, a Montana Republican named Greg Gianforte snarled at a writer for the *Guardian* newspaper that he was a "liberal reporter" and body-slammed the man to the ground. Not everyone was appalled. The next day, people sent more than a hundred thousand dollars to Gianforte's campaign. He pleaded guilty to misde-

meanor assault and agreed to donate fifty thousand dollars to the Committee to Protect Journalists.

The *New Yorker* reported that in Grand Junction, Colorado, a small city where candidate Trump staged a 2016 campaign rally, Erin McIntyre, a writer for the local paper, stood in a crowd of her fellow citizens as they screamed at the out-of-town political reporters, *Hang them all! Electric chair!* In a Facebook post, she wrote, "I thought I knew Mesa County. That's not what I saw yesterday. And it scared me."

Newspapers have had to contend with thin-skinned public officials since ink first dried on newsprint. The Huntsville, Alabama, *Times* printed a story the mayor didn't like, and His Honor threw some punches at the editor and ordered the paper never-ever to print his name again. That was in 1912.

Across the country, officials emboldened to imitate the Trump hostility toward the press are trying to keep public records from reaching the public. In Wisconsin, for instance, the *Baraboo News-Republic* had to sue Sauk County to try to get such documents. Newspapers' lawyers can do battle, but lawyering costs money, and small papers especially haven't many dollars to spare.

Since 1981, the number of daily papers in the country has plunged by more than one-third. Some have gone online; some have just gone. A dispiriting number of them had covered their towns and cities for well over a century. Newspapers are an integrated ecosystem, from the smallest weekly to the great national mastheads. A newspaper folding isn't just some business going to the grave, but another hole in the safety net of neighborhood and community and governance, of facts and accountability.

Peter Hessler, who wrote the *New Yorker*'s story about Grand Junction, reminded the *Columbia Journalism Review* that attacking the local paper as a surrogate for the national news media "doesn't do damage at the national level the way it does at the [local level]. You destroy your local paper, and you don't have anything that serves that role . . .. When you're hurting your own institutions, there's nothing that's going to come in and help you."

Newspapers slash their staffs or disappear even as the need for fact-checked news becomes more acute. Facts disinfect the putrescence of propaganda and twaddle, whether it came from a laptop two blocks from home or a Russian server farm. The Russians didn't need bombs and guns to undermine American democracy. They did it on the cheap, planting malevolently bogus disinformation on Facebook and Twitter, and deriding real news institutions as "fake." More than a half-million Americans followed dozens of Twitter accounts that presented themselves as local news sources, but Twitter found they were bogus, set up by the Kremlin-backed Russian Internet Research Agency.

It's beyond question that finances were killing off newspapers even before the "fake news" barrage and its bizarre, contradictory sidekick, "alternative facts," entered the picture. Newspapers' big money came from advertising, and websites haven't been able to make the same money with online ads. It's positively Shakespearean

The family-run *Oregon Journal* championed political reforms, but like so many afternoon newspapers, it wound up folding—in September 1982.

Demonstrators show some love for the First Amendment and the free press in February 2017 outside the *New York Times* building. The White House, one month into a new administration that had already lied about inauguration attendance figures, had just banned some major news organizations from covering a press briefing.

that, in the decade that advertising has moved from print to the Internet and actual news sources have been elbowed aside by social media, the Newspaper Guild staff at the *San Jose Mercury News,* Silicon Valley's hometown newspaper, has been cut from four hundred to forty-one.

The TV satirist John Oliver took his viewers to the woodshed in 2016 for complaining they should get news for free—news that takes money to produce. "A big part of the blame for this industry's dire straits is on us, and our unwillingness to pay for the work journalists produce."

America doesn't demand much of Americans, but paying serious attention to civic affairs once in a while is certainly one of those obligations. Our economy works like a dollar democracy, and online, every click is like a dollar-vote for something or against something else.

When you click on a gossip website or gobble up preposterous BS masquerading as news but don't bother to read stories about the opioid crisis in your state, then you're click-voting for more celebrity trivia, and less actual news about why your neighbors and relatives are dying. Of course you can read both—but do you? And just because you didn't

bother to read a story doesn't mean hard-working, honest journalists didn't write it.

Something good may be happening, though, since 2016. Millennials have begun casting their news media "votes" by subscribing to magazines and newspapers in bigger numbers, a heartening development for this "legacy medium."

One renowned Millennial evidently has some regard for the standards of old media, too. Edward Snowden, the onetime CIA employee and NSA contractor, leaked mountains of classified information to the *Guardian* and documentarian. One *Guardian* reporter, Glenn Greenwald, told the *New Yorker* that Snowden didn't want his material handled WikiLeaks fashion, which is to say indiscriminately dumped online. "He was vehement. He said, 'I don't want you to dump it. Curate it.'"

The *Tombstone Prospector* wrote in 1897 that journalists, "by devoting the same time, talent, enterprise, and brawn to raising peanuts or making adobes, each and every one would secure a better living, and an insurance on their lives would not be classed as extra hazardous."

Right on every count. In the 1970s, fourteen employees at Tennessee's *Chattanooga News–Free Press* mortgaged their homes to help keep the paper afloat. In 2017, after someone shot out the front windows of her paper, Lexington columnist Teri Carter tweeted what thousands of other journalists could say: "I am threatened weekly, sometimes daily. I am not the enemy."

Public relations is usually a safer job with a bigger paycheck. In 2015, the *Daily Breeze*, a regional daily paper covering southwest Los Angeles County, won a Pulitzer for its investigation into corruption in a local school district. But by then, one of the three prize-winning journalists had moved on, to a foundation PR job that paid him 25 percent more.

Nonetheless, newspaper people persist. Why? *Because newspapers matter.* News stories can change neighborhoods, cities, the world. They can help to get an innocent man out of prison, or start an investigation that imprisons a guilty one. They expose a government policy that's abusive, a business practice that's illegal. They tell us why the hours at the local library will be changing, and what charities in town are looking for volunteers. There's no part of public life, of human life, that a newspaper does not touch.

Gen Michael Hayden ✔
@GenMhayden

Follow ∨

Replying to @jmclaughlinSAIS

If this is who we are or who we are becoming, I have wasted 40 years of my life. Until now it was not possible for me to conceive of an American President capable of such an outrageous assault on truth, a free press or the first amendment.

8:32 PM - 25 Nov 2017

49,193 Retweets   101,069 Likes

This tweet by Michael Hayden, a retired four-star general and former head of the CIA and National Security Agency, was posted after president Donald Trump's tweet lambasting CNN International as a source of fake news.

Newspapers matter because they are force multipliers. Their enterprise reporting sets the agenda for TV network and cable news shows, more than most people realize. Newspapers do not, of course, always get things right. But that is light-years removed from "fake news." That same *Pittsburgh Post-Gazette*'s executive editor noted in his fifteen years in that job, "We have not knowingly published one story, or one paragraph, or one sentence, or one syllable that was not true."

Beyond the particulars of any one day's story is the constant soul-searching it takes to steer the harder course, not to drift into "groupthink," or to take the easy way out on a tough story.

Serious misapprehensions in how newspapers conceive and craft coverage of hugely important stories—like some reporting on the Iraq war and the 2016 election, for instance—can have real consequences in the life of the nation.

Much more often than that, though, newspapers' shortcomings come down to not having enough pairs of eyes, and enough pairs of feet, to monitor all the moving parts in a town, in a city, in state capitals, the nation's capital, and abroad.

Arizona's outgoing Republican Senator Jeff Flake warned against the withering cliche of "fake news" in October 2017:

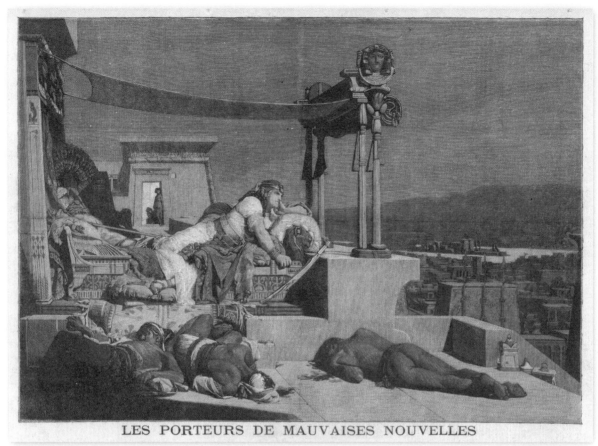

LES PORTEURS DE MAUVAISES NOUVELLES

The Bearers of Bad News, an 1872 painting by Jean-Jules-Antoine Lecomte du Nouÿ, was inspired by a French story of a petulant pharaoh who orders the slaughter of messengers telling him things he doesn't want to hear. Killing the messenger never kills the message.

"We were not made great as a country by indulging or even exalting our worst impulses, turning against ourselves, glorying in the things which divide us, and calling fake things true and true things fake." His Republican Senate colleague, Nebraska's Ben Sasse, who's pointed out the dangers of trying to "weaponize distrust" of the news media, made the case in a New Year's 2018 video that "a republic will not work if we don't have shared facts," and that the nation should "re-teach our kids what the First Amendment is about, and it's not helpful to call the press the enemy of the American people."

As tempting and as satisfying as it would be for newspapers to fling some mud back in the direction whence it came, stooping to the name-callers' level means letting them dictate the rules of journalism. It would mean abandoning facts in order to join a fight, and giving up shining light just for the sake of generating heat. It would change the compact journalists have with citizens to give them clear, principled reportage, the information kit from which they can assemble their own world views.

For three hundred years, newspapers have been the microscope and microphone for Americans. The writers and photographers and editors and publishers are the humans who humanize the place where we live. The newspapers they create are the record of our national life, and their stalwart existence is daily proof, to ourselves and to the world, that the remarkable American democratic undertaking still works.

ACKNOWLEDGMENTS

Beginning at the beginning would mean thanking the drafters of the First Amendment, so I'll skip ahead a couple of hundred years, and say first that I am truly, madly, deeply grateful to my former editor Dean Baquet, who has been Executive Editor of *The New York Times* since 2014, for his stirring and profound foreword. I add my humble thanks to Ken Burns, Norman Lear, Carl Reiner, and Katy Tur for kindly endorsing this effort. I owe thanks, too, to the great newspaper editor Jim Newton for his encouragement, to the archivists and librarians who take delight in sharing the important material in their care, to Tim Thomas, Charles Brown, Meaghan Thomas, Debra Silverman, Stan Piet, Mike Kasper, and Amy Inouye; gratitude and love to Jim, Maria, Becca, Freddie, Aubrey, and to Peter Pepper and Oswald.

SELECTED BIBLIOGRAPHY

Newspaper people spend their careers setting down other people's stories but almost never record their own. I am fortunate to have worked in the *Los Angeles Times* newsroom with men—and a few women—who have covered wars, riots, assassinations, foreign and domestic crises, and to have heard their stories. Their lives and work inspired and informed this book, before I encountered the insightful books listed below. Many of these people are dead and gone now. Three of my colleagues—one a good friend, another a mentor—died on the job: one shot in Iran, one killed by an RPG and machine-gun fire in Central America, and one dead of a heart attack covering the Iraq war. The human stories they lived, the backstories of the Fourth Estate, are as much a part of the country's heritage as the newspaper stories they wrote.

Baldasty, Gerald J. *E.W. Scripps and the Business of Newspapers.* Urbana, Illinois: University of Illinois, 1999.

Bates, Stephen. *If No News, Send Rumors: Anecdotes of American Journalism.* New York: St. Martin's Press, 1989.

Berges, Marshall. *The Life and Times of Los Angeles: A Newspaper, a Family, and a City.* New York: Atheneum, 1984.

Bernstein, Carl, and Bob Woodward. *All the President's Men.* New York: Simon & Schuster, 1974.

Bessie, Simon Michael. *Jazz Journalism: The Story of Tabloid Newspapers.* New York: E.P. Dutton, 1938.

Bingham, Sallie. *Passion and Prejudice: A Family Memoir.* New York: Alfred A. Knopf, 1989.

Broder, David S. *Behind the Front Page: A Candid Look At How the News Is Made.* New York: Simon & Schuster, 1987.

Burns, Eric. *Infamous Scribblers: The Founding Fathers and the Rowdy Beginnings of American Journalism.* New York: Public Affairs, 2006.

Campbell, W. Joseph. *Getting It Wrong: Ten of the Greatest Misreported Stories in American Journalism.* Berkeley: University of California Press, 2010.

Carter, Edward L. *The Story of Oklahoma Newspapers: 1844 to 1984.* Muskogee: Published for the Oklahoma Heritage Association by Western Heritage Books, 1984.

Cash, Kevin. *Who The Hell Is William Loeb?* Manchester, New Hampshire: Amoskeag Press, 1975.

Chancellor, John, and Walter R. Mears. *The News Business.* New York: Harper & Row, 1983.

Chaney, Lindsay, and Michael Cieply. *The Hearsts: Family and Empire.* New York: Simon and Schuster, 1981.

Clayton, Charles C. *Newspaper Reporting Today.* New York: Odyssey Press, 1947.

Clurman, Richard M. *Beyond Malice: The Media's Years of Reckoning.* New York: New American Library, 1990.

Connery, Thomas Bernard. *Journalism and Realism: Rendering American Life.* Evanston, Illinois: Northwestern Univ. Press, 2011.

Cose, Ellis. *The Press: Inside America's Most Powerful Newspaper Empires—From the Newsrooms to the Boardrooms.* New York: William Morrow and Company, 1989.

Creighton, Douglas. *Sunburned: Memoirs of a Newspaperman.* Boston: Little, Brown and Co. (Canada), 1993.

Dary, David. *Red Blood & Black Ink: Journalism in the Old West.* New York: Alfred A. Knopf, 1998.

Douglas, George H. *The Golden Age of the Newspaper.* Westport, Connecticut: Greenwood Press, 1999.

Downie, Leonard, Jr., and Robert G. Kaiser. *The News About the News: American Journalism in Peril.* New York: Alfred A. Knopf, 2002.

Dunford, Earle. *Richmond Times-Dispatch: The Story of a Newspaper.* Richmond, Virginia: Cadmus Publishing, 1995.

Fahs, Alice. *Out On Assignment: Newspaper Women and the Making of Modern Public Space.* Chapel Hill: University of North Carolina Press, 2011.

Felsenthal, Carol. *Power, Privilege, and The Post: The Katharine Graham Story.* New York: Putnam, 1993.

Fink, Conrad C. *Inside the Media.* New York: Longman, 1990.

Forrest, Wilbur. *Behind The Front Page: Stories of Newspaper Stories in the Making.* New York: D. Appleton-Century Company, 1934.

Fowler, Gene. *Skyline: A Reporter's Reminiscence of the 1920s.* New York: Viking Press, 1961.

Fuller, Jack. *News Values: Ideas for and Information Age.* Chicago: University of Chicago Press, 1996.

Gardner, Gilson. *Lusty Scripps: The Life of E.W. Scripps (1854-1926).* New York: Vanguard Press, 1932.

Gies, Joseph. *The Colonel of Chicago: A Biography of the Chicago Tribune's Legendary Publisher, Colonel Robert McCormick.* New York: E.P. Dutton, 1979.

Goulden, Joseph C. *Fit To Print: A.M. Rosenthal and His Times.* Secaucus, New Jersey: Stuart, 1988.

Gramling, Oliver. *AP: The Story of News.* New York: Farrar and Rinehart, 1940.

Halaas, David Fridtjof. *Boom Town Newspapers: Journalism on the Rocky Mountain Mining Frontier.* Albuquerque: University of New Mexico Press, 1981.

Hearst, William Randolph, and Jack Casserly. *The Hearsts: Father and Son.* Niwot, Colorado: Roberts Rinehart, 1991.

Henry, Neil. *Journalism Under Siege in an Age of New Media.* Berkeley: University of California Press, 2007.

Himmelman, Jeff. *Yours In Truth: A Personal Portrait of Ben Bradlee.* New York: Random House, 2012.

Holtzman, Jerome, ed. *No Cheering in the Press Box: Recollections—Personal and Professional—by Eighteen Veteran American Sportswriters.* New York: Holt, Rinehart and Winston, 1973.

Johnson, Marilyn. *The Dead Beat: Lost Souls, Lucky Stiffs and the Perverse Pleasures of Obituaries.* New York: HarperCollins, 2006.

Jones, Alex S. *Losing the News: The Future of the News That Feeds Democracy.* New York: Oxford University Press, 2009.

Karolevitz, Robert F. *Newspapering in the Old West: A Pictorial History of Journalism and Printing on the Frontier.* Seattle: Superior Publishing Company, 1965.

Kindred, Dave. *Morning Miracle: Inside the Washington Post: A Great Newspaper Fights for Its Life.* New York: Doubleday, 2010.

Kluger, Richard, and Phyllis Kluger. *The Paper: The Life and Death of the New York Herald Tribune.* New York: Alfred A. Knopf, 1986.

Kobre, Sidney. *The Yellow Press and Gilded Age Journalism.* Tallahassee: Florida State University, 1964.

Lutes, Jean Marie. *Front-Page Girls: Women Journalists in American Culture and Fiction, 1880-1930.* Ithaca: Cornell University Press, 2006.

Madigan, Charles M., ed. *-30- The Collapse of the Great American Newspaper.* Chicago: Ivan R. Dee, 2007.

Merritt, Davis. *Knightfall: Knight Ridder and How the Erosion of Newspaper Journalism Is Putting Democracy at Risk.* New York: AMACOM/American Management Association, 2005.

Milton, Joyce. *The Yellow Kids: Foreign Correspondents in the Heyday of Yellow Journalism.* New York: Harper & Row, 1989.

Morris, Joe Alex. *Deadline Every Minute: The Story of the United Press.* Garden City, New York: Doubleday, 1957.

Nasaw, David. *The Chief: The Life of William Randolph Hearst.* Boston: Houghton Mifflin, 2000.

Nord, David Paul. *Communities of Journalism: A History of American Newspapers and Their Readers.* Urbana, Illinois: University of Illinois Press, 2001.

Payne, George Henry. *History of Journalism in the United States.* New York: D. Appleton and Company, 1920.

Phillips, Cabell B.H., ed. *Dateline: Washington: The Story of National Affairs Journalism in the Life and Times of the National Press Club.* Garden City: Doubleday, 1949.

Porter, Bruce, and Timothy Ferris. *The Practice of Journalism: A Guide to Reporting and Writing the News.* Englewood Cliffs, New Jersey: Prentice Hall, 1988.

Prichard, Peter S. *The Making of McPaper: The Inside Story of USA Today.* New York: Andrews, McMeel and Parker, 1987.

Pumarlo, Jim. *Bad News and Good Judgment: A Guide to Reporting on Sensitive Issues in a Small-Town Newspaper.* Oak Park, Illinois: Marion Street Press, 2005.

Rittenhouse, Mignon. *The Amazing Nellie Bly.* New York: E.P. Dutton, 1956.

Robertson, Nan. *The Girls in the Balcony: Women, Men, and the New York Times.* New York: Random House, 1992.

Rosenfeld, Richard N. *American Aurora: A Democratic-Republican Returns: The Suppressed History of Our Nation's Beginnings and the Heroic Newspaper That Tried to Report It.* New York: St. Martin's Press, 1997.

Rosenstein, Jaik. *Hollywood Leg Man.* Los Angeles: Madison Press, 1950.

Salisbury, Harrison Evans. *Without Fear or Favor: The New York Times and Its Times.* New York: Times Books, 1980.

Schudson, Michael. *Discovering The News: A Social History of American Newspapers.* New York: Basic Books, 1978.

Seldes, George. *Witness to a Century: Encounters with the Noted, the Notorious, and the Three SOBs.* New York: Ballantine Books, 1987.

Shapiro, Bruce. *Shaking The Foundations: 200 Years of Investigative Journalism in America.* New York: Thunder's Mouth Press/Nation Books, 2003.

Sloan, W. David, and Lisa Mullikin. Parcell. *American Journalism: History, Principles, Practices.* Jefferson, North Carolina: McFarland &, 2002.

Stephens, Mitchell. *A History of News.* New York: Oxford University Press, 2007.

Stone, Gregory N. *The Day Paper: The Story of One of America's Last Independent Newspapers.* New London, Connecticut: Day Publishing Company, 2000.

Swanberg, W. A. *Citizen Hearst: A Biography of William Randolph Hearst.* New York: Charles Scribner, 1961.

Swanberg, W. A. *Pulitzer: The Life of the Greatest Figure in American Journalism and One of the Most Extraordinary Men in Our History.* New York: Scribner, 1967.

Tebbel, John William. *The Compact History of the American Newspaper.* New York: Hawthorn, 1969.

Teel, Leonard Ray. *The Public Press, 1900–1945: The History of American Journalism.* Westport, Connecticut: Praeger, 2006.

Toole, John H. *Red Ribbons: A Story of Missoula and Its Newspaper.* Davenport, Iowa: Lee Enterprises, 1989.

Washburn, Patrick Scott. *The African American Newspaper: Voice of Freedom.* Evanston, Illinois: Northwestern University Press, 2006.

White, David Manning, and Robert H. Abel, eds. *The Funnies: An American Idiom.* New York: Free Press, 1963.

Wilson, Theo. *Headline Justice: Inside the Courtroom: The Country's Most Controversial Trials.* New York: Thunder's Mouth Press, 1996.

Winkler, John K. *William Randolph Hearst: A New Appraisal.* New York: Hastings House, 1955.

NEWSPAPER INDEX

In this index of newspaper names, leading articles (typically, "A" or "The") have been removed for ease of alphabetization, and refer to the newspaper's names at the time of reference. Decades before it was typical for American businesses to merge and consolidate, newspapers were in the habit of changing names, splitting, combining, and merging. The website Chronicling America (chroniclingamerica.loc.gov), produced by the National Digital Newspaper Program and hosted by the Library of Congress, provides access to information about historic newspapers and select digitized newspaper pages.

INDEX

IMAGE CREDITS

Except on the pages noted below, all images in *Don't Stop the Presses!* are from the author's collection.
Please contact the publisher with any comments or questions.

Acme Roto Service, **151**
Agence France-Presse/Getty Images, **84**
Alamy image, **164**
Associated Press, **76** (bottom), **116, 119** (left), **162**
Baltimore Sun, **144** (right), **150**
Chauncey Bailey Project, **40**
Chicago Sun-Times Archives, **46**
Chicago Tribune Archives, **41, 64**
Cleveland Press, **143** (right)
Anestis Diakopoulos, for The *New York Times*, with the kind permission of the photographer, **108** (left)
Everett Collection, **21**
Fairbanks Daily News-Miner, **143** (left)
Getty Images, **27** (right), **89** (right)
Granger, **65, 127** (right)
Honolulu Star-Advertiser, with the kind permission of the newspaper, **121**
Howard University; Moorland-Springarn Research Center collections, **134**
The Huntington Library, Art Collections, and Botanical Gardens, **109** (top)
Kansas Historical Society, **106** (top)
Kusz, Charles L. (Peter Hertzog, ed.) *The Gringo & Greaser* (Santa Fe: Press of the Territorian, 1964), **71**
Library of Congress **32, 33**; Ansel Adams Manzanar War Relocation Center Photographs, **105** (left)
Los Angeles Public Library; *Herald-Examiner* Collection, **128** (left)
Glenn L. Martin Maryland Aviation Museum, **142** (left)
Milwaukee Journal, **36**
National Archives and Records Administration, **39** (bottom)
New York Daily News/Getty Images, **30**
Sunpapers, **158**
Tacoma Public Library photograph collection, **139** (right)
Twitter, **163**
United Press International, **129** (left), **137** (bottom), **145** (left)
United States Postal Service, **83** (left), **130, 135** (right)
University of Missouri–St. Louis; St. Louis Mercantile Library, **42**
U.S. Army Photo Archives, **39** (top)
Nick Ut/Associated Press, **37**
WNYC Archive Collections, **82** (right)

Don't Stop the Presses: Truth, Justice, and the American Newspaper
By Patt Morrison
Copyright © 2018 Patt Morrison

Design by Amy Inouye, Future Studio

ISBN-13 978-1-62640-043-6 (print edition)
ISBN-13 978-1-62640-044-3 (e-pub edition)

Library of Congress Cataloging-in-Publication Data

Names: Morrison, Patt, 1957- author.
Title: Don't stop the presses! : truth, justice, and the American newspaper /
   Patt Morrison ; foreword by Dean Baquet.
Description: Santa Monica, California : Angel City Press, [2018] | Includes
   bibliographical references and index.
Identifiers: LCCN 2018009610 (print) | LCCN 2018014405 (ebook) | ISBN
   9781626400443 (ePub) | ISBN 9781626400436 (hardcover : alk. paper)
Subjects: LCSH: Journalism--United States--History. | American
   newspapers--History. | Freedom of the press--United States. | Newspaper
   publishing--United States--History.
Classification: LCC PN4855 (ebook) | LCC PN4855 .M625 2018 (print) | DDC
   071/.3--dc23
LC record available at https://lccn.loc.gov/2018009610

Printed in Canada

Published by Angel City Press
2118 Wilshire Blvd. #880
Santa Monica, California 90403
+1.310.395.9982
www.angelcitypress.com